Rosie White is Senior Lecturer in Contemporary Literature, Theory and Popular Culture at Northumbria University. She is the author of *Violent Femmes: Women as Spies in Popular Culture* (2007) and the co-editor of 'Acting Up: Gender and Television Comedy', a special edition of *Critical Studies in Television* (2015). She has published essays on Beryl Reid, Roseanne Barr and June Whitfield.

'Admirably smart but eminently readable, topical but informed by a breadth of textual and theoretical histories, Rosie White's book brings new and illuminating insights to bear on how we understand TV comedy and femininity. She cogently shows her readers how these comedies – while typically seemingly "about" heteronormative characters – work to flag the innate strangeness of the binary approaches to gender that heterosexuality pivots on. Drawing on an engaging range of UK and US case studies, from *30 Rock* to *Waiting for God*, from *The Big Bang Theory* to *Smack The Pony*, White's work is a standout moment in the cultural and scholarly drive to recognise the talents and marginalisation of women in comedy, and to unpack the "wobbly scenery" of normative gender identities.'

**Deborah Jermyn, Reader in Film and TV,
University of Roehampton**

'In this startlingly original reading of gender and comedy in transatlantic television, Rosie White persuasively illustrates the inherent queerness of this comedy and reveals how much we lose when we focus on funny performances of gender in a binary way. Her lively discussions of television series and performances sparkle with detail, wit, and theoretical savvy. In the tradition of books that are truly groundbreaking, *Television Comedy and Femininity* will have you nodding in vigorous agreement with its insights. And it will also make you laugh.'

**Linda Mizejewski, Professor of Women's, Gender and
Sexuality Studies, Ohio State University**

'In this illuminating and original book, Rosie White provides deep and detailed understanding of the complex interconnections between comedy, gender and television in order to examine hegemonic identities. Drawing on examples from American and British television, the book offers refreshing insights into landmark comedies and carefully fuses these with analyses of more recent comedies that have yet to be critically explored. This is a must-read for scholars and students in comedy studies, media and communications, gender studies, cultural studies and sociology.'

**Sharon Lockyer, Director of the Centre for Comedy Studies
Research (CCSR), Brunel University London**

Library of Gender and Popular Culture

From *Mad Men* to gaming culture, performance art to steam-punk fashion, the presentation and representation of gender continues to saturate popular media. This new series seeks to explore the intersection of gender and popular culture, engaging with a variety of texts – drawn primarily from Art, Fashion, TV, Cinema, Cultural Studies and Media Studies – as a way of considering various models for understanding the complementary relationship between 'gender identities' and 'popular culture'. By considering race, ethnicity, class, and sexual identities across a range of cultural forms, each book in the series will adopt a critical stance towards issues surrounding the development of gender identities and popular and mass cultural 'products'.

For further information or enquiries, please contact the library series editors:

Claire Nally: claire.nally@northumbria.ac.uk
Angela Smith: angela.smith@sunderland.ac.uk

Advisory Board:

Dr Kate Ames, Central Queensland University, Australia

Prof Leslie Heywood, Binghampton University, USA

Dr Michael Higgins, Strathclyde University, UK

Prof Åsa Kroon, Örebro University, Sweden

Dr Niall Richardson, Sussex University, UK

Dr Jacki Willson, Central St Martins, University of Arts London, UK

**Library of Gender
& Popular Culture**

Published and forthcoming titles:

The Aesthetics of Camp: Post-Queer Gender and Popular Culture
By Anna Malinowska

Ageing Femininity on Screen: The Older Woman in Contemporary Cinema
By Niall Richardson

All-American TV Crime Drama: Feminism and Identity Politics in Law and Order: Special Victims Unit
By Sujata Moorti and Lisa Cuklanz

Bad Girls, Dirty Bodies: Sex, Performance and Safe Femininity
By Gemma Commane

Beyoncé: Celebrity Feminism in the Age of Social Media
By Kirsty Fairclough-Isaacs

Conflicting Masculinities: Men in Television Period Drama
By Katherine Byrne, Julie Anne Taddeo and James Leggott (Eds)

Fathers on Film: Paternity and Masculinity in 1990s Hollywood
By Katie Barnett

Film Bodies: Queer Feminist Encounters with Gender and Sexuality in Cinema
By Katharina Lindner

Gay Pornography: Representations of Sexuality and Masculinity
By John Mercer

Gender and Austerity in Popular Culture: Femininity, Masculinity and Recession in Film and Television
By Helen Davies and Claire O'Callaghan (Eds)

The Gendered Motorcycle: Representations in Society, Media and Popular Culture
By Esperanza Miyake

Gendering History on Screen: Women Filmmakers and Historical Films
By Julia Erhart

Girls Like This, Boys Like That: The Reproduction of Gender in Contemporary Youth Cultures
By Victoria Cann

The Gypsy Woman: Representations in Literature and Visual Culture
By Jodie Matthews

Love Wars: Television Romantic Comedy
By Mary Irwin

Masculinity in Contemporary Science Fiction Cinema: Cyborgs, Troopers and Other Men of the Future
By Marianne Kac-Vergne

Moving to the Mainstream: Women On and Off Screen in Television and Film
By Marianne Kac-Vergne and Julie Assouly (Eds)

Paradoxical Pleasures: Female Submission in Popular and Erotic Fiction
By Anna Watz

Positive Images: Gay Men and HIV/AIDS in the Culture of 'Post-Crisis'
By Dion Kagan

Queer Horror Film and Television: Sexuality and Masculinity at the Margins
By Darren Elliott-Smith

Queer Sexualities in Early Film: Cinema and Male-Male Intimacy
By Shane Brown

Steampunk: Gender and the Neo-Victorian
By Claire Nally

Television Comedy and Femininity: Queering Gender
By Rosie White

Television, Technology and Gender: New Platforms and New Audiences
By Sarah Arnold

Tweenhood: Femininity and Celebrity in Tween Popular Culture
By Melanie Kennedy

Women Who Kill: Gender and Sexuality in Post-Feminist Film and Television
By David Roche and Cristelle Maury (Eds)

Wonder Woman: Feminism, Culture and the Body
By Joan Ormrod

Young Women in Contemporary Cinema: Gender and Post-feminism in British Film
By Sarah Hill

TELEVISION COMEDY AND FEMININITY
Queering Gender

ROSIE WHITE

I.B. TAURIS
LONDON · NEW YORK

To Bill White (1914–2015)

Published in 2018 by
I.B.Tauris & Co. Ltd
London • New York
www.ibtauris.com

Copyright © 2018 Rosie White

The right of Rosie White to be identified as the author of this work has been asserted by the author in accordance with the Copyright, Designs and Patents Act 1988.

All rights reserved. Except for brief quotations in a review, this book, or any part thereof, may not be reproduced, stored in or introduced into a retrieval system, or transmitted, in any form or by any means, electronic, mechanical, photocopying, recording or otherwise, without the prior written permission of the publisher.

Every attempt has been made to gain permission for the use of the images in this book. Any omissions will be rectified in future editions.

References to websites were correct at the time of writing.

Library of Gender and Popular Culture 9

ISBN: 978 1 78453 362 5
eISBN: 978 1 78672 521 9
ePDF: 978 1 78673 521 8

A full CIP record for this book is available from the British Library
A full CIP record is available from the Library of Congress

Library of Congress Catalog Card Number: available

Typeset in Garamond Three by OKS Prepress Services, Chennai, India
Printed and bound by CPI Group (UK) Ltd, Croydon, CR0 4YY

CONTENTS

List of Figures ix
Acknowledgements xi
Series Editors' Foreword xii

Introduction Funny Peculiar: Queering Gender, Comedy
 and Television 1
 Queering Gender 3
 Queering Femininities 11
 Queering Comedy 16
 Queering Television 20

1. Gracie, Martha, Eve and Lucy: Queering Femininity
 in Early American Television Comedy 25
 Queering Space and Time in 1950s American Sitcom:
  The Burns and Allan Show (CBS 1950–8) 26
 Queering Sitcom: *Our Miss Brooks* 35
 Queering the Gaze: *The Martha Raye Show* (NBC 1953–6) 38
 Lucy and Lucille 43
 Queering Suburbia 53

2. Back to the Dollhouse? Queering Postfeminism
 in Contemporary American Sitcom 57
 Postfeminism and the New Comedy 60
 Not Unruly Women? 63
 Sex and the City: Queering Postfeminism 65
 30 Rock 67

'I Want to Go to There' 73
Parks and Recreation 78
Postscript 89

3. ***The Big Bang Theory***: **Queering Masculinity in American Sitcom** 91
   Queer Masculinities in Contemporary American Sitcom 94
   Two and a Half Men 99
   The Big Bang Theory 101
   Race and Ethnicity in *The Big Bang Theory* 107
   Sheldon Cooper: A Third Gender? 111
   Resolving Queer Masculinities 116

4. ***Smack the Pony***: **Feminist Negotiations in British Sketch Comedy** 123
   Contexts: Not a Feminist Sketch Show 125
   Queer Temporalities 129
   Contexts: Postfeminism, Femininity and the 'Norm' 132
   The Grotesque, the Queer, the Monstrous 137
   Feminist Praxis: The Production of *Smack the Pony* 140
   Queerly Desiring Subjects 145
   Speaking and Stunting 148
   Legacies 153

5. **Queering Age: Older Women in British Television Comedy** 159
   Queer Times 161
   Queering Ageing 163
   The Young Old: *The Golden Girls* and *Last of the Summer Wine* 166
   You're Only Young Twice 169
   Waiting for God 179
   Going Forward? 192

Conclusion 199

Notes 207
Bibliography 208
Index 224

LIST OF FIGURES

Figure 1.1 Gracie Allen trims the hedge with George's electric razor (*The Burns and Allen Show*, pilot episode, McCadden Productions/Screen Gems 1950–8). 29

Figure 1.2 Martha sings the opening number in *The Martha Raye Show* (NBC, 1954–6). 41

Figure 1.3 Lucy auditions for the Vitameatavegemin commercial (*I Love Lucy*, 1:30, Desilu Productions, 1951–7). 45

Figure 1.4 The animated opening credits of *The Lucy Show* (Desilu Productions, 1951–7). 52

Figure 1.5 Lucy and Vivian trapped in the shower cubicle (*The Lucy Show*, 1:18, Desilu Productions, 1951–7). 54

Figure 2.1 Liz Lemon as Carrie Bradshaw from *Sex and the City* in 'Do-over' (*30 Rock*, 3:1, NBC, 2008–13). 68

Figure 2.2 Liz talks to Cerie about what she wears to work in 'Jack the Writer' (*30 Rock*, 1:4, NBC, 2008–13). 74

Figure 2.3 Ron under his ex-wife Tammy's spell in 'Ron and Tammy 2' (*Parks and Recreation*, 3:4, NBC, 2009–15). 86

Figure 3.1 Sheldon, Howard, Raj and Leonard confront Kurt in 'The Financial Permeability' (*The Big Bang Theory*, 2:14, Chuck Lorre Productions/Warner Bros Television, 2007–). 106

Figure 3.2 Sheldon hugs Penny in 'The Bath Item Gift Hypothesis' (*The Big Bang Theory*, 2:11, Chuck Lorre Productions/Warner Bros Television, 2007–). 112

Figure 3.3 Sheldon and Amy in bed after their first experience of 'coitus' in 'The Opening Night Excitation' (*The Big Bang Theory*, 9:11, Chuck Lorre Productions/Warner Bros Television, 2007–). 117

Figure 4.1 Competitive lipstick application in *Smack the Pony* (1:1, Talkback Productions, 1999–2003). 135

Figure 4.2 The dating agency sketches (*Smack the Pony*, Talkback Productions, 1999–2003). 146–7

Figure 4.3 'I want to see your tits' (*Smack the Pony*, 2:3, Talkback Productions, 1999–2003). 149

Figure 4.4 The public dance routine (*Smack the Pony*, 1:3, Talkback Productions, 1999–2003). 151

Figure 5.1 Knitting for the baby in 'The Foundling' (*You're Only Young Twice*, 2:5, Yorkshire Television, 1977–81). 173

Figure 5.2 Flora and Cissie rehearse their roles in 'Stranger in Paradise' (*You're Only Young Twice*, 1:1, Yorkshire Television, 1977–81). 175

Figure 5.3 The opening title sequence of *You're Only Young Twice* (Yorkshire Television, 1977–81). 176

Figure 5.4 The residents of Paradise Lodge under Mr King's regime in 'The Deputy' (*You're Only Young Twice*, 2:6, Yorkshire Television, 1977–81). 178

Figure 5.5 Tom Ballard first catches sight of Diana Trent (*Waiting for God*, 1:1, BBC, 1990–4). 180

Figure 5.6 Tom and Diana after they refuse to marry (*Waiting for God*, 5:8, BBC, 1990–4). 192

Figure 5.7 Kim Wilde and Mrs Jenkins in *Going Forward* (1:1, BBC, 2016–). 195

ACKNOWLEDGEMENTS

I would like to thank the Humanities Department at Northumbria University for research support which enabled me to complete this project. This work was made possible by a community of colleagues and postgraduate students, most notably those involved in the Gendered Subjects Research Group and the Gender and Sexuality Research Hub. Victoria Bazin, Julie Scanlon and Mel Waters read draft chapters and offered invaluable advice. Any mistakes are mine.

I would also like to acknowledge the wider support of friends and family in the UK, Ireland and Germany, with particular thanks to Lynn and Ros Edmonds, and to Mel and David Gibson. Chips and curry are sometimes necessary, but not necessarily at the same time.

SERIES EDITORS' FOREWORD

In her seminal work, *Language and Woman's Place* (1975), Robin Lakoff lamented that women were disadvantaged in society as they were socialised to have no sense of humour, in contrast to men who allegedly compete to be the funniest guys in the room. Just as women are regarded as lacking humour, femininity in a comedic context is funny because of its Otherness. As White explores in this book, femininity is aligned with queerness because of that inherent Otherness.

The intersection of female comedy and queer theory is central to White's study, and so resonates with many of the other books in this series where queer studies are deployed in relation to wider popular culture. White argues that gender is performative and that femininity is visibly *différant* in a way that masculinity is not. The female comic is thus couched in the impossibility of a coherent gender, exposing its reiterated masquerade. In television comedy, femininity can be performed by men in drag in the cause of entertainment. Elsewhere, grotesque versions of femininity became television staples in the 1950s through performances by actors such as Lucille Ball and Martha Raye. Such unruly women continue to be found nearly 70 years later in comedies such as *Fleabag* and *Chewing Gum*. As White points out, both British and American television comedy have offered a space in which women can be seen to misbehave, be 'unfeminine,' even if such aberrations are contained by the end of the show. As we find in books throughout this series, the social and historical context of a show's production is vital to unpicking its account of gender and sexual identity. The representation of LBGTQ+ characters is often problematic, yet many early comedies reference queer identities through camp, as well as gesturing to relationships which exceed heteronormative models. Comedy acts as a broken mirror of attitudes towards gender and sexuality, reflecting on contemporary mores and anxieties.

By queering television comedy, White argues that comedy works to destabilise and unsettle our understanding of those categories even as we laugh at them. This is true of several other books in the Library, although the element of laughter is often backgrounded depending on context.

As White points out HBO's *Sex and the City* is one of the most iconic female ensemble comedy shows. Historically placed at the intersection of the Second Wave feminism and postfeminist discourses of empowerment and choice, the show queers heterofemininity. White proposes that more recent ensemble comedies, such as *30 Rock*, *Parks and Recreation*, and *Girls* offer responses to *Sex and the City* that map out a generational journey through feminist and postfeminist contexts. Generational debates about gender and sexual identities may also be seen in shows that depict older and ageing characters, as White shows here and as other books in this series also explore.

This volume is thus in conversation with other books in the Gender and Popular Culture Series in its account of queer theory, ageing femininity and the subversion of stereotypes.

Angela Smith and Claire Nally

INTRODUCTION

FUNNY PECULIAR: QUEERING GENDER, COMEDY AND TELEVISION

In *Women and Laughter* Frances Gray enumerates five ways in which women have been kept away from comedy: the myths that women can't be witty, are prudes, are not sufficiently self-aware, are only 'small potatoes', and, if feminist, are *'ipso facto* humourless' (1994: 8–12). Yet, as Gray and others have repeatedly demonstrated, funny women have a long history of work in comedy theatre, film and television. That history has already been traced, with foundational work by Patricia Mellencamp (1992), Gray (1994) and Kathleen Rowe (1995). These groundbreaking studies from the 1990s address women in television comedy as part of a wider discussion of women in film, stand-up and popular culture. Mellencamp has shaped subsequent debates about women and sitcom, tracking the careers of Gracie Allen and Lucille Ball through vaudeville, radio, film and television (1992, 2003). Her work also brings representations of age to the fore, noting how television comedy contributes to current debates about women and aging (1992, 1999). Gray's *Women and Laughter* is in dialogue with Mellencamp and includes British comedy in the discussion, tracing the different gender dynamics evident in British sitcom and stand-up. Rowe's concept of 'the unruly woman' is a necessary reference in any academic work on women and television comedy, arguing for the subversive feminist potential of such figures. Mellencamp's, Gray's and Rowe's accounts of crazy old ladies, eccentric girls and unruly women have been followed by studies focussing on specific comedy series, such as *Butterflies* (BBC 1978–83) (Andrews 1998; Hallam 2005), *Murphy Brown* (CBS 1988–97) (Rabinovitz 1999), *Absolutely Fabulous* (BBC 1992–2012) (Waddell 1999) and *Kath and Kim* (ABC 2002–7) (Davis 2008), or on particular stars (Horowitz 1997; Lavin 2004; Mizejewski 2007, 2014).

This book extends those discussions about gender and television comedy in American and British traditions. While transatlantic television comedy encompasses very different histories and economies, it also represents a conversation, as stars, shows and formats are borrowed, trialled and reinterpreted for particular national contexts. My analyses focus on some shows that have had little or no academic attention to date; if nothing else, I hope to demonstrate the need for *more* work on women and television comedy. This volume also intervenes in debates about television comedy to propose queer theory as an appropriate lens through which analysis of the medium and the dynamics of humour might usefully unpick gendered identities. The chapters that follow this introduction map a trajectory in conversation with Mellencamp, Gray and Rowe, and the writers that followed them, arguing that gender and television comedy may be fruitfully examined in relation to queer theory. In that regard this book adopts a slightly different approach from those founding studies on women and comedy. My debate addresses television shows that are ostensibly concerned with heteronormative characters, yet these comedies also serve to demonstrate the inherent strangeness of binary accounts of gender that are structured by heterosexuality. Following 30 years of work in queer studies, I examine heterosexuality as a normative discourse whose precarity is repeatedly exposed by television comedy. This approach deploys the strategy of *queering* to unsettle, disturb and worry at any concept of gendered identity as 'normal'. In the last two decades the humanities and social sciences have been transformed by the work of Judith Butler, Eve Kosofsky Sedgewick, Judith Halberstam and many others. As early as 1997 Steven Seidman was writing about 'queering sociology', arguing that it was necessary to examine how the social sciences participated 'in the making of a sexual social system organized around a hetero-homosexual binary and the normative status of heterosexuality' (Seidman 1997: 81–2). In a similar vein, this book addresses the ways in which popular television comedy is built upon *and* exposes normative accounts of gender, inviting its viewers to examine the peculiar particularities of heteronormative gender roles.

Queering Gender

Gender is a funny thing. The more you examine it the less clear any binary understanding of it becomes, so that gender under scrutiny is deeply peculiar. One can say the same thing about comedy, a field patrolled by the truism that the more you examine it the less funny it becomes. So this volume is perched on a paradox. If you want to examine comedy you destroy its sense of humour (which may be a bad thing), but if you want to examine gender you destroy its certainties (which, I propose, is a good thing). One thing that gender and television comedy have in common is that the labour which goes into constructing them is often invisible. That is why examining comedy and gender is simultaneously destructive and instructive, because it exposes the mechanics of their construction. Examining gender *in* comedy throws up new problems and paradoxes, as comedic performances of gender often deconstruct our binary understandings of it. Comedy is essentially playful but hegemonic identities are constituted upon the notion of absolute certainties, however fictional those absolutes may be. Judith Butler memorably names this as the '*heterosexual matrix*' in *Gender Trouble* (1990), later 'heterosexual hegemony' in *Bodies That Matter* (1993). Drawing on the work of Monique Wittig and Adrienne Rich, Butler deploys this term:

> to characterize a hegemonic discursive/epistemic model of gender intelligibility that assumes that for bodies to cohere and make sense there must be a stable sex expressed through a stable gender (masculine expresses male, feminine expresses female) that is oppositionally and hierarchically defined through the compulsory practice of heterosexuality (1990: 151)

The chapters in this book examine how television comedy has the potential to destabilise that intelligibility, upsetting heteronormativity as a compulsory practice and even gesturing toward other possibilities regarding gender identities and sexual desires.

There is a long tradition of disrupting heteronormative hegemony in stage and screen comedy. Mark Simpson notes how, for male comedy duos such as Laurel and Hardy, Jerry Lewis and Dean Martin, or Morecambe and Wise, the shared bed 'was the contradiction at the heart of the genre, managing somehow to accommodate the audience's curious ambivalence towards non-heterosexuality – both fascinated by it and loathing it' (1998: 138). Simpson argues that the shared bed signified the innocence of these pairings, but also their *queerness* (1998: 138). Such queerness is compounded by the popularity of double acts such as Lewis and Martin or Morecambe and Wise. These were not avant-garde entertainments but family variety shows, at the centre of television schedules around public holidays such as Thanksgiving and Christmas. The image of two men in bed together is represented as the epitome of intimate friendship and yet emphatically *not* gay. If they are not gay, however, they are not straight either, calling upon a tradition of playfulness within the comic field that allows for such transgression (Simpson 1998: 139). Simpson ascribes this, in part, to their particular historical context. Evading the legibility of gay male identities that emerged after the legislative change demanded by gay rights campaigners in the 1960s, these homosocial double acts embody a queer doubletalk, a fluidity that encompasses both/and rather than either/or. This may be a nostalgic account of queer history, yet it resonates with Judith Halberstam's proposal that some of the queerest figures are now to be found in children's animation, a genre which likewise plays upon a fluidity of identity where gender and sexuality are not fixed or certain (2011: 1–52).

The concept of gender as performative is a grounding assumption of this study. Performativity is a doubly problematic term when applied to material that is itself all about performance. Judith Butler was critiqued for an alleged confusion between performance and performativity following the publication of *Gender Trouble* in 1990. That debate was addressed in her subsequent volume, *Bodies That Matter* (1993):

> Butler's position could be said to be anti-voluntarist, particularly in *Bodies That Matter*, insofar as she emphasises that performativity is not something the subject does, but is a process through which the subject is constituted, and that gender is not something that can be put on or taken off at will. This distinction between

voluntarism and anti-voluntarism is most often understood by commentators as the difference between performance and performativity (Sullivan 2003: 89)

In short, performativity refers to the way in which we are socially constructed, whereas performance is an elective choice. So, for example, an individual may be performatively masculine but may elect to perform femininity through cross-dressing or drag. Even this brief example reveals the problematic nature of such distinctions as we may question whether cross-dressing is a completely elective choice where it involves aspects of desire. None of this is straightforward; indeed, it lends its philosophical and linguistic *queerness* to the discussion in interesting ways. Yet it is necessary to consider questions of performativity and performance when examining femininity and television comedy. It is tempting to propose that all comedy performance radically undermines the social construction of gender. But this is clearly not the case, as theatre, film and television comedy all have histories of misogyny and homophobic stereotyping. Recent examples such as the much-debated *Little Britain* demonstrate the ambivalences of television comedy in this regard (Lockyer 2010b). The distinctions between performativity and performance, as between anti-voluntarist and voluntarist appropriations of identity, are not absolute or simple (Sullivan 2003: 90). Nevertheless, I will attempt to map some of the dynamics at play where women perform comedy on television, taking June Whitfield as an example. Readers not familiar with Whitfield's work should feel free to substitute the name of any well-known female comedy actor.

Here is one model of how it works: the identity of June Whitfield (as a social subject) is performatively constituted in and through discourses of gender, sexuality, class, race and so on. The star persona of 'June Whitfield' the actor is discursively produced and self-fashioned as an extension of that performative subject, so that the characters that June Whitfield chooses to perform reflect upon both June and 'June'. June Whitfield is not an originary or authentic figure in this dynamic. One can say that she is constituted in and through the discursive formations which make possible her star persona 'June Whitfield' and her comedy performances, for example as Edina Monsoon's mother in *Absolutely Fabulous*. June Whitfield performs the role of Mother but this does not emerge from a 'real' stable identity which is merely overlaid by professional and social performances; rather, her career as a comedy actor has the potential to make evident the 'stylized repetition of acts' (Butler 1990: 140) that serve to form the *illusion* of gendered identity. Whitfield's performances on screen thus reflect upon the performativity of her identity as a social subject, and on the construction of identity per se.

That comic performance offers a potential space for reflexive accounts of identity is hinted at in *Gender Trouble*, where Judith Butler addresses the comedy of heterosexuality:

> The ideal of a coherent heterosexuality that [Monique] Wittig describes as the norm and standard of the heterosexual contract is an impossible ideal, a 'fetish' as she herself points out. A psychoanalytic elaboration might contend that this impossibility is exposed in virtue of the complexity and resistance of an unconscious sexuality that is not always already heterosexual. In this sense, heterosexuality offers normative sexual positions that are intrinsically impossible to embody, and the persistent failure to identify fully and without incoherence with these positions reveals heterosexuality itself not only as a compulsory law, but as an inevitable comedy (1990: 122)

In this passage heteronormativity is proposed as a comic position because it is founded upon a paradox. More specifically, the notion of a 'norm' in sexual terms is constituted here as a fictive and contradictory position, only sustainable in relation to a ghostly other – the 'lesbian', the 'gay man' and so on. Television comedy is one arena in which the 'persistent failure' of coherent heteronormative identities is exposed and played upon, presenting viewers with a range of gender and sexual identities which are visibly tenuous and always already unstable. Comedy is often produced through the very exposure of such impossible identities, making the comedy of gender and its relation to heterosexuality visible and *funny*.

Critical work on comedy has addressed this with regard to work which explicitly stages gender *as* a performance. Henry Jenkins and Kristine Brunovska Karnick discuss moments in Hollywood comedy where characters within the filmic narrative *become* performers – by impersonating someone else, for example:

Such moments of layered performance are central to a large number of comic films within both the comedian comedy and the romantic comedy tradition, where these diagetic performances invite our awareness of the construction and maintenance of social and personal identities (1995: 151)

Yet this applies primarily to the drag performances of male comedy actors – Dustin Hoffman in *Tootsie* (Sydney Pollack, 1982) or Robin Williams in *Mrs Doubtfire* (Chris Columbus, 1993) – where we are reassured by the star persona and acting chops of the actor that it is all just an act and that there is a 'real' man under the costume (Tasker 1998: 31–5). For female comedy actors, 'our awareness of the construction and maintenance of social and personal identities' is always already present because of our cultural understanding of femininity *as* artifice. For women in comedy, the impossibilities of coherent gender identity are framed by Western discourses of femininity as masquerade (Riviere 1986; Doane 1991).

The Hollywood legacies of this dynamic can be mapped through the queered performances in *Some Like It Hot* (Billy Wilder, 1959), where Tony Curtis and Jack Lemmon spend much of the film dragged up as Josephine and Daphne. Marilyn Monroe's performance as Sugar Kane is equally *about* performance, yet within the diegesis she is presented as 'naturally' female (Stott 2005: 67–8). In contrast to the male characters, Sugar is shown to play out her emotions on stage when she sings 'I'm thru with love' after being dumped yet again. Sugar is unable to separate herself from her onstage persona. The song expresses her inner anguish, so that heterofemininity is performed as flatly representing the self, without depth or layers. Monroe as Sugar Kane is stereotypically (and 'authentically') feminine because of her proximity to and identification with her emotions, whereas Curtis and Lemmon as Josephine and Daphne are cognitively superior, their masculinity paradoxically – and comically – confirmed by their plot-driven voluntarist appropriation of feminine disguise. Within the film, Sugar's *lack* of disguise, her visible inability to lie and dissemble as the woman who always gets the 'fuzzy end of the lollipop', gives her a childlike innocence which *Some Like It Hot* appears to endorse. At the same time Sugar is the most carefully framed and presented visual presence. Monroe's star billing attests to her headlining power, and the film does all it can to endorse the 'Marilyn' brand. Sugar Kane's Oscar-winning outfits carefully frame Monroe's physical attributes, most notably in the two stage costumes which are carefully lit and shot to make her appear semi-naked.

The visual aesthetic of the film thus contradicts its narrative, opening a fissure in its account of 'real' heterofemininity. In its overstatement of Monroe's star persona, *Some Like It Hot* presents femininity as drag too. There are no real women here. The women's orchestra that Curtis and Lemmon join in order to escape homicidal gangsters represents a transgressive working-class femininity, most clearly in the train journey where the 'girls' are riotous, squeezing into Lemmon's bunk with crackers and booze for a midnight party. Sweet Sue and her Society Syncopators offer an unruly account of femininity. Despite their stereotypical blondeness, even the women in the background of this cinematic narrative are contradictory. Sue is not 'sweet' and her musicians are not 'society girls'. Their willing acceptance of two drag queens as 'real' girls underlines the fluidity of gender identities in the film. Within this context Marilyn cuts an even more peculiar figure.

The infamous punchline that concludes the movie is Osgood's response to Daphne's revelation that s/he's 'a man': 'Nobody's perfect'. Yet *Some Like It Hot* has spent nearly two hours attempting to reify Monroe's 'perfection' within the Hollywood continuum as the ultimate 'natural' child-woman. To believe the love story narrative between Tony Curtis's and Marilyn Monroe's characters is to ignore the significant intercutting of their love scenes with Jack Lemmon and Joe E. Brown's passionately comic tango, and it is also to disavow the labour that went into Monroe's performance. If we take Sugar/Marilyn at face value and buy into the Hollywood image, we deny the skill with which her performances were constructed (Gray 1994: 9–11; Mulvey 2017). As Jenkins and Karnick observe, romantic comedies like *Some Like It Hot* and *The Seven Year Itch*, are 'self-conscious about the process of staging a performance', yet also 'invite our familiarity with the extratextual images of stars, with the problem of constructing and maintaining a coherent image, with the mechanics of masquerade and impersonation' (1995: 166–7). Monroe's skill is to make us believe that Sugar is also Marilyn, a masquerade built upon Hollywood studios' investment in the mythic contiguity between actors' roles and their 'real' lives. In *Gender Trouble* Butler addresses Garbo's star persona, asking 'is "the body" itself shaped by political forces with strategic interests in keeping that body bounded and constituted by the markers of sex?' (1990: 129). Looking at classical Hollywood (and the studios' subsequent investment in television production) one has to answer in the affirmative. Monroe, like other studio-era stars, was an asset, her body a prime piece of symbolic real estate. Even as she fulfils the terms of her contract, however, Monroe tests the boundaries of the heterosexual economy within which we understand her. Laura Mulvey speculates that in her later films – including *Some Like It Hot* – Monroe 'was beginning to perform the showgirl dilemma', to the extent that she 'might have produced a "theoretical" reflection on the lived nature of "to-be-looked-at-ness"' (2017: 208). A skilled comedy actor whose shtick is all about femininity, she exposes the comic impossibility of the sex/gender system. Placing Monroe alongside Curtis and Lemmon, her 'drag' appears even more skilled as it throws all authenticity into question. When he first sees Sugar sashaying along the railway platform, Lemmon/ Daphne asks: 'How do they do that? [. . .] It's a whole different sex!', confirming that sex/gender is not something that you are but something that you *do*.

Women in comedy on screen have more at stake than men because comedy roles are not marked out as traditional for woman. In *Some Like It Hot* Monroe is framed by the central romantic narrative in an attempt to secure her performance within normative heterofemininity. Lemmon as Jerry/Daphne is the most unruly figure regarding gender because his performance disturbs the terms of hegemonic masculinity. If men in drag are funny, they are not supposed to become so rapidly naturalised. Jerry as Daphne is too large and too masculine to be safely framed as feminine yet his rapid accretion of stereotypically 'feminine' desires as the gold-digging fiancé of Osgood Fielding III places him within a genealogy of Hollywood women in comedy, character actors who have traditionally played the sidekick from Eve Arden to Joan Cusack (Roof 2002). Women in comedy roles in classical Hollywood are out of step with *proper* femininity.

That sideways account of heterofemininity is what makes women in comedy so interesting. If identity is performative, and culture is a process through which we make and remake our identities, then comedy performance harbours the potential to make that process visible by affording a moment when the curtain falls back and the wobbling scenery is revealed. Comedy performance exposes the citationality of gender acts, allowing a misperformance of gender and making it *funny*:

> The loss of the sense of 'the normal' [...] can be its own occasion for laughter, especially when 'the normal', 'the original' is revealed to be a copy, and an inevitably failed one, an ideal that no one *can* embody. In this sense, laughter emerges in the realization that all along the original was derived (Butler 1990: 138–9)

Comedy performances may thus make heterofemininity visible through a range of techniques: by *over*performing and revealing the masquerade of hegemonic femininity; by deploying physical comedy to transgress and expose the limits of heteronormative behaviour; by juxtaposing 'appropriate' and 'inappropriate' femininities; and by performing the female body as excessive, ageing – *différant*. Many of these techniques are embedded in traditions of theatrical, cinematic and television performance, yet to have a female actor deploying such skills remains an exceptional act rather than a gesture which confirms tradition. Standard comedic tropes such as direct address to the camera – the conspiratorial look, the raised eyebrow – have been widely used by male comedy performers such as Charlie Chaplin and Eric Morecambe but are less often deployed by women on screen. As with the voiceovers of classic film noir, women in comedy are rarely given the authority of a narrative point of view, either as central protagonists delivering the final punchline or through direct address to camera. Some recent British sitcoms, such as *Miranda* (BBC 2009–15), *Chewing Gum* (Channel 4 2015–) and the critically acclaimed *Fleabag* (BBC 2016–), deliberately buck this trend. Female comedy protagonists are thus 'unruly women' and that unruliness opens a window onto the construction sites of femininity (Rowe 1995).

Television comedy situates such misperformances of gender within a more domesticated arena. What happens when such acts are framed by the small screen in a 30-minute show rather than sustained for over an hour in the cinema? The economics of the medium are clearly different: television is a cheaper form than film-making. The cultural costs of performance are, however, very similar. Women in television comedy are often queered, their gender and sexuality thrown into question. They are rarely seen as 'sexy', unless they are providing the background for a male comedian's joke, as with Benny Hill and his legion of unnamed, generic

'Hill's Angels' (Gray 1994: 21–2). Sarel Eimerl, writing for *Mademoiselle* in 1962, followed a long tradition of regarding women in comedy as 'at best, unglamorous; at worst, fairly gruesome [...] or generally ugly' (cited in Martin and Seagrave 1986: 17). Such debate continues into the twenty-first century. Linda Mizejewski begins her 2014 book *Pretty/Funny: Women Comedians and Body Politics* with an account of Christopher Hitchens's infamous *Vanity Fair* essay, 'Why women aren't funny' (2007). Hitchens's opinion piece provoked a range of responses in the popular press at the time and the essay continues to reverberate online (Lang 2017; Zarum 2017). In the April 2008 issue of the same magazine, Alessandra Stanley responded to Hitchens's essay by profiling a number of contemporary 'Queens of Comedy', including Kristen Weig, Maya Rudolph and Tina Fey, yet the feature perversely served to repeat anxieties about the sexual appeal of funny women (White 2010). Back in 1962 Eimerl concluded her article in an unequivocal manner, deciding that 'real' women were simply not funny or, if tempted to be witty, cannily repressed their skills: 'Those who didn't [...] would lose out with men and would be labelled "odd women"' (cited in Martin and Seagrave 1986: 19).

This book is about the oddness of women who do not repress their skill and wit in order to conform to heterofemininity but rather deploy it to expose the contradictions and limitations of normative gender identities. Within twentieth- and twenty-first-century Western capitalism, television comedy is one space in which female performers may trouble the boundaries of normative heterofemininity by indicating the cost of discourses of 'choice'. This is particularly important at a moment when choice is a key constituent of neoliberal Western identity: 'norms associated with traditional femininity operate to cordon off particular choices which threaten the coherence of its boundaries including choosing to be a lesbian, childless, single or a feminist' (Budgeon 2011: 286–7). Making the 'wrong' choice in these times is difficult and even dangerous.

Queering Femininities

Steve Neale and Frank Krutnik cite Elder Olson's *The Theory of Comedy* (1968) during their exploration of the dynamics of humour in popular film and television:

For Olson, 'the basis of the ridiculous and the ludicrous [...] is the unlike'. All instances of the comic involve a departure from a norm, whether the norm be one of action, appropriate behaviour, conventional dress, or stereotypical features. However, the unlike must be tempered by the like, for as 'we approach the wholly unlike, we approach the monstrous, and the monstrous is never ridiculous'. There must in other words be a degree of normality in the abnormal, a degree of the appropriate in the inappropriate, a degree of the logical in the illogical, and a degree of sense in the otherwise nonsensical (1990: 67)

This definition proposes comedy as intimately concerned with normative behaviours, dress, features and so on, but also notes how comedy plays upon the thin tissue separating 'normal' and 'abnormal'. Although Neale and Krutnik are not specifically discussing femininity, it haunts this passage. Femininity is often constituted as 'monstrous' (Russo 1986; Creed 1993), as other to a perceived norm, and thus by extension femininity cannot be funny. This odd logic produces stereotypes such as the deviant, monstrous and humourless feminist. Yet there is a long genealogy of women on stage and screen who have made careers in comedy, and several encyclopaedic studies map that history (Martin and Seagrave 1986; Banks and Swift 1987; Unterbrink 1987; Silverman 1999; Spangler 2003). What about them? Funny women complicate the dynamic mapped by Neale and Krutnik because for the female comedy performer the monstrous is ever-present. Being funny is dangerous for women precisely because it positions them as 'abnormal', 'inappropriate', 'illogical' and 'nonsensical'. Mary Russo remarks on the dangers of 'making a spectacle of oneself' as 'specifically feminine' (1986: 213) and proposes that for a woman to be 'other' or 'deviant' is to transgress the borders of heterofemininity. For women, then, being funny ha-ha also entails being funny *peculiar*.

This dangerous position challenges the invisibility of gender norms: 'A norm is not the same as a rule, and it is not the same as a law. A norm operates within social practice as the implicit standard of *normalization*' (Butler 2004: 41). The implicit quality of gender norms is a substantial aspect of their power. They are naturalized and invisible, managing and guiding social performances and our understanding of those performances

INTRODUCTION 13

as always only either 'masculine' or 'feminine'. Gender norms present themselves as outside history, as incalculably linked to biological or cultural eternities, as *just how it is*:

> If gender is a norm, it is not the same as a model that individuals seek to approximate. On the contrary, it is a form of social power that produces the intelligible field of subjects, and an apparatus by which the gender binary is instituted. As a norm that appears independent of the practices that it governs, its ideality is the reinstituted effect of those very practices. This suggests not only that the relation between practices and the idealizations under which they work is contingent, but that the very idealization can be brought into question and crisis, potentially undergoing deidealization and divestiture (Butler 2004: 48)

Can television comedy work to bring gender norms 'into question and crisis'? Might comedy expose the ways in which we invest in gender identities? Could it work to undermine the ways in which femininity is performed, idealised and made intelligible?

'Funny peculiar' is the title of this introduction, so as a means of expanding on my understanding and usage of the term 'queer' I would like to explain what I understand by 'funny peculiar'. When I was growing up, if you said that someone was 'funny' you might be asked if you meant that they were *either* 'funny peculiar' *or* 'funny ha-ha'. This meant defining someone as either odd/weird/queer or a laugh a minute. Such a binary understanding of 'funny' is, like most of the other binaries upon which our mediatised culture relies, flawed. For something to be 'funny ha-ha' it often addresses the oddness that passes as normal. In stand-up comedy this is one way in which observational humour works, by pointing out surreal or ridiculous aspects of the everyday. The shows and performers I address in this volume veer toward 'funny peculiar' as a way of being 'funny ha-ha'. Funny peculiar is thus one way of understanding funny women: that they are always already odd, other and out of step with the fiction of hegemonic femininity.

My usage of 'queer' thus falls in line with Alexander Doty's definition of queer as 'a quality related to any expression that can be marked as contra-, non-, or anti-straight' (1993: xv). As Butler asserts above, heteronormativity is something of a fiction, a dominant trope that proves remarkably elusive when you try to pin it down. The essence of 'straight' is hard to find, despite its social and political hegemony, just as hegemonic femininity and masculinity are ultimately elusive. Yet we still tacitly understand what constitutes the kind of femininity that is *not* coded as peculiar, odd or queer. Even in academic feminist writing the subject of hegemonic femininity has proved elusive:

> There has been, to our knowledge, no investigation of 'hegemonic femininity', yet a wealth of writing about 'hegemonic masculinity'. What new questions [...] might the notion of femininities allow us to ask? What new insights or possibilities might it open up? (Gill and Scharff 2011: 2)

In their examination of postfeminism, Rosalind Gill and Christina Scharff propose that 'a postfeminist sensibility includes the notion that femininity is increasingly figured as a bodily property', for a body that is self-regulating, self-contained and sexualised primarily in terms of its capital within consumer culture (2011: 4). This volume builds upon existing work on women and television comedy but also registers the potential for television comedy to expose hegemonic femininity, both before second-wave feminism and within a postfeminist landscape. Female comedy performers in contemporary television, as in early cinema or in burlesque and vaudeville theatres, tend not to conform to the physical imperatives of heterofemininity to be small, slim, still and sexy, to not take up too much space, to not make too much noise and to not desire too little, too much or the 'wrong' object. Instead they deploy their appearance, through size, costume and make-up, and their verbal and physical skills, through clowning, to perform a femininity that is transgressive, queered, unruly.

Some of the debate around the usage of 'queer', politically and academically, is about its potential elision of lived LGBTQ experience (Jagose 1996: 3). It is important to be suspicious of any term that claims to be all things to all people, but for the purposes of this study 'queer' is mobilised as a means of understanding the gender trouble that women and television comedy can evoke. Doty's definition of queer as 'a quality related to any expression that can be marked as contra-, non-, or anti-straight' (1993: xv) appears to set up a broad binary – that queer is most definitely *not* about heterosexuality. His subsequent desire to 'construct "queer" as something other than "lesbian", "gay", or "bisexual"; but I can't say that "lesbian", "gay" or "bisexual" *aren't* also "queer"' (1993: xvii) makes evident the manner in which queer debate offers a means of discussing gender and sexuality that acknowledges the slipperiness of those categories. British and American television comedy is predominantly heteronormative, but often addresses the peculiarities of heterosexual identities, inadvertently defamiliarising the 'norm'. In this sense television comedy echoes Judith Butler's account of queer theory as engaged in exposing determinist understandings of the sex/gender system:

> The dissonance between gender and sexuality is thus affirmed from two different perspectives; the one seeks to show possibilities for sexuality that are not constrained by gender in order to break the causal reductiveness of arguments that bind them; the other seeks to show possibilities for gender that are not predetermined by forms of hegemonic heterosexuality (2004: 54)

The shows addressed in this volume are offered as examples of that 'dissonance': they address and expose the fiction of heteronormative identities, even gesturing toward possibilities beyond hegemonic gender roles. This underpins my argument that television comedy can offer a space in which women may move beyond the normative bounds of heterofemininity. In comedy women often speak too much or too loudly, deploying verbal wit. Roseanne Arnold and Hylda Baker are notable examples from both sides of the Atlantic, each deploying not only the shock of a raucous female voice but also the accents of working-class women (Rowe 1995: 63–4; Medhurst 2007: 77–82). These are queer characteristics in relation to hegemonic white middle-class norms, which require women to be silent or softly spoken. As Lear says of Cordelia: 'Her voice was ever soft, / Gentle and low – an excellent thing in woman'. Cordelia, the faithful daughter, is an 'excellent' woman only in the past tense, when she is silenced by death and presented as a tragic addendum to her father. Such imperatives remain current in contemporary media. Anne Karpf's work on women and radio notes the exclusion of women's voices from key broadcast roles, and the tendency for women newsreaders to employ a lower tone of voice in order to be heard as authoritative (Karpf 2013).

Women are often more physically mobile in comedy than in traditionally feminine genres, such as melodrama or romance. From Lucille Ball to Michelle Gomez, women in television comedy have employed vaudeville and clowning techniques to wrestle hegemonic femininity into the spotlight and expose its ridiculous limits. Women on screen, as in middle-class society, tend to be physically continent, trained not to take up too much space. In contemporary parlance, we have manspreading but not womanspreading. Movement on screen (as in sport or social arenas) involves women visibly occupying space and potentially becoming the protagonist rather than a 'to-be-looked-at' object (Mulvey 1989). Laura Mulvey's classic essay addresses the static female stars of classical Hollywood, framed by the 'male gaze', but women in comedy have tended to be physically *in*continent, disrupting their environment. An early comic film, directed and produced by its star, Florence Turner, exemplifies this tradition. In *Daisy Doodad's Dial* (1914) Turner plays the title character, who competes with her husband for prizes in face-pulling competitions. When she practises pulling faces in a train carriage on the way to a competition, Daisy is arrested for disturbing the peace; even the police are shocked by her faces. Bailed out of jail by her husband, she dreams about her grotesque faces and in the final sequence her distorted visage fills the frame. That comic legacy may be seen in Lucille Ball's prodigious gurning on the *Lucy* shows, where skilled clowning deliberately unpicks her Hollywood celebrity.

Queering Comedy

Alexander Doty begins his analysis of George Cukor's *The Women* (1939) by writing about the queer pleasures of mass culture: 'the queerness of comedy consists of far more than humorous representations of queerness. Let's face it, as a genre comedy is fundamentally queer since it encourages rule-breaking, risk-taking, inversions and perversions in the face of straight patriarchal norms' (2000: 81). Doty proposes that comedy defies closure and thus offers a slippery, queered account of the status quo: 'the fact remains that queerness is the source of many comic pleasures for audiences of all sexual identities' (2000: 81). This volume follows Doty's proposal, viewing the 'fundamental queerness' of television comedy as a space in which binary accounts of gender may be examined, deconstructed and challenged. This is not to propose that comedy is a politically radical genre, or that television comedy offers a radically subversive medium, but rather that the 'rule-breaking, risk-taking inversions and perversions' at the heart of much comic performance can disturb the ground upon which our understandings of gender rest.

In a similar vein to Doty, Steve Neale and Frank Krutnik note the ambiguity of stereotypes in comic narratives, proposing that characters must be recognisable but also 'other' to perceived norms, and that comedy relies on the transgression of such norms to produce laughter:

> comedy necessarily trades upon the surprising, the improper, the unlikely, and the transgressive in order to make us laugh; it plays on deviations both from socio-cultural norms, and from the rules that govern other genres and aesthetic regimes. In the case of comedy, therefore, generic conventions demand both social and aesthetic indecorum (1990: 3)

For much of its history, British and American television comedy has relied upon stereotypes even as it might be seen to expose and thus undermine them. Much early work on television comedy was preoccupied with establishing whether sitcom, in particular, could be understood as a transgressive or conservative format (Grote 1983; Feuer 1986; Marc 1989). Yet this approach, itself rooted in a binary model of progressive/reactionary, good/bad, sidesteps more interesting questions about what happens when television comedy addresses gender and sexuality. In the BFI dossier on *Television Sitcom*, Andy Medhurst and Lucy Tuck note British sitcom's obsession with sex and gender roles, arguing that 'Sitcom cannot function without stereotypes' (1982: 43). They also observe, however, the double bluff of camp stereotyping: 'The merciless ridicule that the idea of feminine men has been subjected to shows how threatening such an idea has been to the prevailing sexual ideology and must make us wary of dismissing those types out of hand' (1982: 50). Retrograde stereotypes of LGBTQ identities are thus understood not only as politically problematic but also as indicating how mainstream popular culture attempts to deal with difference by simultaneously acknowledging its existence and attempting to deny its power. In Foucauldian terms this is a discursive strategy which creates a visible and coherent identity even as it attempts to control it.

Television comedy is one popular form with the potential to destabilise binary accounts of gender and thus to queer heterofemininity, to throw it into question. More specifically the queer analysis which this book pursues is based on the understanding of 'Queer [...] as a deconstructive practice that is not undertaken by an already constituted subject, and does not, in turn, furnish the subject with a nameable identity' (Sullivan 2003: 50). Queer is thus invoked not as a noun but as a verb which does not call upon a stable identity or destination (for sexuality or for gender) but is rather a practice and a process – *queering*. The indeterminacy of television comedy performance and its effects is part of its queer practice and potential. Comedy is not secure in its effects: what seems funny to one person may appear offensive, incomprehensible or just not funny to another. It appears almost too logical to address gender and sexual identities in television comedy through a queered lens, where the traditions of that comedy work to destabilise and unsettle our understanding of those categories even as we laugh at them. 'The merciless ridicule [...] of feminine men' (Medhurst and Tuck 1982: 50), of masculine women and of eccentric individuals of any gender is an aspect of television comedy that merits further attention and debate, not least for its role in policing social conventions regarding gender. The television comedy stereotype of the camp man – the performances of Frankie Howerd, Larry Grayson and John Inman on British television in the 1960s and 1970s, for example – are potentially homophobic in their reiterations of homosexuality as effeminate, but also constitute *visibility*. Andy Medhurst maps the contradictory tradition of English 'effeminate queens', noting that in the 1970s, when LGBTQ politics were in their infancy, figures such as Howerd and Inman were regarded as 'reactionary and damaging', yet they may also be understood as 'an index of defiance, an embodiment of survival, and a fabulous refusal to conform and behave – proof that poofs endure' (2007: 87–8).

At the same time, producing queered readings of television comedy does not render popular culture a utopian space in which we are 'free' to play any role. As an overtly 'playful' form it offers no certainties for academic critique. There is no finitely correct reading of a comedic performance, because comedy is constantly on the move, inviting contradictory responses from critics and audiences. Yet television comedy appears compelled to address complex issues of identity such as class, sexuality, race and gender. In her examination of social class in *Little Britain* (BBC 2003–6), Sharon Lockyer observes that characters such as Vicky Pollard may be read as both a celebration of the 'unruly woman' and 'an extension of chav vilification' (2010a: 108). Close analysis of viewers' responses confirms that the effect of comedy is always a contested field. Sally Shaw's work on audience responses to *Love Thy Neighbour* (ITV 1972–6), a sitcom about a white couple's response to their black neighbours, uncovered a 'complicated and ultimately unresolved dialogue between audiences and institution [which] has much to tell us about cultural responses to the challenging racial landscape of 1970s Britain as mediated through a popular text' (2012: 75–6).

Comedy is a lightning rod for contemporary concerns, fears and debates, and thus an ideal place to examine hegemonic femininity in British and American popular culture. Feminism itself is now part of that contradictory cultural field, so much so that arguably 'most feminism in the West now happens in the media, and for the majority of people their experience of feminism is an entirely mediated one' (Gill 2007: 40). The mediated feminism that appears on our small screens is part of the queered femininity that comedy continues to produce. What could be queerer than a feminist on popular television? Although television comedy may not be politically feminist, it has the potential, through its queer accounts of gender, to make visible the performance of heterofemininity, to make evident the peculiar labour that performance entails, as well as its limits and gaps.

Despite the attention paid to television comedy since the early excursions of academic critique in the 1970s, it has often been the poor cousin to more 'legitimate' objects of analysis such as realist drama, quality television and news programming (Marc 1989: 13; Gray 1994: 19). Nevertheless a canon of work on comedy television has emerged, as has a subsidiary body of material on gender and television comedy. This latter material has tended to focus on femininity, as gender is still understood as referring primarily to the subordinate 'other'. Much of the critical work on gender and television comedy thus comes from a feminist perspective specifically informed by 50 years of theory and praxis since the 'second wave'. This book examines some moments in that longstanding discussion, asking questions about how gender *works* in television comedy by examining how femininity is constituted, dealt with and sometimes unpicked in this medium. Television comedy, with its roots in theatre, music hall and vaudeville, represents a continuing, anxious debate about how gender can be, should be and could be performed and understood.

Queering Television

Can television itself be understood as a queer medium? In her contribution to *High Theory/Low Culture*, Tania Modleski posits mass culture as 'feminised' through its association with consumption (1986: 39), while in the same volume Laura Mulvey notes how 'Television revolutionized the conditions of spectatorship associated with mass entertainment' (1986: 80), transforming the cinema audience into domestic consumers. Television is thus situated as a domestic object providing consumable pleasures for the female viewer *and* as a mass medium for producing images and narratives, shaping heterofemininity. Television has 'always had its eye on women' (Spigel and Mann 1992: vii). Patrice Petro takes the feminisation of television a step further, proposing that the 'place' of television studies with regard to the older, more established field of film studies, is similarly gendered (1986). More recent work continues to situate television studies as marginal even in relation to newer fields such as celebrity studies (Bennett and Holmes 2010). Popular television is thus 'feminized' as a consumer product, as a medium and as an academic subject. It is identified with the subordinate category of femininity within the patriarchal landscape of popular media:

> Television embodies contradictions – rather than the 'either/or' logic, one of 'both/and', an *inclusive* logic of creation/cancellation in which mimicry and simulation are stolid cornerstones rather than lofty embellishments. [...] A model of difficult inclusion, unlike the exclusionary tactics of binarisms and irrevocable differences, is promising (Mellencamp 1992: 5)

Television's subaltern position may thus be regarded as its queerly productive advantage, offering the difficulties of contradiction rather than the certainty of binary absolutes. Its programme formats are multiple and open-ended, making television 'a heterogeneous medium, never one thing or another, but rather a patchwork of different forms and genres' (Wheatley 2016: 12). This patchwork of formats, styles and genres affords television a queered vocabulary with space for more various pleasures and more varieties of identification. The chapters which follow range across such pleasures and identifications, examining women – and men – in television comedy who play upon those productive contradictions.

The volume is divided into two sections, addressing television comedy in the United States and Britain as distinct but related traditions. Chapter 1 reviews key female performers in early American television comedy: Gracie Allen, Martha Raye, Eve Arden and Lucille Ball. Television formats such as sitcom were being established in the early 1950s but were not securely framed, still emerging from theatrical variety shows and radio comedies. How did these women's early work in the new medium of television comedy examine and satirise what Betty Friedan would later call 'the feminine mystique'? Lynn Spigel's foundational work on women and television in the 1950s notes how the 'layered realism' of early sitcom offers a commentary on the fantasy of postwar white middle-class domesticity (1992b: 159). This chapter is also in part a literature review, returning to early critical work, such as that of Theodor Adorno and David Marc, as well as discussing writing which addresses the queer potential of women in comedy, such as that by Patricia Mellencamp, Alexander Doty and Judith Roof. Although American television comedy was toned down and tidied up as the 1950s ended, early seasons of sitcoms such as *The Burns and Allen Show* and *I Love Lucy* retain the messy indeterminacy that Mellencamp describes above, thus lending itself to queer interpretation.

Chapter 2 brings the discussion of women in American sitcom up to date with *30 Rock* (NBC 2006–13) and *Parks and Recreation* (NBC 2009–15). These shows are exceptional because they feature female stars who are also showrunners. Tina Fey and Amy Poehler are part of a new generation of women working in popular television: female performers who write and produce their own shows. Fey's and Poehler's work is emblematic of what appears to be a postfeminist moment in American comedy, where one could imagine that gender equality is already achieved. As these comedies demonstrate, however, inequities remain. Just as Chapter 1 discusses 1950s femininity before the second wave, so this chapter engages in contemporary debate about postfeminism and popular culture, addressing complex intersectional identities that have become increasingly visible in the twenty-first century. *30 Rock* and *Parks and Recreation* build their comedy around privileged white women who struggle to cope with the demands of their professions and their own desires. The queered communities which feature in *30 Rock* and *Parks and Recreation* trouble any simple happy ending, so that these comedies expose the exigencies of women working in corporate culture or in public office. Such comedies ask what constitutes success in postfeminist popular culture and at what cost it is achieved.

Chapter 3 continues to examine the cost of success by discussing the gender politics at work in *The Big Bang Theory* (CBS 2007–), one of the most popular contemporary sitcoms on television. Although this show initially represented a range of queered masculinities through its four leading male characters, that dynamic has been unpicked. Leonard, Howard, Sheldon and Raj have gradually been ushered toward more heteronormative identities. Ethnic stereotypes such as the Jewish mother or the feminised Oriental are deployed within the show, so that the ostensibly liberal politics which the sitcom promotes become cover stories for more traditional accounts of gender and identity. *The Big Bang Theory*'s female characters have been quietly drafted into misogynist stereotypes: the ditsy blonde, the nagging wife, the sexually voracious spinster. The political potential of queering masculinity is thus confounded in *The Big Bang Theory*, its characters fitted into stereotypical frames. The *costs* of heterosexual hegemony are apparent in *The Big Bang Theory*, while enormous profit has been made from the syndication and distribution of this long-running hit sitcom across an international market.

In the second section of the book, Chapter 4 moves across the Atlantic to examine a British millennial sketch show, *Smack the Pony* (Channel 4, 1999–2003). *Smack the Pony* deploys sketch comedy to interrogate heterofemininity at the height of postfeminist popular culture. The queer temporality of the sketch format, together with the show's scrutiny of feminine behaviours and desires, affords a space for women's voices and a deliberately indefinable silliness. Several of the sketches in *Smack the Pony* offer monstrous depictions of femininity which draw attention to heterosexual hegemony, thus queering gender by doing violence to 'proper' versions of it. Other sketches employ surreal and camp modes of performance which gesture toward a utopian elsewhere, produced through comic stunts and playful interventions. Many of these performances speak to and of a feminist anger regarding the postfeminist focus on women's bodies, executed with professional skill and an evident delight in transgressing such control.

Chapter 5 turns to British sitcom, examining how representations of age and ageing can be understood as queering gender. *You're Only Young Twice* (Yorkshire Television 1977–81) and *Waiting for God* (BBC 1990–4) are set in private retirement homes and feature communities of older women and men. The cast of *You're Only Young Twice* is almost entirely female; a timely platform for a generation of female character actors. This comedy, which seems entirely conventional and inoffensive, is paradoxically infused with a camp sensibility that indicates the radical potential of communities beyond the nuclear family. *Waiting for God* stars the British comedy actors Stephanie Cole, as Diana Trent, and Graham Crowden, as Tom Ballard, in a sitcom which follows a narrative of late-life romance. Although this trajectory might appear to accede to a heteronormative model, that structuring narrative is repeatedly confounded. Diana and Tom engage in a battle of wits with the neoliberal manager of their retirement home, intervening in debates about how the elderly should behave. This series directly engages with different discourses of ageing, indicating that 'waiting' is not the best strategy. Having examined these two sitcoms from the late '70s/early '80s and the early '90s, the chapter concludes with a brief examination of a more recent sitcom about life in late life. Jo Brand's *Going Forward* (BBC 2016), a sequel to *Getting On* (BBC 2009–12), is a far less hopeful vision of getting old. Here there is no retirement community but rather older people marooned in their own homes, anxiously waiting for a hurried visit from Buccaneer 2000 carer Kim Wilde (Brand). This is care at its most minimal level and, despite Wilde's best attempts, her frail and elderly 'clients' are lonely, isolated and disenfranchised. *Going Forward*, which Brand co-wrote with Geoff Atkinson, offers a searing critique of discourses of 'successful ageing' in neoliberal times.

My examination of television thus tracks an eccentric course through American and British television comedy from the mid twentieth century into the twenty-first. The first three chapters investigate the history of American sitcom, together with some of its most successful recent iterations, in order to unpick the heterosexual hegemony it is often seen to represent. The fourth chapter examines the queer potential of television sketch comedy, as a format which can expose and examine the exigencies of heterofemininity. Finally, Chapter 5 examines two British sitcoms about elderly communities which demonstrate how ageing can queer heteronormative identities. This is not a historical overview and nor is it meant to be. My choice of subject has been driven by pleasure and curiosity: like Alice I have found the process of studying television comedy curiouser and curiouser. As with any object of academic scrutiny, the more television comedy is examined the stranger it appears. This is an investigation into the queer times and places of television comedy and gender, questioning the borders and hinterlands of hegemonic identities.

CHAPTER 1

GRACIE, MARTHA, EVE AND LUCY: QUEERING FEMININITY IN EARLY AMERICAN TELEVISION COMEDY

This chapter is in part a literature survey, retracing formative work on American television comedy and gender to examine how aspects of this emerging format queer heterofemininity. Gracie Allen, Martha Raye, Eve Arden and Lucille Ball are key figures in the development of television comedy performance whose work has been closely examined and critically mapped. Such performances chart the strategies and traditions that inform early American television comedy and its queered representations of gender. Lucille Ball, in particular, is an exceptional figure. Her performance in *I Love Lucy* (CBS 1951–7), *The Lucille Ball Show* (CBS 1957–60), *The Lucy Show* (CBS 1962–8) and *Here's Lucy* (CBS 1968–74) embodies a contradictory account of femininity. If Lucy was an aspiring but unsuccessful klutz, Lucille Ball was a star performer and producer. Ball established a production company with her then husband and co-star, Desi Arnaz, in order to produce the first season of *I Love Lucy*, becoming a powerful player in Hollywood while playing a lovable failure on the small screen (Landay 2010). This chapter examines women in television comedy in the light of such contradictions. Even where female performers are not in control of the production process, the characters they portray are often wildly at odds with their professional careers. Many female comedy performers act out failure even as they succeed in their field, and thus embody some of the contradictions inherent in white Western heterofemininity.

Queering Space and Time in 1950s American Sitcom: *The Burns and Allan Show* (CBS 1950–8)

In *In a Queer Time and Place* Judith Halberstam proposes that 'Queer uses of time and space develop, at least in part, in opposition to the institutions of family, heterosexuality, and reproduction' (2005: 1). Halberstam's work deconstructs heterosexual hegemony, deploying popular examples to examine queer alternatives that expose the peculiarity of perceived norms. Her work investigates 'strange temporalities, imaginative life schedules, and eccentric economic practices', with examples drawn from 'subcultural practices, alternative methods of alliance, forms of transgender embodiment, and those forms of representation dedicated to capturing these wilfully eccentric modes of being' (2005: 1). This does not appear to lend itself to sitcom, often regarded as one of the most limited, conservative and unimaginative television formats (Mills 2009). In its early years, however, American sitcom was an uneasy creature. Restless, uncertain and willing to experiment with form, early sitcom offers a remarkable vision of queered domesticity, eccentric women and nervously camp men. In the early 1950s, television comedy was a queer place and time, as sitcom exceeded the limits of the studio set and attempted to situate raucous variety performances within a domestic narrative.

Situation comedy on American network television in the late 1940s frequently replicated shows which had proved successful in radio. *Mary Kay and Johnny* (Dumont, NBC and CBS, 1947–50), widely cited as the first television sitcom, was adapted from radio and led the way (Marc 1989: 50; Morreale 2003b: 1). *The Burns and Allen Show*, one of the most successful sitcoms of its era, made the move from radio to television in 1950, building upon George Burns and Gracie Allen's prior success as a husband and wife act in vaudeville (Mellencamp 1992: 315–16). The half-hour television show drew upon the theatrical comedy variety show, a format which had been established on radio, and was recorded in front of a live audience (Spigel 1992b: 136–80). Early sitcom thus offers an interstitial moment between the theatrical spaces of vaudeville and the incorporated technologies of radio and television. As television sitcom became established during the 1950s it inherited traditions from vaudeville and variety shows that worked to queer gender, class and ethnicity on the small screen.

Lynn Spigel charts the development of the format, arguing that its uneasy combination of vaudeville traditions and 'realist' narrative opened a window onto the heterosexual pairings that it depicted: 'Torn as it was between theatricality and naturalism, the family comedy seemed unable to resist reflecting back on the paradox of its own form' (1992b: 159). This reflexivity may be one feature of television comedy that made such shows particularly appealing to a female audience. A 1953 *Television Magazine* survey of 'The audience – a profile of TV owners, their habits and preferences' found that 'the highest number of women before the TV receiver is earned by comedy variety shows, with quiz-audience participation, drama and musical variety close behind' (Mann 1992: 65). As the 1950s rolled on, however, early sitcoms which dealt with urban working-class ethnicities were replaced by comedies based in the white middle-class suburbs: the 'WASP-com' (Marc 1989: 54). *I Love Lucy* bridged the urban-to-suburban and ethnic-to-WASP movement of American sitcom across the schedules (Morreale 2003b: 4). The early seasons of *I Love Lucy* represent a compromise between vaudeville or 'vaudeo' (Murray 2002: 103) television variety shows such as *The Colgate Comedy Hour* (NBC 1950–5) and the emergent genre of television sitcom, which it helped to establish as a visual and narrative form (Landay 2010: 23–35). *I Love Lucy* thus occupied an interstitial space in early American television, at a moment when styles and formats were being established. It was a show that referenced vaudeville and the queer spaces that tradition afforded its subjects (White 2016).

I Love Lucy did not emerge from a vacuum, however; the vocabulary of vaudeville was evident across television comedy. Watching *The Burns and Allen Show* or *The Martha Raye Show* (NBC 1953–6) in the twenty-first century, one is struck by their fluidity. These programmes move swiftly between variety acts featuring a dance troupe or an impressionist and a recognisable sitcom narrative. During its first two years *The Burns and Allen Show* framed its stars within that vaudeville tradition. Each episode begins and ends in front of a theatrical curtain in a live television broadcast which replicates Burns and Allen's stage work (Unterbrink 1987: 55; McCracken 2002: 57). George Burns has three roles within the show: he is the extradiegetic narrator, a character within the sitcom and an old stager, introducing and interacting with variety acts that interrupt the domestic narrative. As 'George', Burns performs the character role established in the couple's vaudeville, film and radio work, reiterating that history in the pilot episode of *The Burns and Allen Show*:

> Burns and Allen funnelled their 1926 marriage, vaudeville, radio, and film routines and characters/stars into an upper-middle-class situation comedy format and style – a historical agglutination suggesting that what is monolithically termed popular culture is a process: a collection of discourses, scenes, or turns recycled from various media and contextualized within historical moments. (Mellencamp 1992: 316)

That 'historical agglutination' is clearly evident on screen. Many contemporary viewers would have known Burns and Allen from their previous work and *The Burns and Allen Show* references that history, while demonstrating the different aesthetic potential of television. In contemporary terms this could be seen as post-modern bricolage *avant la lettre* – Burns's improvisations, in particular, are a means of accounting for mistakes within a live broadcast show – but these 'agglutinations' and mistakes are also moments of possibility within a heavily regulated medium which allow for other, queerer times and spaces to emerge. At this interstitial moment in television comedy we catch a glimpse of 'wilfully eccentric modes of being' (Halberstam 2005: 1).

This is evident in the pilot episode. Following the opening titles George emerges from the side of a theatrical stage, with a curtain and proscenium arch. He introduces himself as 'Gracie Allen's husband' and proceeds to describe the dynamic of their act, with his role as 'the straight man', famous for his pauses, reactions and repetitions, which he demonstrates. This opening sequence not only breaks the fourth wall, it also unravels the professional skill of vaudevillian comedy, revealing the mechanics of the straight man within a double act – although as Patricia Mellencamp notes, 'George [...] was never *just* a straight man' (1992: 321). This sequence also establishes George as narrator of the onset action which frequently interrupts a story he is about to tell. The transitions between George's to-camera stand-up monologue, the variety acts and the sitcom narrative expose the workings of television as a modern medium. *The Burns and Allen Show* constantly references the artificial geographies which separate audience and performer, set and studio, diegetic and extradiegetic narrative. From the outset this is a comedy about television, performance and domestic space.

Finally the curtain sweeps open to reveal George and Gracie's home. Burns's voice-over narration takes us on a tour of 'the outside' and 'the inside', ironically noting the lack of distinction between the two as the set moves to accommodate the camera and actors. The studio audience and viewers at home are taken through the house as if we are neighbours meeting a couple newly arrived in the neighbourhood. The sequence ends outside a large window at the front of the property which is opened by Gracie Allen. She is framed by the proscenium that George was leaning against, but also by the enormous window, underlined by a hedge in a window box which Burns says she has planted herself. This combination of suburban idyll and theatrical staging hyperbolises the domestic home, making it strange. After opening the window, Allen pauses to acknowledge applause from the studio audience before producing a man's electric razor and efficiently trimming the top of the hedge, to much laughter from the audience (Figure 1.1).

Burns pauses to let the laughter ease before saying 'That's my Gracie. [pause] That's my razor too.' This sequence is an example of the exquisite

Figure 1.1 Gracie Allen trims the hedge with George's electric razor (*The Burns and Allen Show*, pilot episode, McCadden Productions/Screen Gems 1950–8).

comic timing that Allen and Burns brought to television from their years of stage experience. Gracie's appropriation and misuse of domestic goods – in this case George's razor – signal that this comedy has scant regard for the conventions of heteronormative time and place. Throughout its run *The Burns and Allen Show* will offer 'strange temporalities, imaginative life schedules, and eccentric economic practices' (Halberstam 2005: 1). The domestic idyll is clearly artificial. The comic pauses that Burns and Allen deploy do not just allow for the laughter but also mark the space between what is happening on screen and what is happening in viewers' homes. While the domestic sitcom purports to mirror the suburban idyll of middle America, this is a distorted reflection and, as such, a commentary which disturbs the 'taken-for-granted heterosexuality' of the home (Browne 2009: 42).

Critical work on *The Burns and Allen Show* has noted its overtly artificial account of suburban domesticity. Alison McCracken argues that the show's use of space is a commentary upon contemporary discourses of the housewife at a time when women's roles within the white middle class were under intense scrutiny:

> Only George could escape the diegesis, going beyond that curtain directly to address the audience. Gracie was thus confined within the boundaries of the stage set, like a madwoman in a cage. As audience members, we are invited by her husband George to observe her through the windows he provides for us. He both protects her and exhibits her, thus demonstrating traditional middle-class gender roles (wives are to be protected and displayed), but also directly linking this kind of marriage display with the freak show. (2002: 57)

The freakish display of Gracie, together with the show's reflexive commentary on the *business* through which it reproduces a vision of the domestic couple, makes for a queered account of heteronormativity in a decade when sexuality and gender were anxiously policed. As McCracken notes, *The Burns and Allen Show* constantly punctures the illusion of domesticity. For Burns, if not for Allen, the boundaries of the stage did not exist and his performance draws upon vaudeville and vaudeo traditions where entertainers moved out beyond the curtain and even into the audience. Burns casually hops between the sitcom set and out beyond the curtained proscenium, offering a physical demonstration of the relationship between vaudeville and television comedy which repeatedly confounds any attempt to install a realist account of domestic normativity.

David Marc calls this 'punching a hole through the proscenium' and credits the series with 'a surrealistic confusion of presentation and representation' as it switches between the diegesis of sitcom narrative and the extradiegetic stand-up mode of direct address by Burns to the audience (1989: 21). Lynn Spigel goes further, arguing that the 'layered realism' of such shows offer a commentary on the theatrical artifice of postwar white middle-class domesticity (1992b: 159; see also 1992a). Such layered realism is evident in the advertising that was laced through the sitcom's storyline. In 'Harry Morton's private secretary' (1:4), Bill Godwin (introduced in the pilot as 'America's most loved announcer') suddenly hijacks the narrative to demonstrate how to use Carnation as a substitute for cream or milk at a fraction of the price. The commercial imperative of consumer culture is front and centre; as Frances Gray states, sitcom is 'addressed to woman *as consumer*' (Gray 1994: 42). Yet the advertising segments are treated with irreverence. In the pilot Burns responds to a similar spiel by Godwin with the retort 'Are you finished?', and then directs him to walk through the door rather than straight out of the set, stating with some sarcasm: 'We gotta keep this believable'. There is little attempt to deny the artifice of the television studio in these sequences; indeed the exposure and transgression of realist artifice in visual entertainment is part of the show's comedic shtick. In this way *The Burns and Allen Show* offers its audience a knowing, sophisticated urban entertainment.

The fluid, ironic and transient space of *The Burns and Allen Show* stages a particularly queered account of gender because it exposes the 'taken for granted' aspects of heteronormativity (Browne 2009: 42). George and Gracie are a married couple within the show – just as Burns and Allen were in a longstanding Hollywood marriage – and their relationship is a central tenet of the scripts, yet it is framed within a visibly fictional arena, positing a tension between the 'real' marriage of Burns and Allen and the scripted comedy of George and Gracie. All sitcoms are fictional but few are so keen to point at their scaffolding. George and Gracie's affection for each other is unshakeably tolerant yet it constantly pecks at those heteronormative foundations through surreal comedy and theatrical business. If early sitcom provided a forum in which social and sexual tensions at odds with postwar suburban homogeneity might be expressed, so the surreal style of *The Burns and Allen Show* exposes the exigencies of middle-class dreams of white America (Marc 1989: 21). Karen Halttunen traces this back to Victorian parlour theatre: 'The message of parlor theatricals was simply this: middle-class social life was itself a charade' (1982: 185). Sociological studies were already drawing attention to the artifice that characterised postwar suburbia, and television comedies in the early 1950s acknowledged such performativity, licensing a humour which satirised suburban domesticity even as it was exploited as a normative trope. As Lynn Spigel explains, shows like *I Love Lucy* and *The Burns and Allen Show* 'welcomed viewers into a simulated neighbourhood where everyone was putting on a show' (Spigel 1992b: 165). Not only was suburbia lampooned for its artifice, but sitcom characters often became entangled in the theatricality of performance and television programming, taking part in quiz or talent shows, or auditioning to perform in advertisements.

The queered dynamic of early American sitcom reaches its apogee in Gracie Allen's famous linguistic chaos: 'a kind of bottomless pit in which audiences were caught in an endless quagmire of metarealities' (Spigel 1992b: 166). In one sense this can be read as a stereotypical division of gender roles. As the female partner Gracie is less physically mobile than George and more firmly situated within the sitcom narrative. She rarely ventures beyond the confines of their sitcom home set, apart from their closing farewell in front of the curtain (McCracken 2002: 57). Yet this does not fully explain the gender dynamic within the show. Allen's transgressive role within the double act had been established in their earliest work. When they began working together in vaudeville they conformed to the traditional roles in a husband and wife act. Burns had been the comedian with Allen as the straight, reactive partner, but the laughter that her reactions produced inspired a change of role where Allen got the funny lines and Burns was the straight guy. Burns and Allen thus represent a contradictory dynamic that accedes to a heteronormative model even as it parodies and undermines it. As Burns states in the pilot: 'You see, to be a straight man you have to have a talent. You have to develop this talent. [pause] Then you gotta marry her, like I did.' Burns, in character as George, is thus cast as Gracie's keeper and manager but not the bigger star; Gracie is the 'talent'. Although George here credits Gracie as the 'talent', he always frames the transgressive potential that she represents and is thus a reassuring presence as the man in charge (Mellencamp 1992: 321; McCracken 2002: 57).

Allen's transgressive fluidity is evident in her speech, that 'quagmire of metarealities' (Spigel 1992b: 166). Gracie often mixes metaphors or understands language too literally: 'Gracie ruptures the language of patriarchal common sense, operating in terms of a linguistic and social code more complex and exotic than the everyday' (Gray 1994: 55; see also Mellencamp 1992: 317). The contradiction inherent in this character role is that Gracie is fastidiously logical: 'it was language and its learned conventions that were arbitrary, vague, and confusing, not Gracie, who did not play by conventional rules' (Mellencamp 1992: 316). Gracie's performance accedes to *and* unpicks binary stereotypes of masculine logic and feminine irrationality. It is thus not surprising that gender and sexuality are unfixed by Gracie's logic. In one episode Gracie launches into a muddled rant about 'Men' when she thinks that her neighbour's husband is having an affair with his secretary. When George complains, she states: 'You're my husband: I don't think of you as a man.' Gracie later meets the (male) secretary after misidentifying another (female) guest as the femme fatale; she pragmatically berates the neighbour's husband: 'What do you want to chase him for? She's much prettier' (1:4). The situation of this comedy is resolved through reinstating heteronormative order – that women are 'prettier' – but it also implies that men can be pretty too, thus disturbing the absolutes of a binary world where men are handsome and women are pretty. The situation retains the echo – reiterated through Gracie's apparent acceptance of such a possibility – that the male secretary might *also* be an object of desire for his male employer. This continues throughout the episode; when George and Gracie's son says that he has the lead in *Romeo and Juliet* Gracie asks which one he is to play. George can also challenge the gender line. During a to-camera monologue about the shift in women's roles, he complains that women are wearing trousers, disrupting binary understandings of gender: 'The other day I gave my seat to a man [pause] and he said "Thank you madam" and took it' ('Politeness Never Pays', 6:18). Such playful comedy on heteronormative logic offers a queer perspective on this suburban idyll.

Despite such disruptive moments, the gender dynamic of the Burns and Allen double act fed into more conventional patterns of behaviour. Gracie was not given the final line or the authority of direct address to the audience in *The Burns and Allen Show*. That was George's part, underlined by his narrative role and the ever-present cigar. Gracie's power was equivocal and queerly suggestive in its evasion of finite conclusions. Her unshakeable serenity and confidence in her own worldview was *funny* but also suggested other possibilities (Gray 1994: 53–7). Patricia Mellencamp notes Gracie Allen's 'enigmatic quality', fostered through a consistent public persona which did not trouble her character role, because Gracie always stayed in character (1992: 316). Allen did not develop an extradiegetic celebrity persona in interviews or through autobiography. As in their onscreen partnership, she left that to George, so that, just as he narrates *The Burns and Allen Show*, he narrated their off-set lives. While this can be seen as a capitulation in terms of conventional hetero-femininity – that she let her husband and partner take the lead on stage as in their career – there is little doubt that Gracie was the engine which drove their comedy, and the absence of a 'real' Gracie Allen lends itself to her evasive refusal to be defined. Mellencamp finds this paradox problematic:

> the contradiction of the programme and the double bind of the female spectator and comedian – woman as both subject and object of the comedy rather than the mere objects that they are in the Freudian paradigm of jokes – are dilemmas which, for me, no modern critical model can resolve. (1992: 321)

One critical solution to this dilemma is to embrace Gracie's refusal of logic and Allen's enigmatic public persona as similar strategies. This refusal of common sense, of the taken-for-granted-ness of heterosexual reason, offers a powerful potential for queer readings of gender and sexuality. Gracie's attention to the minutiae of everyday speech – the semiotic terrorism of her comic repartee – makes her an effective *guérillère*, deconstructing the respectable middle-class heteronormativity in which *The Burns and Allen Show* is set. Her refusal of common sense, of the language in which the other characters blindly swim, makes sense and language both visible and questionable. By being 'stupid' Gracie is very smart. It is this, together with George's loaded pauses and the show's anti-realist aesthetic, that makes *The Burns and Allen Show* a queer place and time at a moment when sexuality and gender were nervously monitored.

Queering Sitcom: *Our Miss Brooks*

Television sitcom may be understood as a queer medium, because of its subaltern status, and its ability to 'embod[y] contradictions – rather than the "either/or" logic, one of "both/and"' (Mellencamp 1992: 5). This is even evident in some of the more standard 1950s sitcoms – and in the critical work around them. Sitcom has a history of derogatory analyses: 'it is a genre often perceived to be of less worth, of less invention and of less social value than many more "serious" forms of programming' (Mills 2009: 2). Theodor Adorno's 1954 essay, 'How to look at television', offers a scathing account of *Our Miss Brooks* (CBS 1952–6) as 'a shrewd method of promoting adjustment to humiliating conditions by presenting them as objectively comical and by giving a picture of a person who experiences even her own inadequate position as an object of fun apparently free of any resentment' (Adorno 1991: 143–4; see also Greene 2008: 33). This show focusses on a high schoolteacher, Miss Brooks (Eve Arden), and her attempts to romance a colleague while evading the strictures of the school principal. Adorno's reading of the sitcom is predicated upon an understanding of television as a flatly realist medium and its viewers as passive consumers. He does not credit the television audience with any ability to read *Our Miss Brooks* as a critique of the schoolteacher's 'inadequate position'. Nor does Adorno acknowledge the ambiguities of Eve Arden's performance as Miss Brooks. He remarks on the character's 'intellectual superiority and highspiritedness' only to propose that they invite audience identification (1991: 143).

Examination of the production context might have thrown more spokes in Adorno's wheel as *Our Miss Brooks* was produced and filmed at Desilu Studios, the production company set up by Lucille Ball and Desi Arnaz. The Oscar-winning cinematographer Karl Freund worked on both *I Love Lucy* and *Our Miss Brooks*. Freund had worked with German Expressionist directors such as Fritz Lang; he developed many of the

Desilu innovations which established the sitcom format (Landay 2010: 27–32). In a piece for *Art Photography* magazine (December 1953) Freund describes the camera techniques he developed for television sitcom, stating that 'The public acceptance of "I Love Lucy" and "Our Miss Brooks" has been a source of great inspiration for me.' Sitcom thus has a genealogy which includes not only the 'low' theatrical traditions of vaudeville but also the 'high' art of German Expressionism. Although *Our Miss Brooks* grew out of the cultural hegemony of Hollywood, it was developed at a moment when the formats and visual aesthetics of the small screen were being established. Adorno's critique of *Our Miss Brooks* echoes postwar concerns about the effect of popular media on the American family, where television was paradoxically regarded both as a means to cement the white middle-class suburban family and as a dangerous medium for new ideas which might attack 'family values' (Spigel 2001: 4). *Our Miss Brooks* thus offers a more interesting case study than Adorno's account would indicate.

Television in the 1950s provided a harbour for female character actors; Judith Roof cites Eve Arden as a performer who never headlined a film but made a career playing secondary characters, presenting her as 'an odd mixture of perversity, middleness and implied queerness' (2002: ix). Roof's examination of supporting turns deconstructs the heteronormative imperative of Hollywood cinema, focussing on the middle part of the narrative where the comic sidekick is most visible, before they fade into the background when the heterosexual couple is united at the end of the film: 'They are the site where minor, middle, and perverse overlap, undoing narrative as they do it and showing us another way to look' (2002: 3). Such analyses disrupt the trajectory of heteronormative romantic narrative, exposing the shadows of other possibilities which haunt that dominant story: queer sexualities, feminine communities, hedonistic fun. What happens when this approach is applied to television? Although Hollywood film and television are intimately connected, they represent very different aesthetics. In contrast to the more hermetic economy of Hollywood film, television formats are leaky vessels, with potential for long-running narratives and rapid generic mutation. Television offered Hollywood performers another space, one in which they could extend their careers (as did Lucille Ball and Eve Arden) and perform across a range of formats such as drama, sitcoms, chat shows and game shows.

Television itself thus constitutes a queer medium which is all 'middle', most visibly in serial forms of television narrative such as soap opera where an ending is always provisional or deferred: 'The television apparatus works against logical notions of causality and closure' (Feuer 1986: 102). David Marc describes sitcom as 'An art of the middle' (1989: 26), albeit addressing its politics rather than its narrative form. In Marc's work the radical potential of direct audience address in stand-up comedy is privileged over the conservative politics of mass-produced sitcom. Like Adorno, Marc regards the sitcom as a capitalist instrument: 'The sitcom [. . .] is the technology of the assembly line brought to art' (1989: 13). While there is no doubt that sitcom is an industrial form, rooted in the economies of Fordist production and consumption, it is the contradictory consumerist mandate for novelty and innovation which makes it a potential arena for non-normative identities to be rehearsed even as they are curtailed. Roof argues that, in Hollywood cinema, 'female comic seconds are degendered, masculinized, or queered; they are removed from any salient action in any role except as facilitator or wise fool, even though their presence still hints at perverse alternatives of nonmarriage, independence, and business success' (2002: 10). In 1950s Hollywood film, 'perverse alternatives' were kept to the margins, but in television that secondary role could become the central character, as it did for Lucille Ball in *I Love Lucy* or for Eve Arden in *Our Miss Brooks*.

Women in Hollywood whose voice or physical presence were deemed not appropriate for A-list films could headline B-movies (Ball) or forge a career as the eternal sidekick on the big screen (Arden); or they could strike out into the wider spaces of television, even if in doing so they had to produce their own shows and take on the studios at their own game. The Desilu production company established by Desi Arnaz and Lucille Ball in order to produce *I Love Lucy* eventually bought out Ball's former Hollywood studio, RKO. At the height of its success, Desilu owned more studio and office space than MGM or Fox (Horowitz 1997: 27). George Burns and Gracie Allen also had their own television production company, the McCadden Corporation (*New York Times*, 29 August 1964: 21). In this way early television comedy offered a transitional, queer medium, harbouring a complex range of performers and styles and often reflecting upon the hegemony of heteronormative gender roles. The comedy variety shows hosted by Martha Raye offer a salient example of this.

Queering the Gaze: *The Martha Raye Show* (NBC 1953–6)

Martha Raye is a very different television star from Gracie Allen or Eve Arden. Like Allen, Raye had a background in vaudeville and worked her way through film and radio before arriving in television. Her mother was touring the vaudeville circuit in 1916 when Martha (née Margaret) was born. Her parents had a husband and wife comedy act and Martha joined them on stage when she was three years old: 'singing, mugging and making clown faces' (Martin and Seagrave 1986: 237). That infant performance characterised her stage persona through much of her career. Raye's trademark was her 'big mouth', deploying slapstick physical comedy and mugging to the camera. This did not make for unalloyed success, and her film career was short-lived. From 1936 to 1940 she was under contract with Paramount but after the first two years they only cast her in three films (Martin and Seagrave 1986: 240). Raye's vaudeville style did not translate well to film and responses to her work on screen were mixed. When Chaplin cast her as one of the serial killer's intended victims in *Monsieur Verdoux* (Charles Chaplin, 1947) she won praise from critics but audiences were less impressed; the film was a flop at the box office (Martin and Seagrave 1986: 240). Raye's entrée to television came from the established vaudeo star Milton Berle, who featured her as a guest on his variety shows. After a number of successful appearances on NBC variety programmes, the network finally commissioned *The Martha Raye Show*, first broadcast in December 1953. This monthly hour-long programme showcased Raye's vaudeville style, and achieved excellent ratings in the 1954–5 season, albeit not reaching the heights of *I Love Lucy* (Martin and Seagrave 1986: 241).

Martha Raye's stage persona was the opposite of Gracie Allen's witty verbal comedy; she was loud, zany and physically boisterous, cutting across proper white middle class femininity. Mary Unterbrink describes *The Martha Raye Show* as 'physical humour, with Martha roughing up the guest stars and her sidekick, former boxer Rocky Graziano' (1987: 111). The show inserted variety acts and stand-alone sketches into an ongoing sitcom narrative featuring Martha and her onscreen boyfriend, played by Graziano. The pace was far more manic than *The Burns and Allen Show*, emulating the Jewish *toomler* tradition which influenced early television variety programmes hosted by golden age stars such as Ed Wynn, Sid Caesar and Milton Berle (Marc 1989: 38–9). Raye's work drew heavily upon vaudeville, most particularly the violent 'New Humour' that had emerged at the turn of the century. In the 1890s a faster, more visceral style of physical comedy appeared:

> While older forms of cerebral, moralistic and thoughtful humour were associated with the supposedly more refined and edifying sensibilities of Protestant middle-class values and the so-called genteel traditions of literary comedy, the new emotional styles of low or broad and unrestrained comedy were viewed as products of the working classes, the new immigrant masses, and African Americans, all of whom, it was believed, laughed mainly at what shocked and surprised their nervous systems. (Glenn 2000: 43)

The latter was precisely what Raye's show cited, toned down for television. Martha Raye embodied the tradition of ethnic working-class humour on the less regulated vaudeville circuit, a background evident in her earlier work in film.

In Raye's first feature film, *Rhythm on the Range* (Norman Taurog, 1936), she performed the hit comedy number 'Mr Paganini (you'll have to swing it)', which juxtaposes conventional Hollywood song with bluesy ragtime and dance moves to match. In the Hollywood-style verses Raye is static, using only her hands and face to comically overemphasise the lyrics, but once the chorus breaks into ragtime jazz she cannot keep her body still, employing a 'blackvoice' style of singing reminiscent of Sophie Tucker (Glenn 2000: 53). The song was closely associated with Ella Fitzgerald, who first recorded it in 1936, the same year that *Rhythm on the Range* was released. The lyrics narrate an encounter between the Paganini of the title (probably a reference to the Italian composer and virtuoso violinist) and an enthusiastic member of the audience who wants him to play her tune – or 'swing it'. The song thus marks an exchange between European white 'high' culture and African American popular culture. Fitzgerald interspersed the lyrics with her famous scat improvisation and Raye follows that lead. This white appropriation of African American culture is problematic but illustrates the complex racial history of vaudeville (Glenn 2000: 49–56). Many vaudeville acts drew upon the blackface tradition of minstrelsy, and white female comedians tended to cite African American traditions as a means of performing 'cultural excess'. Female vaudevillians thus deployed physical comedy, size and transracial performance to deliver what Susan A. Glenn terms their 'comic girth' (2000: 49–50, 47). In this way the vaudeville tradition allowed female comedy performers to take up space on stage, but only via complex discourses which often engaged misogynist and racist stereotypes (Allen 1991; Jenkins 1992: 245–76).

Raye's film and television work reaches back to vaudeville's 'New Humour', aligning her with its early women comics, those 'newcomers in grotesquerie':

> Like the serious actress Sarah Bernhardt, these adventurous women won their claims to fame by going overboard, violating gender norms through their excessiveness. As one theatre critic put it, with the 'flurry of their dances', the 'strenuousness of their music', their tremendous displays of physical energy, and their 'insinuating appeals to the senses', these 'clever women do not hesitate to sacrifice all the vanities of their sex – looks and grace – to evoke laughter from their audience.' (Glenn 2000: 46)

Raye was by no means unattractive but her routines included making distorted faces to camera, deploying her famously large mouth to comic effect. Her mouth, together with her blues-style singing, made her comedy distinctive but also 'unfeminine' in 1950s America. Aspects of this alleged lack of appropriate femininity were entangled with racism and misogyny in contemporary reviews. *The New York Times* reported that she had sued a magazine to stop them comparing her to a chimpanzee, while another critic wrote that her mouth 'stretched to a gargantuan shape, the mouth of an ape or a cow' (cited in Martin and Seagrave 1986: 245). Martha Raye's comedy was thus framed as not properly feminine and not properly white. The liminality of her gender and racial identity is consequently aligned with the fragmented aesthetic of early television variety programmes, themselves inflected by the 'low' heritage of vaudeville, which offered a patchwork of contemporary references, styles and genres (Stober 2007).

The first episode of *The Martha Raye Show* begins with a group of female dancers who introduce the star. Raye then appears (Figure 1.2) with a troupe of male dancers whose routine comically disrupts her delivery of the opening number. The compère comes on and welcomes

Figure 1.2 Martha sings the opening number in *The Martha Raye Show* (NBC, 1954–6).

the audience to 'Gino's basement café, where celebrities meet to eat under the street' (1:1). He introduces an impressionist who delivers a series of Hollywood characters, ending with Edward G. Robinson in *Little Caesar* (Mervyn LeRoy, 1931). A camera which starts from the point of view of the café audience, with the backs of their heads in the foreground, follows Edward G. Robinson himself emerging from the crowd to attack the impressionist because he is driven mad by everyone doing Little Caesar impressions wherever he goes. Robinson is restrained and the police are called; they recognise him and launch into a Little Caesar routine so that Robinson attacks a policeman. Robinson is arrested, bailed out by show regular Caesar Romero, and seeks a bed for the night in Martha's apartment, where she is nursing a bad cold. All of this takes place in the first ten minutes. The easy slippage between television studio variety show, comedy sketch, vaudeville performance, Hollywood celebrity and sitcom narrative, all loosely tied together in a hectic smorgasbord of pace and *chutzpah*, make evident the queerness in Martha Raye's performance. Nothing here is certain. Her star persona, which combines her talent for big-screen song and dance routines with an apparent compulsion to mug to camera, compounds the frenzied, chaotic style.

The excessive proliferation of genres, styles and camera shots in this opening sequence contradicts Laura Mulvey's account of the female star in Hollywood cinema as a static figure whose 'to-be-looked-at-ness' is framed by the combined 'male gaze' of the camera, the (male) protagonist and the (masculine) audience (1989). Raye's mobile and frenetic character destabilises such cause and effect. Television scholarship has challenged the application of such a unified gaze to the small screen:

> the television variety show helped arbitrate the contrasts in lifestyle between the Hollywood screen siren and the average woman by bringing the performative aspects of vaudeville (its direct address and mugging for the camera) into conflict with the cinema's 'illusionist' conventions, challenging as well, the passivity inherent in the cinema's representation of the woman in her object-like-ness. (Mann 1992: 42)

Early television scholarship was quick to note differences between viewing film and television, deploying the notion of the 'glance' and the possibilities of a less concentrated viewing dynamic in the domestic space as opposed to the immersive environment of the cinema (Caughie 1981; Ellis 1982; see also Smit 2015: 893). The multiplicity of *The Martha Raye Show*'s address, its attention to the fragmentary gaze of its diverse audience, offers a queerly unstable point of view in an entertainment programme where everything is transitory and mutable. There is little room here for the situated dynamic of the 'male gaze'.

Unlike *The Burns and Allen Show*, where Gracie is framed and contained by George, *The Martha Raye Show* knows no boundaries in its frenetic pace and camp incorporation of Hollywood stars, often placed in incongruous situations or costumes, such as Edward G. Robinson and Caesar Romero in short toga outfits doing a high-kicking dance routine with Martha. Raye's hyperactive screen persona was forged in vaudeville and debuted in Hollywood cinema but was given fuller rein on television. While 1950s television did not offer a utopian space of free play for women in comedy, it did represent an arena in which cinematic conventions, its stars and visual stylings, could be parodied, examined and exposed. The proliferation of the television set brought the 'contradictions and challenges of a rapidly transforming society' into the family home and made them the object of debate (Howard-Williams and Katz 2013: 16). The glossy surfaces of television comedies attempted to elide such contradictions but this young medium nevertheless staged emerging social transformations, often placing women at the centre of the narrative. Denise Mann's analysis of *The Martha Raye Show* demonstrates how television comedy represented a domestic arena in which Hollywood stars were undercut even as its female protagonists offered mediating accounts of the 'average girl' as starstruck fan (Mann 1992). The ethnically diverse sitcoms of the early 1950s render heterosexual hegemony as a mutable field. This is evident even in the most successful shows, such as *I Love Lucy*.

Lucy and Lucille

I Love Lucy continues to circulate in reruns, box sets, on demand and online; Lucy is a cultural phenomenon. Lucille Ball began her career as a fashion model for Hattie Carnegie in 1930s New York, later becoming a contracted studio player in Hollywood (Kanfer 2003: 30–8). She had been a B-list star before her success on radio and television, so that when Ball created Lucy Ricardo she brought to the role a star persona which already featured in Hollywood gossip columns and cinema magazines. Alexander Doty notes the contradictions which early episodes of *I Love Lucy* exposed between Lucille Ball's star image and 'drab, ditzy, no-talent Lucy Ricardo' (Doty 1990: 14). He argues that the early 1950s was a period when American television offered a platform to identities beyond straight WASP America: 'Ball and her collaborators fashioned a situation comedy character who seemed (at least during the series' first three or four seasons) constantly on the verge of becoming deconstructed by the movie-vaudeville performer who played her' (Doty 1990: 15; see also Landay 1998: 155–96). Like Gracie Allen, Eve Arden and Martha Raye, Lucille Ball was a skilled actor and comedienne, so that Lucy's alleged *lack* of talent was contradicted by Lucille's evident abilities in show business (Mellencamp 1992: 329; Landay 2010: 44–5). In that space between success and failure, *I Love Lucy* exposes contradictions and fault-lines within white heterofemininity.

Judith Halberstam advocates the queer potential of failing as a means of opening up new possibilities for gendered performance: 'Where feminine success is always measured by male standards, and gender failure often means being relieved of the pressure to measure up to patriarchal ideals, not succeeding at womanhood can offer unexpected pleasures' (2011: 4). Lucy is always failing to 'measure up' in this regard, and her escapades offer viewers many 'unexpected pleasures', not least the contradictions between Ball's celebrity and professional skill in delivering highly complex comedy about 'failure'. Through 'failing' so skilfully as Lucy, Lucille Ball succeeded far beyond many of her peers in television. The studio system of classical Hollywood replicated fantasies of heteronormative perfection, yet Lucy embodied *failed* heterofemininity on the small screen. She was chaotic, excessive, sometimes drunk. Ball's performance of intoxication was a regular routine in the television series she headlined and she shared this vaudevillian schtick with Martha Raye, who also deployed a 'drunk' act in film and television work. The figure of the drunken woman is always already outside white middle-class respectability. These comic performances of female inebriation are thus a form of grotesque, the moment of intoxication licensing aberrant behaviour which undercuts heterosexual hegemony. Such routines offer carnivalesque moments within the television narrative where women become too loud, too physical, too amorous, too much.

One of the most famous examples in the first season of *I Love Lucy* enacts a significant unpicking of 1950s heterofemininity. In 'Lucy does a TV commercial' (1:30), Lucy is yet again trying to escape her domestic role, this time auditioning for the 'Vitameatavegemin Girl' in a live television commercial during Ricky's show (Figure 1.3). She presents herself as Lucille McGillicuddy, because Ricky, as usual, does not know what she is up to and has not sanctioned her application. The job involves a set script and a demonstration performed to camera, advertising a new tonic called Vitameatavegemin, which (it is revealed to the audience but not to Lucy) has an alcohol content of 23 per cent. The Vitameatavegemin routine bears some examination as a representation of the medicalisation of femininity through the '50s. As middle-class families moved out to the suburbs, white femininity became the focus of a burgeoning advertising and medical industry which sought to sell housewives newly available domestic goods alongside the alleged benefits of pharmaceutical solutions to their problems. Housewives were told by popular 'experts' and the medical profession that they needed to subsume their desires to those of their family, and that those who challenged the heteronormative ideal were in some way defective or even

Figure 1.3 Lucy auditions for the Vitameatavegemin commercial (*I Love Lucy*, 1:30, Desilu Productions, 1951–7).

insane (McCracken 2002: 51–4). Vitameatavegemin is clearly designed to enable middle-class women with disposable income to conform to the bright and 'peppy' WASP ideal of heterofemininity. In her first audition as the Vitameatavegemin Girl Lucy follows the set script:

> Hello friends. I'm your Vitameatavegamin girl. Are you tired, run-down, listless? Do you poop out at parties? Are you unpopular? The answer to all your problems is in this little bottle. Vitameatavegamin. Yes, Vitameatavegamin contains vitamins, meat, vegetables and minerals. Yes, with Vitameatavegamin, you can spoon your way to health. All you do is take a great big tablespoonful after every meal. Mmm ... It's so tasty, too! Tastes just like candy! So why don't you join all the thousands of happy peppy people and get a great big bottle of Vitameatavegamin tomorrow! That's Vita-meata-vegamin! [wink]

Vitameatavegemin obliquely references the mass consumption of tranquillisers such as prescription drugs and alcohol by women in suburban America during the 1950s. During the rehearsal Lucy is asked to take a spoonful, after saying 'It's so tasty, too', with her subsequent response giving the lie to the script. She shudders at the taste of it, yet after several takes the liquid begins to taste *much* better.

Ball's performance exposes the gap between the advertisers' spiel and the 'real', adding another layer of irony as *I Love Lucy* was sponsored by Philip Morris cigarettes and Lucy is shown earlier in the same episode pretending to advertise that brand. How that contradiction may be understood is debatable. Lori Landay proposes that this is 'cultural hegemony in action', using celebrity endorsement to sell cigarettes (2010: 16). Lynn Spigel examines the Philip Morris cartoon sequence which introduces this episode, featuring Lucy and Desi characters and a cigarette box which becomes a theatrical curtain. She argues that the hyperreal *mise-en-abyme* structure of the promotional cartoon reflects upon the artifice of 'family' that domestic sitcoms offer their audience (1992a: 17–18). Such contradictory dynamics are at the centre of Ball's celebrity and her performance as Lucy. Lucy and Lucille are neither conformist *nor* subversive, but simultaneously known *and* unknown, familiar *and* unreachable. This underpins Ball's queer appeal as Lucy: a disruptive force which is at the same time entirely explicable and safe. 'Lucy does a TV commercial' offers a reflexive commentary on television, consumer culture and femininity. Lucy's inebriation becomes increasingly evident, licensing more 'unfeminine' behaviour and raising laughs in the studio – as it does in the classroom when I show this clip to third-year undergraduates.

The Vitameatavegemin routine follows Lucy's drunken disarticulation of the script – 'Do you pop out at parties? Are you unpoopular? Well?? ARE YOU?' – and her appropriation of the screen, as she eventually gives up trying to pour out a spoonful and chugs the liquid straight from the bottle. Having had a short nap the still-inebriated Lucy subsequently wanders into shot as Ricky is performing his first number and disrupts the live television show, following him around the stage as he tries to escape and drowning out his singing with her raucous imitation. Lucy's disruption of Ricky's songs were a regular feature of the first season owing to a contractual restriction on Desi Arnaz's performances which meant that they had to be worked into the narrative of the show in order to take place at all (Landay 2010: 42–3). Lucy thus brings performative disorder to the space of the television studio, interjecting Lucille Ball's skilled physical clowning and discordant voice, albeit a disorder that was carefully choreographed and produced (Doty 1990; Mellencamp 1992: 322–33; Gray 1994: 46–52; Landay 1998: 155–96; Landay 2010: 37–52). Lucy's inebriation undercuts the consumer imperative lodged within 1950s femininity. David Marc argues that in postwar America: 'Television was a medium committed to happiness, and it had little time for comedians or anyone else who refused to share in the joys of material consumption. "We" were an audience, one nation under Bob Hope' (1989: 45). Yet Lucy satirises the joys of 'happy peppy people' in her Vitameatavegemin routine, even as she is sponsored and framed by the tobacco giant Philip Morris. This may be 'cultural hegemony in action' but its workings are exposed (Landay 2010: 16).

Time after time, through her failed attempts to escape domesticity, Lucy enacts what Mandy Merck calls a 'deconstruction of the unacknowledged perversity of the public sphere' (2005: 188). Lucy's desire to exceed her domestic role indicated that the home might not be quite as satisfying as 1950s advertisers, sociologists and psychiatrists were telling women that it should be. In this respect, she echoed the contradictory discourse evident in 1950s women's magazines which traced 'a celebration of nondomestic as well as domestic pursuits and a tension between individual achievement and domestic ideals' (Meyerowitz 1993: 1465). Annamarie Jagose writes that 'queer describes those gestures or analytical models which dramatise incoherencies in the allegedly stable relations between chromosomal sex, gender and sexual desire' (1996: 3). Just as Lucy queered heterofemininity in the sitcom, so the star persona of Lucille Ball embodied a queer dynamic in the context of 1950s celebrity culture. Lucille Ball, the television star, and the series of 'Lucy' characters which she performed, disrupts the smooth exterior of hegemonic heterofemininity, placing queered identity at the centre of the television schedule.

That tension between Lucy and Lucille extends to the series as a whole. Part of the appeal for viewers was that Lucy and Ricky Ricardo mirrored the marriage of Lucille Ball and Desi Arnaz; viewers were aware that the ditzy housewife on screen was a wealthy and glamorous figure off screen. The merchandising and publicity surrounding the series offered viewers a doubled pleasure, knowing that *I Love Lucy* was both real and not-real. Any insight into the 'real' lives of Ball and Arnaz was always already framed by discourses of show *business*. Lucille Ball's 1940s film star persona was translated into a more domestic and intimate 1950s television celebrity, whose fluidity and apparent tangibility added to her appeal (Spigel 1992b: 222). The identification between Lucille and Lucy was most remarkably played out in the incorporation of the birth of Desi Arnaz Jr into the show's second season. The birth of 'Little Ricky' upstaged the inauguration of President Eisenhower in January 1953 (Mellencamp 1992: 329; Kanfer 2003, 161; Landay 2010: 65–76). *I Love Lucy*'s popularity is indisputable. The CEO of Philip Morris, O. Parker McComas, called the show: 'the all-time phenomenon of the entertainment business. On a strictly dollars-and-cents basis, it is twice as efficient as the average nighttime television show in conveying our advertising message to the public.' Revenue from peripherals around the Ricardo baby were expected to top $50 million (Andrews 1976: 81, citing McComas). This is the contradiction at the heart of *I Love Lucy*: that even as Lucy exposed 'the unacknowledged perversity of the public sphere' she was making huge profits for corporate America (Merck 2005: 188).

I Love Lucy offers a queerly refracted account of domesticity in an era when the home was enshrined at the centre of the American dream. Most 1950s suburban sitcoms attempted to normalise white middle-class values and to reposition women as wives and homemakers (Haralovich 2003). Although early 1950s sitcoms such as *The Goldbergs* (CBS 1949–55), *Mama* (CBS 1949–56) and *Amos 'n' Andy* (CBS 1951–3) had dealt with ethnic, black working-class families, American sitcoms tended to depict white middle-class leisure in the suburbs rather than urban labour later in the decade (Morreale 2003b: 1–5). The first season of *I Love Lucy* focussed on an as-yet childless couple whose primary relationship is with their landlords, the Mertzes, who live in the same building. The final season had the Ricardos moving to the suburbs in Connecticut, while *The Lucy Show* also placed Lucy in the suburbs. Lucy's comic zaniness, her queer heterofemininity – as a figure who is both contained and unconfined – is significant in a postwar America where women were being encouraged to forsake the workplace for the pleasures of maternity and domesticity. Lucille Ball as 'drab, ditzy, no-talent Lucy Ricardo' (Doty 1990: 14) acted out contradictions within 1950s femininity: that not all women wanted to stay in the home and that not all of them did:

> The series typified the both/and logic and the paradox of women and comedy (and work) – the female performer/spectator caught

somewhere between narrative and spectacle, always having two effortless jobs, historically held as a simulation between the real and the model. (Mellencamp 1992: 323)

Lucy represents this liminal, queered femininity *as* comedy, as a performance which is apparently effortless and yet carefully crafted. Comedy offers a commentary on gender here, in that *being* funny can destabilise hegemonic gender identities. Joanna Rapf proposes that Jerry Lewis is an involuntary feminist in his surreal representations of 'curiously androgynous' masculinities: 'His persona is both child and man, both male and female, and even both mother and son' (Rapf 2003: 148). Lucy is equally 'curious' in her representation of femininity, even though her disruptions are contained at the end of each episode.

Like Lewis's mobile masculinities, Lucy's identity is equivocal in *I Love Lucy*. She frequently employs disguises, donning baggy suits and moustaches in performances that reference working-class, ethnic masculinities. Alexander Doty remarks on the queer pleasures that Lucy and Ethel's double act could offer:

Moments such as Lucy's imitating Tallulah Bankhead's gender-transgressing deep voice or her cross-dressing masculine or butch, and her butch-femme role-playing with Ethel (as reporters, as a male–female vaudeville team, Lucy as the writer-director of an operetta in which Ethel is the soprano star, as cowboys in a homemade Western film, Lucy as a baseball player) often work to reinforce those fundamentally queer pleasures in the narrative for certain viewers by evoking lesbian cultural codes and references. (1993: 46)

Such performances reference burlesque and vaudeville traditions of cross-dressing and gender play. By 1952 male stars, such as Milton Berle, who had emerged from that tradition, were being toned down in response to concerns about the effect of such performances on the family audience (Spigel 1992b: 148). For a short time television comedy variety formats had offered a revival of vaudeville in television 'vaudeo' variety shows, promoting the Jewish, 'borscht belt' roots of its stars (Murray 2002: 102). The ethnic masculinity of major players such as Berle, Sid Caesar and George Burns, like Gracie, Eve, Martha and Lucy's deconstructive femininity, worked to unravel the middle-class heteronormativity of white America. As the 1950s proceeded, however, the Yiddish traditions which informed vaudeo were carefully repackaged and domesticated, making room for more conventional female characters in the curtailed arena of domestic sitcom. Lynn Spigel argues that the merger of domestic comedy and vaudeville humour 'allowed people to enjoy the rowdy, ethnic, and often sexually suggestive antics of variety show clowns by packaging their outlandishness in middle-class codes of respectability' (1992b: 151). This, once again, is the both/and logic of comedy.

In this context Lucille Ball's physical comedy troubles the friable boundaries of heterofemininity. Lucy's cultural excess is constituted through the deployment of her body as an object. Ball frequently uses clowning techniques that denote a childlike naivety rather than a fully adult persona. By the fourth season the Ricardos are in Hollywood and Lucy reproduces the famous mirror routine from *Duck Soup* (Leo McCary, 1933) with guest star Harpo Marx. She literally and discursively aligns herself with one of the most famously childlike male character comedians in a sequence where she is once again cross-dressed and clowning ('Lucy and Harpo Marx', 4:27). Ball's physical comedy frequently undercuts Lucy's sexual identity. Spigel argues that within 1950s sitcom this de-eroticised androgyny made space for different accounts of femininity outside the Hollywood binary of virginal good girl or femme fatale (1992b: 154). Lucy's childishness contributes to the gender trouble within *I Love Lucy*. Katherine Bond Stockton notes that the child is a queer figure, representing a 'sideways' trajectory which contradicts the linear chronology of heterosexual time (Bond Stockton 2009; Halberstam 2011: 73). Performers whose work represents a child in an adult body – like Lucille Ball, Harpo Marx and Jerry Lewis – offer a disruptive account of time, linearity and heteronormativity. Despite Lucy's marriage to Ricky, their small-screen relationship tends to play out as that of child and parent rather than that of fully sexualised man and woman, with Lucy as the androgynous, naughty kid.

Long before *I Love Lucy*, Ball's femininity had come under question with regard to her star persona. Hollywood studios found her difficult to place; while they recognised that there was a 'Lucille Ball type', they didn't know what to do with her. Talking about her early career Ball states:

I had to start as a model because I looked like a model. And I had to start [in Hollywood] as the 'other woman' or the 'career girl' because I had a lousy voice. I have a deep, guttural voice that has no softness or romanticism. It's aggressive. I've always had it, no matter how I try to dolly it up. (cited in Horowitz 1997: 23)

Ball's voice marked her as working class or deviant: 'exceed[ing] the gender of the body from which it proceeds. That excess confers upon it a privileged status vis-à-vis both language and sexuality' (Doty 1993: 120). Ball's 'lousy voice' denoted a contradiction between how she looked and how she sounded. In Henry Hathaway's noir film *The Dark Corner* (1946) Ball plays a tough career girl who helps the protagonist and her voice is inconsistent: sometimes shrill, sometimes husky. She employs her voice to better effect in *What's My Line?* (CBS 1950–67), appearing as the 'mystery guest' six times on the American panel quiz, a record which attests to her celebrity. In her first appearance Ball responds to the blindfolded panel's questions with a version of the queer 'Martian' nonsense language that Lucy and Ethel developed in 'Lucy is envious' (3:23) when they were dressed as aliens to promote a film (*What's My Line?*, 21 February 1954; see Doty 1993: 46–7). In her third appearance Ball answers the question 'Are you male' with a baritone 'Mostly no' (*What's My Line?*, 1 January 1961). This is not to suggest that Ball was 'unfeminine' but that her physical comedy and her voice did not sit neatly within normative 1950s white middle-class femininity. She problematised hegemonic heterofemininity with something more complex, contradictory and inconsistent. Her voice was an asset in television comedy, where her performance followed the traditions of ethnically marked vaudeville. Despite Lucille Ball's Anglo-Saxon identity, her comedy vernacular was distinctly 'other'.

The heterosexual partnership at the centre of *I Love Lucy* was also marked as transgressive. Ball and Arnaz were regarded as an inter-racial couple, with Desi Arnaz's heavily accented Cuban American a frequent joke within the show. Lori Landay provides an incisive reading of how *I Love Lucy* negotiated Ricky's ethnicity by situating his 'otherness' in complex and contradictory ways (2010: 76–86). The 1950s WASP marriage is thus problematised in *I Love Lucy* by compromised authority figures. Ricky Ricardo and the grumpy, ageing Fred Mertz offer a contrast to the youthful all-American fathers of later suburban sitcoms. This equivocal heterosexuality is further undercut by the queer alliance of Lucy and Ethel and the close friendship of Lucille Ball and Vivian Vance, which produced rumours of a lesbian affair (Doty 1993: 39–40; Landay 2010: 58–60). In *The Lucy Show* (CBS 1962–8), Lucy Ricardo became Lucy Carmichael, a widowed mother of two who has moved out to the suburbs and is once again with Ethel in the casting of Vivian Vance as divorcée Vivian Bagley.

The animated credit sequence for the first season features stick-figure Lucy and Vivian repairing the title letters with a hammer, initially in skirts but rapidly running off to change into trousers and collect a ladder. Finally they shake hands as the letters all fall down again (Figure 1.4). Contemporary commentators were quick to spot the absence of significant male characters and some made homophobic comments about the 'Dyke sans Dick show', referring to *The Dick Van Dyke Show* (CBS 1961–6) (Kanfer 2003: 236).

There is certainly the potential for a lesbian reading here: the Lucy–Ethel partnership as readable in terms of Adrienne Rich's 'lesbian continuum' (discussed in Doty 1993: 41–6). Rich proposes the lesbian continuum not simply as a means of identifying queer histories but also as a means of challenging the dominance and limitations of heteronormativity. The homophobic rumours and comments may be

Figure 1.4 The animated opening credits of *The Lucy Show* (Desilu Productions, 1951–7).

understood as indicative of this: that the characters (and the actors who play them) are perceived as 'not normal', as 'peculiar', because they disturb the smooth facade of gender binaries and exceed its bounds. Naming them as 'dykes' is a frantic attempt to reinstate those boundaries by constituting Lucy and Ethel as irrevocably 'other', just as it evidences cultural anxieties about the possibility of women working together without men. The power of such performances is in their refusal to be named and delimited within the bounds of the normative, the respectable, as appropriately heterofeminine.

Queering Suburbia

There is a critical consensus that American sitcoms were tidied up during the 1950s. Working-class, ethnic, urban sitcoms were replaced by bland, de-ethnicised white middle-class nuclear families living in the suburbs (Brook 1999; Haralovich 2003; Morreale 2003b). Although suburban sitcoms such as *Father Knows Best* (CBS and NBC 1954–60) and *Leave It to Beaver* (CBS and ABC 1957–63) reified the normative white family, predicated on the centrality of fathers and sons, other series questioned the perceived limitations of the American suburban idyll. By the 1960s sitcoms that included fantasy elements – housewives who were witches or genies, for example – worked to defamiliarise the American dream:

> We are [...] made to question the 'naturalness' of middle-class existence. We are asked to hesitate in our beliefs about the normative roles of gender, class and race that so pervade the era's suburban lifestyles. In this sense, the fantastic unmasks the conventionality of the everyday. (Spigel 2001: 123)

Shows such as *Bewitched* (ABC 1964–72) and *I Dream of Jeannie* (NBC 1965–70) offer a supernatural commentary on suburban femininity but more realist sitcoms could also address the shifting social landscape. In *The Lucy Show* and *Here's Lucy*, broadcast from the early 1960s to the mid-1970s, Lucy is widowed, working and bringing up children on her own. Those homophobic comments about the relationship between Lucy and Vivian indicate that a significant shift in white suburban femininity is in process. If the last season of *I Love Lucy* moves Lucy and Ricky out to the suburbs, *The Lucy Show* depicts a single parent (Lucy) and a divorcée (Vivian), muddling along. Lucy finally goes out to work. There is no Ricky to hold her back and, like most single women, she needs to earn a living. The patriarchal role is taken up by her bad-tempered boss, Mr Mooney (Dale Gordon), whose business as a Hollywood agent facilitates interactions between Lucy and a number of television guest stars, such as George Burns, Milton Berle and Jack Benny.

The suburbs now become a dysfunctional domestic arena, where Lucy and Vivian are hapless in their attempts to survive the heterosocial idyll. In 1963 their attempt to put in a shower results in them flooding the bathroom with water, Lucy and Vivian clownishly trapped within the fish tank they make of the shower cubicle (Figure 1.5; *The Lucy Show*, 1:18). They are out of their element, and it is *funny*. The Lucy shows continue to comment upon gender and sexual identity. An episode of *Here's Lucy* featuring Carol Burnett has Lucy and Carol entering a beauty pageant. Dale Gordon camps it up, teaching them to walk like beauty queens, while Lucy and Carol parody femininity with clownish glee in the swimsuit round (2:24). That episode was originally broadcast in March 1970 and in November 1970 the Miss World Contest was

Figure 1.5 Lucy and Vivian trapped in the shower cubicle (*The Lucy Show*, 1:18, Desilu Productions, 1951–7).

famously attacked by feminist activists, who infiltrated the Royal Albert Hall in London to throw flour bombs and shake football rattles, disrupting Bob Hope's misogynist routine as compère. This action followed similar protests at the Miss America pageants in 1968 and 1969. Lucy is not a feminist activist but her queer parodies of heterofemininity from *I Love Lucy* to *Here's Lucy* were remarkably prescient.

The normative frame of suburban sitcom is broken in these series. If the suburb is a space from which queer identity must flee, lesbians and gay men migrating to more visible and hospitable queer spaces within urban conurbations, it is also a space that has created them and which is capable of harbouring a queer perspective. In her book on queer suburban imaginaries, Karen Tongson maps the suburbs of southern California, the location of much American network television production. Southern California is usually depicted as a wealthy, white suburban fantasy, in series such as *The OC* (Warner Bros 2003–7), despite its ethnically mixed population. In sitcom, however, the contradictions of Californian suburban life seep through:

> From the ideal nuclear families who glowed in exemplars on shows like *Ozzie and Harriet* (1952–1966) and *Leave It to Beaver* (1957–1963), to their bizarro Goth doubles on *The Munsters* (1964–1966) and *The Addams Family* (1964–1966), TV has grappled with the social transformations of a suburbia that it played a tremendous role in creating. Nothing is impossible in the suburbs on American television. (Tongson 2011: 22–3)

American films and television series have played upon the uncanny camp kitsch of suburbia, from the suburban fantasies of Pee-Wee Herman, *Edward Scissorhands* (Tim Burton, 1990) and *Suburgatory* (ABC 2011–14) to the suburban gothic of *Buffy the Vampire Slayer* (Fox 1997–2003) and *Desperate Housewives* (ABC 2004–12) (Doty 1993: 81–95; Murphy 2009). In such narratives the suburbs represent a queer liminality, a campy no-place between the rural and the urban, fantasy and reality. The hegemonic heteronormativity of bourgeois white suburbs is translated into a shadow world where eccentricity, deviance and the supernatural are just below the surface. As in David Lynch's *Blue Velvet* (1986), there is always the possibility of finding something nasty lurking behind the white picket fence.

Like television, suburbia is culturally marked as domestic and feminine. Like television, this is often expressed in derogatory terms, with suburbia depicted as the dreary 'temporal zone of the everyday in which people follow tedious and unthinking routines in a cyclical round of continuous repetition' (Giles 2004: 30). As in *Suburgatory* and *Desperate Housewives*, however, television sitcom can transform the everyday into a hyperreal fantasy with women at its centre. American suburban sitcoms in the twenty-first century offer technicolour wardrobes and sets which reference their '50s predecessors with post-modern irony. In this neoliberal, post-everything era it appears that suburbia is still where we rehearse ideas about gender: 'Suburbia, as much as the city against which it is often defined, is therefore both a product of modernity and a space in which the dilemmas and contradictions of modernity can be articulated' (Giles 2004: 31). Gracie, Martha, Eve and Lucy offer complex and contradictory accounts of femininity on television, echoing traditions which reach back into the nineteenth century and which continue to resonate into the twenty-first. These characters do not escape their television narratives but make the perverse restrictions of heteronormativity more visible, deconstructing the ideal femininities of their era. This chapter has addressed early television sitcom and variety formats as comedies which can harbour eccentric, aberrant and queered heterofemininities. The next chapter considers more recent sitcoms which also centre on female protagonists. Can television comedy in the twenty-first century represent queer femininity in postfeminist times?

CHAPTER 2

BACK TO THE DOLLHOUSE? QUEERING POSTFEMINISM IN CONTEMPORARY AMERICAN SITCOM

This chapter examines women in contemporary American sitcom, particularly *30 Rock* and *Parks and Recreation*. How do these twenty-first-century shows navigate postfeminism and the gravitational pull of Hollywood romance? Television comedies which centre on female protagonists have become increasingly visible in the post-network era, targeting niche audiences and offering multifaceted narratives that reward close observation and faithful viewing. Yet the politics of how women are represented on television remain complex and contradictory. Women in the new comedies of the 1990s offered a narrative sophistication informed by all that television and film could afford. Amanda Lotz hails *The Days and Nights of Molly Dodd* (NBC 1987–8, Lifetime 1988–91) as a forerunner of series such as *Ally McBeal* (Fox Network 1997–2002) and *Sex and the City* (HBO, 1998–2004), shows which: 'blend drama and humor and break from realist traditions by incorporating devices that draw attention to their status as texts' (2006: 90). American sitcom had been 'drawing attention to [its] status as text' from the early days when George and Gracie stepped out beyond the curtain at the end of *The Burns and Allen Show*. Nevertheless, the narrative complexity introduced in the 1980s and 1990s registered a shift in American television comedies based around female characters that merits further examination, not least because they represent a problem for feminist television criticism in a postfeminist era:

> It is impossible to argue persuasively that these series are either feminist or antifeminist because of their contradictory nature and their sophisticated use of narrative devices, as well as the complexity of their textual form and the programming context in which they circulate. [...] Although one might prefer clear unassailable findings, scholarship must acknowledge the ambivalence that results from textual or contextual complexity rather than willfully disregarding such confounding variables (Lotz 2006: 98–9)

Such 'confounding variables' make queer analyses of these comedies all the more apposite: the multivalent dynamics of performance, narratives, intertexts and programming contexts offer themselves for queer appraisal. What do these comedies *do* with gender and sexuality? One thing they clearly do not do is take any identity category *straight*. The new comedies are postfeminist, just as they are post-modern, post-network and poststructuralist in tendency. Gender, sexuality and race are at the forefront of the new American sitcom and this chapter focusses primarily on two popular series that offer variously queer views on postfeminism: *30 Rock* (NBC 2006–13) and *Parks and Recreation* (NBC 2009–15). The rationale for these choices is threefold; they are successful, they have garnered popular and academic attention for their focus on female protagonists, and they feature women in the professional sphere. These series are also relevant for this study owing to their queerly resistant account of postfeminist popular culture, a resistance that quietly undermines heteronormativity. *30 Rock* is set behind the scenes of a television comedy show, offering a commentary on popular media and postfeminism via its focus on Liz Lemon (Tina Fey) as showrunner. *Parks and Recreation* examines the contradictions and negotiations of heartland America, as Leslie Knope (Amy Poehler) and her colleagues engage in civic politics in the small-town setting of Pawnee, Indiana.

These comedies are at the forefront of a perceived boom in popular female-centred series, with female writers, showrunners and stars (Harris 2011; Williams 2013). One marker of this shift appeared in the

April 2008 issue of *Vanity Fair*, where Alessandra Stanley addressed the old chestnut that 'women aren't funny' in the wake of Christopher Hitchens's attack on funny women in the same publication. Hitchens's earlier 'provocation' asserted that, while some exceptional women were funny they were also 'hefty or dykey or Jewish, or some combo of the three' (2007). Hitchens rolls out the 'dyke' word, insulting lesbians as well as Jewish women and 'hefty' women, in order to make his point and reiterating the pejorative link between queer and Jewish identities that emerged in Cold War America (Jakobson 1998: 524–5). He links ('normal') women's lack of humour to their 'natural' power, rooted in their ability to bear children:

> the explanation for the superior funniness of men is much the same as for the inferior funniness of women. Men have to pretend, to themselves as well as to women, that they are not the servants and supplicants. Women, cunning minxes that they are, have to affect not to be the potentates (Hitchens 2007)

This remarkable worldview, which pitches women as the movers and shakers while men stand in the corner and nervously make jokes, proposes that funny women are 'like Dr. Johnson's comparison of a woman preaching to a dog walking on its hind legs: the surprise is that it is done at all' (Hitchens 2007). The misogyny of this 'provocation' reiterates the gender dynamic outlined in the introduction to this volume: the continued perception of funny women as 'peculiar'. Reading through this deliberate offence, one can discern the queer identity imposed on any woman with the temerity to make a career in comedy.

Alessandra Stanley's response to Hitchens acknowledges the continuing shelf-life of such misogyny, closing with a statement from Tina Fey, writer, producer and star of *30 Rock*, that '"You still hear it [. . .] It's just a lot easier to ignore"' (Stanley 2008). Stanley, Fey and others argue that the culture of comedy has shifted in response to a wider cultural shift in gender relations. Yet concerns around comedy and femininity remain. Stanley's article raises the weary ghost of the man-hating, ugly and humourless second-wave feminist, while focussing on the new comedy's poster girls: Tina Fey, Amy Poehler, Kristen Wiig, Maya Rudolph and Sarah Silverman (White 2010). These performers defy longstanding misogynies about funny women by being visibly heterofeminine – pretty *and* funny – yet this also means that they tread a complex path (Mizejewski 2014: 1–29). As performers, producers and writers, such women step outside conventional gender roles. Although the new women in comedy are funny *and* sexy, perhaps because of this they are still perceived as odd and exceptional, *still* funny peculiar. Contemporary female stars in American sitcom thus offer a queered account of heterofemininity. By being pretty *and* awkward, girlish *and* potty-mouthed, Fey's and Poehler's work resonates with academic debate regarding feminism and postfeminism, addressing the contradictions and inconsistencies of white heterofemininity in the twenty-first century.

Postfeminism and the New Comedy

Susan J. Douglas maps the emergence of postfeminism in the 1980s as advertising agencies employed feminist discourse to market products to young single women with disposable income:

> The message was that women were capable of remaking themselves and that this remaking required not only intelligent consumption but also hard work. Thus could women be, simultaneously, self-indulgent consumers, buying high-priced exercise shoes and spa memberships, and self-denying producers who were working hard to remake something – their bodies (1994: 263)

Postfeminism's focus on the female body as a cultural project has shifted up several gears since the 1980s. Whereas *Roseanne* was informed by a second-wave feminism which satirised the 'domestic goddess' (Rowe 1995: 50–91), twenty-first-century sitcom is in conversation with the overwhelming onslaught of postfeminist media.

This shifting political context is accompanied by a shifting aesthetic. It is no coincidence that much of the new comedy follows a 'comedy vérité' style rather than the standard multi-camera format of studio sitcom. Instead of the limited domestic sets and heightened colour palette of traditional American comedies, these shows borrow from the aesthetics of documentary, with the visual idiom of a single, hand-held camera. Comedy vérité also offers a particular mode of narration:

> these programmes don't just ape the factual aesthetics of docusoaps and factual programming; they deliberately employ them in order to question and critique the supposed objectivity and access which documentaries offer, and which distinguishes them from such 'fictional' programming as sitcoms (Mills 2008: 89)

In this way, shows like *The Office* (BBC 2001–3, NBC 2005–13) represent a comedy founded on irony that 'simultaneously undermines and reinforces the ideals, dreams, and realities of the post-millennial American middle class' (Detweiler 2012: 730). Comedy vérité is part of a broader move across television and film since the 1990s, which may be understood as a response to the challenge of the internet and new media technologies: a shift 'toward narrative complexity in television storytelling that blurs distinctions between episodic and serial narratives, that exhibits a heightened degree of self-consciousness, and that demands a higher intensity of viewer engagement' (E. Thompson 2007: 63; see also Mittell 2006). The new comedy assumes a knowing 'blue-chip' audience: 'upscale, well-educated, urban-dwelling, young viewers advertisers so desire to reach' (R. Thompson 1996). This is an audience which looks for and 'gets' complex visual and verbal references, an audience that will watch the series online, or buy the box sets, because it is not 'just' regular television but a show which rewards repeated viewings (Thompson 1996). The new comedies reference a range of quality television indicators, offering a cinematic aesthetic and intertextual references to popular media, and targeting niche audiences who are in on the joke rather than a broad demographic targeted via 'least objectionable' programming (Lotz 2006: 27; Cardwell 2007).

The new comedies also address a postfeminist vision of liberation constituted almost exclusively for the white middle class, and predicated on neoliberal economies. Women are a desirable demographic in the post-network era, where broadcasters are looking for a niche audience to bolster advertising revenue, simply because they constitute an identifiable and sizeable statistical target (Lotz 2006: 24). This postfeminist era of female-centred television is thus about commercial imperatives more than liberal politics:

> Female audiences may see their lives reflected in more complex and sophisticated ways as a result of their new inclusion in dramatic

narratives, but pursuing these pleasures transforms them into commodity audiences for advertisers who seek them through their tastes and preferences (Lotz 2006: 35)

The revolution is being televised and sold back to us by smart technologies that track our viewing and shopping. If you watched *that* you might like *this*. Post-network television thus employs feminist discourse while carefully defusing its politics, once again aligning the new comedy with postfeminism, because postfeminism rests on the fantasy of equality for all in the face of evident social and economic inequity. Angela McRobbie calls this the fantasy of an 'equality norm', that we are all somehow equal, even as the evidence all around us says otherwise (2011). Rosalind Gill and Christina Scharff echo Susan J. Douglas in their description of a 'postfeminist sensibility', where:

> femininity is increasingly figured as a bodily property; a shift from objectification to subjectification in the ways that (some) women are represented; an emphasis upon self-surveillance, monitoring and discipline; a focus upon individualism, choice and empowerment; the dominance of a 'makeover paradigm'; a resurgence of ideas of natural sexual difference; the marked resexualization of women's bodies; and an emphasis upon consumerism and the commodification of difference (2011: 4)

Even as the new comedy may be aligned with the dynamics of such 'postfeminist sensibility', however, television comedy has also become a prime means of exposing the exigencies of postfeminism. *30 Rock* and *Parks and Recreation* address the sensibility that Gill and Sharff describe by parodying it, undercutting its effects. This is not to say that these are overtly feminist comedies, but that the shows' writers and performers address postfeminism as a discourse which is unavoidable in broadcast media. It is increasingly normalised, and much of these series' comedy is based around the exposure and examination of the sheer craziness of postfeminist sensibility in the twenty-first century.

Linda Mizejewski's work on key female figures in contemporary American comedy traces the postfeminist contradictions of 'pretty/ funny' women, mapping the different strategies of performers such as Sarah Silverman, Margaret Cho and Wanda Sykes. Now, more than ever, she argues, 'the status of the female body itself – its visibility, availability, and presumed heterosexuality – is intrinsic to women's comedy even at its most transgressive' (Mizejewski 2014: 19). As Mizejewski notes, however, 'Comedy is a rich site for queer performance' (2014: 16). Liz Lemon in *30 Rock* and Leslie Knope in *Parks and Recreation* problematise the 'successful femininities' thrown up in debates around third-wave feminism, an iteration of feminist politics that claims to navigate the complexities of late modernity with its multiplicity of sexual and gender identities (Budgeon 2011). In particular, *30 Rock* and *Parks and Recreation* satirise the disconnect *between* generations of women which continues to be debated within feminist praxis (Winch, Littler and Keller 2016). These comedies thus puncture the notion that second-wave feminism is defunct or that women can afford to ignore the inequities that continue to structure our lives.

Not Unruly Women?

The complex landscape of television comedy and postfeminist popular culture in the twenty-first century challenges many of the grounding assumptions of early academic work on gender and comedy. In *The Unruly Woman* Kathleen Rowe examines 'how the figure of the unruly woman – too fat, too funny, too noisy, too old, too rebellious – unsettles social hierarchies' (1995: 19). Rowe proposes Miss Piggy, Roseanne Barr and Mae West as emblematic examples of unruly women, mapping the politics of their gendered performances in relation to the Bakhtinian carnivalesque. Rowe also notes the anger which unruly women express through comedy, citing Marleen Gorris's feminist film *A Question of Silence* (1982) as a touchstone. She identifies eight signifiers of female unruliness:

1. The unruly woman creates disorder by dominating, or trying to dominate, men. She is unable or unwilling to confine herself to her proper place.
2. Her body is excessive or fat, suggesting her unwillingness or inability to control her physical appetites.
3. Her speech is excessive, in quantity, content, or tone.
4. She makes jokes, or laughs herself.

5. She may be androgynous or hermaphroditic, drawing attention to the social construction of gender.
6. She may be old or a masculinized crone, for old women who refuse to become invisible in our culture are often considered grotesque.
7. Her behavior is associated with looseness and occasionally whorishness, but her sexuality is less narrowly and negatively defined than is that of the femme fatale. She may be pregnant.
8. She is associated with dirt, liminality (thresholds, borders, or margins), and taboo, rendering her above all a figure of ambivalence (Rowe 1995: 31)

Even as this list was published it was already becoming historical, as *Roseanne* ended its run in 1997, and *Friends* debuted on NBC in 1994. Aside from category four, the current crop of sitcoms with female leads do not ostensibly correspond with Rowe's 'unruly woman'. These are comedies about *good* girls. Characters like Liz Lemon and Leslie Knope are young, middle-class, heterofeminine women succeeding in a corporate environment. The comedy focusses on their struggles in the tradition of American work-based comedies such as *The Mary Tyler Moore Show* (CBS 1970–7). The new funny women reveal unruly tendencies, such as Liz Lemon's predilection for 'night cheese' or Leslie Knope's fondness for unfeasible amounts of whipped cream, but these peccadillos do not affect their professional lives; arguably they are symptomatic of the stresses such lives entail. While these shows harbour a queer perspective on contemporary heterofemininity they do not constitute the overtly unruly politics of shows like *Roseanne*, because they speak to a different generation of American television and a different political landscape.

As Kathleen Rowe and others have asserted, *Roseanne* constituted a seismic shift in television comedy but it is difficult to see a direct successor to that blue-collar family sitcom based around a female star. *Roseanne* was understood as a sitcom which was self-evidently informed by second-wave feminism, deploying a realist aesthetic predicated on audience identification and radical politics (White 2017). Jane Feuer argues that the 'unruly woman' is often a female clown, citing Lucille Ball, Jennifer Saunders and Jenna Elfman as examples, and maintaining an opposition between the surreal comedy of shows such as *Absolutely Fabulous* and 'more "realistic" comedies such as *Roseanne*, with its proletarian setting and more lifelike characters, [which] may be seen as providing a better critique of domesticity in its very believability' (2008a: 83). By the 1990s, however, American sitcom was moving from proletarian, family-based comedy to friends-as-family shows set in urban centres, which developed complex and often surreal storylines to engage their desired audience. The success of *Friends* on NBC shifted the networks' focus to a younger demographic, where family is replaced by young, upscale, 20-something singles in the big city (Morreale 2003b: 248–9).

The preponderance of sitcoms starring, written and produced by women which have emerged in the twenty-first century are thus notably different in tone from *Roseanne*. *Roseanne* centred on a blue-collar family and a working-class housewife but *30 Rock* and *Parks and Recreation* address single professional women: privileged 'girls' struggling to find their feet in the world. Their desires and ambitions are conventional. Like their network forebears they are overwhelmingly heterosexual and white. Their bodies are, at most, slightly plump (or what passes for normal outside Hollywood), and rigorously policed by the characters themselves. Their world is bounded by the media. This is television speaking to television and social media, addressing a cultural landscape which is fragmented and contradictory, where identity is an intersectional field and audiences are likely to be spending more time online than in front of a television set (Morreale 2003b: 249). Such comedies deliver punchlines by the dozen, referencing a range of media and demonstrating little allegiance to political figures or particular agendas. These shows are aware of second-wave feminism but inhabit a postfeminist milieu. The most notable example is *Sex and the City*, a television show about female friendship and postfeminist consumption which continues to haunt its successors (Munford and Waters 2014: 46–53).

Sex and the City: Queering Postfeminism

Sex and the City is a significant marker with regard to women in contemporary television comedy, because it demonstrated that there was an audience for comedy featuring a female ensemble cast. The series privileged 'the homosocial world of women' by foregrounding female friendship in a manner that looked back to the politics of the second wave, while marketing a consumerist fantasy of Manhattan that continues to sell bus tours and merchandise (Jermyn 2009: 45). Most significantly, *Sex and the City* brought a 'queer sensibility', packing its storylines with 'transgressive moments [...] that undermined normative categories of gender and sexuality'. It made the link between single straight women and gay male sexuality that positioned both as 'outsider' figures with regard to heteronormativity (Jermyn 2009: 62–3). The queered postfeminism on show in *30 Rock* and *Parks and Recreation* can be traced back to *Sex and the City*.

Critical accounts of *Sex and the City* have noted that it substitutes queer knowledge for feminist insight, because the show refuses to acknowledge the need for social change or sexual politics even as it troubles heteronormativity through its protagonists' constant discussion of sex (Gerhard 2005). Liberation and equality are thus translated into conversations about 'funky spunk' in glossy cocktail bars by women sporting high-end fashion. The show instead traces the complexity of contemporary femininities through a generational discourse: 'The relationship, then, between 70s feminism, postfeminism and popular queerness is tangled up in *Sex and the City* in ways that testify to just how hard it is to learn from our (feminist) elders' (Gerhard 2005: 39). Jane Gerhard argues that *Sex and the City* offers a 'narrative queerness' that reflects upon the protagonists' heterofeminine identities. In a show ostensibly predicated on postfeminist aesthetics, where the body is the (only) site of liberation – a body seemingly free of historical and political context – the queer tendency of *Sex and the City* privileges women's relationships with other women over the romantic narrative that dominates the programme (Jermyn 2009). Such a strategy 'alters the representations of their heterosexuality, drawing it out from the shadow of its hegemonic closet. The women's heterosexuality functions as a site where postfeminism and queer mass media interact' (Gerhard 2005: 43). One significant feature of this queer postfeminism is the constant discussion about sex and relationships: 'The women's talk provides an account of the "dissonance" the characters experience between ideas about heterosexual romance and their experience of straight sex' (Gerhard 2005: 45). While Carrie, Samantha, Miranda and Charlotte may experience heterosexual 'dissonance' they are also focussed on the search for a compatible 'Mr Right', so any disturbance of heterosexual hegemony is carefully contained by the narrative impetus of the show. *Sex and the City* is discursively aligned with the 'heterosexual imaginary' (Ingraham 2005:

4), despite the extent to which that imaginary is disturbed by the variations that *Sex and the City* exposes within heterosexual practice. Later comedies featuring female leads have expanded upon such narrative queerness and heterosexual dissonance even as they too are drawn back to the 'heterosexual imaginary'. *30 Rock* and *Parks and Recreation* (and subsequently Lena Dunham's *Girls*, HBO 2012–17) may thus be understood as discursive reactions to the legacy of *Sex and the City*, unpicking its fantasies of fashion, romance and female friendship.

Where Roseanne Connor was overtly confrontational, a verbally and physically unruly woman, these queered postfeminist comedies are covertly subversive, challenging dominant norms by exposing the uneven fictions of heteronormativity. Carrie, Charlotte, Miranda and Samantha celebrate the fantasy of choice in a consumerist cityscape, but Liz Lemon and Leslie Knope are visibly unable to live up to the *Sex and the City* dream. They are geekish, socially inept and unfashionable. *30 Rock* and *Parks and Recreation* satirise the unattainable postfeminist lifestyles which are relentlessly iterated across contemporary consumer culture. It is notable that *Sex and the City*'s golden era preceded the 2007–8 financial crisis in American markets and the resulting credit crunch. More recent comedies, such as *Two Broke Girls* (CBS 2011–) and *Girls*, are more in keeping with the pessimism of the economic downturn and its effects on a younger generation. *30 Rock* and *Parks and Recreation* were produced and broadcast as the credit crunch took hold; both shows are caught between the consumer excesses which preceded the 2007–8 crash and the reconstruction of neoliberal agendas which succeeded it. Liz Lemon and Leslie Knope thus reflect upon realities for white middle-class women in the professions: women who struggle to get there and, once there, struggle to deal with the isolation, self-doubt and misogyny they face on a daily basis (Gill 2009; Scharff 2016). Liz and Leslie are not role models. They do not speak to a feminist understanding of the woman in comedy as a transgressive figure who overtly challenges the system, but they do address the queered dynamics of women in comedy and women at work.

30 Rock

The comic genealogy outlined above may be observed in the opening of *30 Rock*'s third season. In the pre-credit sequence Liz Lemon walks down a New York street in imitation of Carrie Bradshaw (Sarah Jessica Parker) in the opening credits of *Sex and the City* (Figure 2.1). A large black limo pulls up and a voice says 'Hello Pussycat', referencing Carrie's longstanding romance with 'Mr Big' (Chris Noth). Initially abusing what she takes to be a kerb crawler, Liz is delighted to discover the occupant of the car is Jack Donaghy (Alec Baldwin), her former boss who is back to reclaim his old job ('Do-over', 3:1). The camera pans to a shot of the New York skyline before the opening credits roll.

Like *Sex and the City*, *30 Rock* is located in a mythic New York. Scenes are often shot in the city streets and the credit sequence features Rockefeller Plaza, where the fictional television show *The Girly Show* is produced and the real National Broadcasting Company (NBC) has its headquarters (hence '30 Rock'). There are constant narrative references in *30 Rock* to 'the actual city' (Nussbaum 2013). Later in season three, Liz suggests to her current boyfriend that they resolve their relationship by meeting on Brooklyn Bridge, in imitation of Miranda and Steve in the first *Sex and the City* film (Michael Patrick King, 2008; *30 Rock*, 3:7, 'Señor Macho Solo'). The screen histories of New York are thus constantly invoked in *30 Rock* as a means of demonstrating how Liz attempts to live the *Sex and the City* dream and how that fantasy is failing her.

Sex and the City's title sequence itself references *That Girl* (ABC 1966–71), *The Mary Tyler Moore Show* (CBS 1970–7) and *Rhoda*

Figure 2.1 Liz Lemon as Carrie Bradshaw from *Sex and the City* in 'Do-over' (*30 Rock*, 3:1, NBC, 2008–13).

(CBS 1974–8), so that *30 Rock* is situated within a genealogy of women in television sitcom (Jermyn 2009: 41–4). Yet Liz Lemon is not a feminist heroine nor a postfeminist fantasy. As Jenna (Jane Krakowski) points out, Liz is not one of the *Sex and the City* women but rather 'the lady at home who watches it' ('Cleveland', 1:20). She is bad-tempered, bitter and compromised at work and in her personal life. Defending Liz Lemon against a Twitter backlash in 2012, Emily Nussbaum succinctly outlined the character's appeal in *The New Yorker*:

> Unlike some other adorkable or slutty-fabulous characters I could name, Liz only superficially resembled the protagonist of a romantic comedy, ready to remove her glasses and be loved. Beneath that, she was something way more interesting: a strange, specific, workaholic, NPR-worshipping, white-guilt-infected, sardonic, curmudgeonly, hyper-nerdy New Yorker. In the first episode, Jack nails her on sight as 'a New York third-wave feminist, college-educated, single-and-pretending-to-be-happy-about-it, over-scheduled, undersexed, you buy any magazine that says "healthy body image" on the cover and every two years you take up knitting for [. . .] a week.' Even Liz had to admit he scored a point. (2012b)

Throughout *30 Rock*'s seven seasons, Liz Lemon's strangeness and specificity mark her emphatically as *neither* a groundbreaking feminist role model who speaks truth to power, like Roseanne Connor, *nor* a fantasy postfeminist gal pal, like Carrie Bradshaw.

The irony is that *30 Rock*'s writer, executive producer and star, Tina Fey, is indeed a feminist groundbreaker in American television comedy. She changed *Saturday Night Live* (NBC 1975–) as the show's first female head writer (1999–2006), intervened in national politics with her uncanny impression of Sarah Palin, and broke into Hollywood both as a writer (*Mean Girls*, Mark Waters, 2004) and as a star (*Admission*, Paul Weitz, 2013; *Date Night*, Shawn Levy, 2010; *Baby Mama*, Michael McCullers, 2008) (Mizejewski 2012; Patterson 2012: 233–4). In Fey's autobiography she gives her reply to questions about Jerry Lewis or Christopher Hitchens saying 'women aren't funny', by quoting the response of her friend Amy Poehler to a male *Saturday Night Live* colleague's comment that one of her jokes wasn't appropriately feminine: 'We don't fucking care if you like it' (Fey 2011: 144).

Fey can certainly be categorised as an 'unruly woman': one has only to watch her hosting the 2013–15 *Golden Globes* with Poehler for evidence of this. Eleanor Patterson argues that: 'Fey's star text highlights the dialectical nature of postfeminism, where opposing meanings coexist and are negotiated, and ultimately points to the limits of postfeminism by negating a reality in which gender equality has been achieved' (2012: 233). The contradiction between the 'successful' postfeminist narrative of Fey's career – displayed in glossy magazine interviews and photoshoots, chat show appearances and award ceremonies – and the onscreen 'failures' of Liz Lemon works to queer postfeminist heterofemininity. Tina Fey as Liz Lemon offers a troubling account of contemporary femininity by demonstrating how the postfeminist fantasy of professional success – 'having it all' – is complex and compromised by depicting 'a feminist TV writer complicit in profit-driven, sexist mainstream media and [...] exploring the messy ways feminist ideals actually play out in institutions and in popular culture' (Mizejewski 2012: para 4). That gender trouble is made evident by *30 Rock*'s complex relation to the real contexts in which it is produced and broadcast.

30 Rock is set in the studios of a television comedy show similar to *Saturday Night Live*. Liz Lemon is the showrunner of *The Girly Show*, which struggles in the ratings until her new boss, Jack Donaghy, forces her to accept a different lead performer, the African American comedian 'crazy' Tracy Jordan (Tracy Morgan). Jordan rapidly becomes the star of a renamed *TGS with Tracy Jordan*, ousting Lemon's friend, Jenna, for whom she originally wrote the show. In fact, Fey originally wrote the part of Jenna as a vehicle for her colleague and friend on *Saturday Night Live*, Rachel Dratch, but following the pilot Jane Krakowski was cast as Jenna, leaving Dratch to play a number of eccentric secondary characters during the first season (Dratch 2012). *30 Rock*'s repeated exposure of the pressures and compromises involved in making network comedy grounds the series in industrial reality. It is rooted in the comedy tradition of a show-about-a-show, like HBO's *The Larry Sanders Show* (1992–8), and workplace comedies such as *The Office*. This reflexive intertextual relation to television and popular culture make *30 Rock* an emblematic new comedy with a palimpsestic relation to the real, playing upon the celebrity personae and career histories of its cast and guest stars.

30 Rock also follows a change in American television comedy which Jane Feuer identifies as a move towards queer humour:

Just as in the earlier sitcoms, Jewish humour became American humour; nowadays it might be that 'queer' humour is American humour, that the 'camp' sensibility long cherished by closeted gay men has now become part of mainstream American humour. Following a definition of 'camp' as a 'gay sensibility', we can say that 'queer humour' embraces both identification and parody, that it paradoxically combines into one sensibility the most extreme feelings of empathy and the bitchiest kind of detached amusement (2008b)

Such humour informs *30 Rock*, satirising Liz Lemon's struggles to secure a romantic partner and adopt a child but not ignoring the pathos which those struggles entail. From the outset, Liz's gender and sexual failures are central to the comedy. As Emily Nussbaum noted, Liz Lemon is not the standard romantic comedy heroine, but something more strange and interesting (2012b). She confounds the trajectory of Hollywood romcom, that postfeminist narrative which follows women on their journey to gain independence, struggle with the pressures of 'having it all' and finally find a happy-ever-after with a nice New Man (Glitre 2011: 19). *30 Rock* extends the terms of romantic comedy from its first season by placing gender and sexual orientation at the centre of its scripts and treating all identities as potentially queer.

Liz's heterosexuality is examined in the first season though a date with another woman. Whereas in *Friends* such a scenario might produce a hysterical reaction — what Margo Miller calls 'ironic dismissal' (2006: 148) — here it addresses Liz's loneliness as a single professional woman, opening the debate out into a broader discussion of sexual identity. In 'Blind date' (1:3) Liz is in her usual bad temper and Jack, correctly diagnosing that she has 'not been touched' recently, offers to set her up with his friend Thomas. Liz initially refuses, but after choking on a TV dinner while alone in her apartment kitchen she is scared into agreement. Heterosexual romance is thus immediately problematised by the implication that Liz is driven as much by fear of dying alone as by any desire for a significant other. Preparations for the date parody the Cinderella narrative of romantic comedy. Liz is not intending to change out of her work clothes but Jack gives her cash to go shopping in her lunch hour, telling her to 'find something in a *women's* clothing store'. Her subsequent glamorous departure through the writers' room is greeted with wolf whistles from male colleagues at this makeover from ugly duckling to swan. So far, so postfeminist. The comic twist to this romance is that the date turns out to be with *Gretchen* Thomas (Stephanie March), as Jack has assumed that Liz is a lesbian.

When Gretchen asks if anyone has made this mistake before, a series of flashbacks show the younger Liz Lemon being mistaken for a boy or a lesbian. The joke attests to the limitations of heteronormative femininity in a postfeminist era. *30 Rock* repeatedly addresses Hollywood's narrow definition of heterofemininity and in this episode lesbian identity is neither derided nor dismissed. Gretchen asserts that she is not interested in straight women but they agree to have dinner and meet up again as friends. A range of lesbian stereotypes are lampooned. Gretchen conforms to a glossy configuration of lesbian identity informed by series such as *The L Word* (Showtime 2004–9), but Liz is the one who reels out clichés, planning trips to IKEA together. When Gretchen ends the friendship because she is in danger of becoming romantically involved, Liz again voices an offensive scenario, suggesting that in 25 years' time if they are both still alone they should move in together and, if it would 'help' Gretchen, Liz would let her 'do stuff' to her. At this point Gretchen makes an exit, saying: 'I can't be around you anymore.' Liz regretfully notes that this is 'what the guys always say'. Jack Donaghy and the men in the writers' room appear more broadminded than Liz in this instance, Jack encouraging Liz to meet Gretchen again and identifying Liz's shoes as 'bi-curious'. The writers' room advocates her new relationship, albeit because Gretchen 'is hot'. Pete, Liz's friend, encourages her to consider it, despite Liz's annoyance that men just think women can 'flip a switch' with their sexual preferences. When Liz retaliates by asking if Pete would consider having a relationship with their colleague Frank, Pete is surprisingly open-minded. The episode sails close to offence at several points, but proposes sexuality as more fluid and less predictable than Liz Lemon is willing to acknowledge. Such storylines situate *30 Rock* in relation to discourses more often associated with third-wave feminism, navigating the contingency of multifaceted identities in late Western modernity (Budgeon 2011: 280).

30 Rock repeatedly exposes the narrative tropes of romantic comedy, undermining happy endings and revealing the extent to which such fantasies saturate postfeminist popular culture. In 'The head and the hair' (1:11), an ideal date turns out to be Liz's third cousin; in

'The Bubble' (3:15), a handsome neighbour, Dr Drew Baird (Jon Hamm), proves impossible to date because he is completely incompetent but lives in a 'bubble' where everyone is nice to him because of his looks. As Liz states: 'He is a victim of our culture's obscene cult of superficiality'. In the final season, Liz gets married and adopts a child but she refuses to have a conventional wedding and almost fails to notice the success of her adoption owing to the threatened cancellation of her television show. *30 Rock* offers a critique of Hollywood's heteronormative happy endings. Katherine Glitre notes the postfeminist confusion of pleasure with empowerment: '"Popular feminism" is feminism without protest, politics replaced with pleasurable self-indulgence in the personal problems of the privileged few' (2011: 28). *30 Rock* queers postfeminism by making those personal problems and pleasurable self-indulgences visibly ridiculous. These are not protagonists we want to identify with, but protagonists whose struggles and discomforts quietly burst the bubble of prettier, straighter, romantic comedies.

'I Want to Go to There'

Liz Lemon acquires a number of stock phrases in *30 Rock*, such as 'What the what?!', 'Bleurgh', 'Shut it down' and 'I want to go to there'. This last statement, based on Fey's daughter's first reaction to the Disney World website, is deployed as a wistful evocation of desire, whether that be for a particular person or for a type of food (see jlucas8's comment on Davies 2013). 'I want to go to there' effectively describes the Lacanian desire to desire, the impossible fulfilment that Hollywood narratives have historically deployed as a means of selling heteronormativity and branded goods. 'I want to go to there' also posits a childlike, *randomly* desiring subject which undercuts the normative sexual and gender identities posited by Hollywood romance (Best 2005). This random configuration of desire and identity opens up queer readings of *30 Rock*.

The comedy vérité aesthetic of *30 Rock* is a logical style for a television show about a television show. Accordingly, one might expect it to play out the tension that Ros Gill observes in poststructuralist analyses of popular media: 'in the last few years, images that for some commentators represent crude and offensive stereotypes have been reclaimed as ironic, playful or even subversive comments or send-ups'

(2007: 13). *30 Rock*, however, comments on that 'ironic' reclamation of stereotypes, by placing the liberal politics of Liz Lemon in a setting where the intersectionality of identity is overwhelming. This is evident in the relationships between women on the show and, most significantly, in the inability of different generations of women to communicate effectively with each other. Cerie Xerox (Katrina Bowden) is the beautiful but incompetent production assistant on *TGS*. As her name implies, she is a cypher, epitomising a postfeminist millennial: the 'girl' (Projansky 2007).

In 'Jack the Writer' (1:4), the men in the writers' room are ogling Cerie in one of her many revealing and inappropriate outfits, recapped in a montage of flashbacks, most of which resemble underwear. Liz decides to have a quiet word with Cerie about this, assuming that she intends to work her way into the industry, but is taken aback when Cerie says that she does not want to work in television but rather to 'marry rich and then design handbags' (Figure 2.2). Cerie's main concern throughout the series is that people treat her as pretty. Like Dr Drew Baird, she lives in 'the bubble', benefiting from the superficiality of media culture. Instead of perceiving herself as a disadvantaged or exploited object of the male gaze, Cerie pities Liz, often commenting on her greater age and repeatedly assuming that Liz is divorced.

Figure 2.2 Liz talks to Cerie about what she wears to work in 'Jack the Writer' (*30 Rock*, 1:4, NBC, 2008–13).

Jenna Maroney, on the other hand, is jealous of Cerie's youth, frequently attempting to follow her style in an attempt to be 'cool' and anxiously policing her own appearance for signs of ageing. Jenna is an older and more professionally ambitious version of Cerie, who only deploys feminist discourse when it is to her advantage. In 'Believe in the stars' (3:2), Jenna and Tracy Jordan try to settle a dispute about who is the more oppressed, a white woman or a black man, by swapping roles in a deliberately offensive melange of cross-dressing and blacking-/whiting-up. In these comic interactions feminism is played against postfeminism, age against youth, race against gender, exposing limited assumptions on both sides, but also privileging the point of view of Liz Lemon. As the central protagonist, Lemon has the most call on audience identification, so that we are invited to critique Cerie's vapidity and Jenna's self-absorption. The post-modern irony that the show calls upon thus only goes so far. *30 Rock* mocks the excesses and egos of show*business*, commenting upon the dubious politics of corporate America and exposing the contradictions of postfeminist popular culture.

Liz Lemon is an 'unruly woman' but only in the context of twenty-first-century hyperfemininity. Cerie Xerox represents a postfeminist discourse that only sees *proper* femininity as a young, white straight woman evacuated of all politics. Such limited accounts of gender continue to damage and restrict women. Going back to Kathleen Rowe's definition we can see how, in relation to this extreme image of postmillennial femininity, Liz Lemon is indeed unruly. She refuses to 'confine herself to her proper place', as she runs *The Girly Show*. She *is* 'androgynous or hermaphroditic' according to Jack Donaghy, while Cerie views her as 'old or masculinized'. Liz is frequently spattered with whatever food she has consumed that day, thus associating her with 'dirt, liminality (thresholds, borders, or margins), and taboo, rendering her above all a figure of ambivalence' (Rowe 1995: 31). Liz Lemon differs from earlier unruly women, however, in that she appears fully cognisant of the costs and possibilities such unruliness entails. She suffers for her difference, but also employs and embraces it, so that unruliness is not embodied in this character but rather enacted in a self-consciously performative manner. Citing Judith Halberstam's work on female masculinity, Eleanor Patterson remarks how 'Liz's masculinity exceeds to the point that she becomes a straight drag king. [. . .] Liz's aggressive and unpolished behaviour further masculinizes her, and troubles the dominance of hegemonic male masculinity' (2012: 243). Patterson cites the season four episode 'Black light attack' (4:10), where Liz sports a moustache, but also notes how the show depicts her as 'ugly and lower class' because she does not conform to a mainstream heterofemininity which is young, groomed and silent (2012: 243). This ambivalent queering of gender performance, celebrating otherness while at the same time framing it within a distinctly heteronormative culture, permeates *30 Rock*.

That complex rendering of identities is also evident in the show's examination of queer sexualities. In 2011 *30 Rock* won a GLAAD award for the episode 'Klaus and Greta' (4:9) featuring Liz Lemon's gay cousin. GLAAD (formerly the Gay and Lesbian Alliance Against Defamation) campaigns against homophobic media representations of LGBTQ people and hosts an annual Media Awards ceremony to: 'recognize and honor media for their fair, accurate and inclusive representations of the lesbian, gay, bisexual and transgender community, and the issues that affect our lives' (GLAAD n.d.). Tina Fey attended the 2011 event to receive the award, and has been clear about *30 Rock*'s commitment to diversity and equality. Later that year, however, the show was at the centre of a controversy following a homophobic stand-up routine by Tracy Morgan, who plays Tracy Jordan in *30 Rock*, in which he 'joked' that if his son was gay he would kill him. Morgan went on to work with GLAAD, and a public apology was issued by Tina Fey and the NBC executive Bob Greenblatt. Fey's statement was quoted on the GLAAD website:

> I hope for his sake that Tracy's apology will be accepted as sincere by his gay and lesbian coworkers at *30 Rock*, without whom Tracy would not have lines to say, clothes to wear, sets to stand on, scene partners to act with, or a printed-out paycheck from accounting to put in his pocket. The other producers and I pride ourselves on *30 Rock* being a diverse, safe, and fair workplace (Kane 2011)

In January 2012 *30 Rock* screened a double episode which addressed Tracy Morgan's 'rant' by placing Tracy Jordan in a similar scenario, with GLAAD's evident approval (Ferraro 2012).

An awareness of LGBTQ issues is evident throughout the show's six-year run, as *30 Rock* frequently addresses sexual politics in a queerly playful manner. In 'Cougars' (2:7), Liz is asked out by a much younger man. Jamie, the coffee delivery boy, initially says that he is 25 and Liz lets him believe that she is 29, whereas in fact he is 20 and she is 37. Jenna approves of their liaison, aligning herself with Liz as a 'cougar', and immediately acquiring a boyfriend who is even younger than Jamie. This episode exposes the double standard regarding age, gender and 'normative' desire. It also addresses the limits of heteromasculinity when Frank, one of the writers, falls for Jamie too. Frank is stereotypically straight through much of the series, ogling Cerie, watching porn and generally behaving like an adolescent. His baseball cap displays unlikely mottos, and he is overweight, unshaven and slovenly. Nevertheless, in 'Cougars' Frank goes 'gay for Jamie', challenging his character's established heteromasculinity, admitting 'I want to kiss him on the mouth' and practising a 'gay' look by donning a vest and neckerchief and attempting to rotate his hips. Frank's colleagues do not find his new identity shocking, but question its validity. Liz's comment that 'You can't be gay for one person [...] unless you're a lady and meet Ellen' underlines the transgressive aspect of Frank's new sexual identity. Whereas female sexuality is often regarded as malleable (as Liz observed in 'Blind date'), male sexuality is perceived as more fixed, predicated upon hegemonic masculinity. 'Cougars' also parodies the stereotype of the groomed gay man with the portly, scruffy Frank, thereby troubling homonormative and heteronormative masculinities. At one point Frank tells an uninterested Jamie: 'We're just two straight guys who want to enjoy each other's bodies'. In a sequence after the final credits, he is shown dancing wildly at a gay disco in a pink baseball cap with the motto 'Power tool', before admitting to his two dance partners 'This is not working; I'm not gay gay.' Frank's desire for another man reiterates the philosophy of 'I want to go to there' by having an otherwise hyper-heteromasculine character suddenly encounter, and acknowledge, same-sex desire. This episode is one of many in *30 Rock* which question the hegemony of identity, whether it be sexuality, gender, race or class.

The epitome of *30 Rock*'s queered heterofemininity is Jenna Maroney, whose insecure, ambitious and theatrical persona mines a history of camp. Like Samantha Jones on *Sex and the City*, Jenna is effectively a drag queen (Adkins 2008: 118–19, Jermyn 2009: 64–5). It is no surprise that, when Jenna decides to acquire an entourage, it is populated by camp gay men rather than other women ('Secrets and lies', 2:8). Jenna's off-kilter film projects and amoral willingness to do anything to become famous establish her at the core of *30 Rock*'s camp aesthetic. Her motives are never authentic:

> Frank: You're a big phoney ... everything about you is fake. Your tan's fake, your hair's fake –
> Jenna: Not the front!
> Frank: You've never done or said anything real or genuine the whole time I've known you. ('Up All Night', 1:13)

Jenna's lack of heteronormative, authentic subjectivity embodies the 'I want to go to there' aspect of *30 Rock*. This comedy aesthetic speaks to a queer sensibility:

> Following Marx's definition of critical theory as 'the self-clarification of the struggles and wishes of the age', we might think of queer theory as the project of elaborating, in ways that cannot be predicted in advance, this question: what do queers want? (Warner 1993: vii)

Echoing the Freudian question 'what do women want?', Michael Warner poses this question about queer desire as a rhetorical strategy, in order to elaborate on queer theory and identity as rejecting 'a minoritizing logic of toleration or simple political interest-representation in favour of a more thorough resistance to regimes of the normal' (1993: xxvi). In a similar manner, *30 Rock* depicts unspecifiable queer desires and undermines secure heteronormative identities. Gender and sexuality are 'highly unstable' in *30 Rock* as the show unpicks Hollywood romance and presents characters who do not sit securely within heteronormative or homonormative identities (Halley 1993: 83).

Parks and Recreation

If *30 Rock*'s queered characters are situated in an urban, liberal, media industry setting, *Parks and Recreation* addresses queer possibilities in the more conservative arena of rural civic politics. Introduced as a mid-season replacement of six initial episodes, the series was critically panned even before it was broadcast, and the second season underwent a shift in emphasis (Martin 2009). From the outset, however, *Parks and Recreation* examines gender, power and sexual identity in the context of recent shifts in American politics. The show's creators researched the show by sitting in on local government meetings in Los Angeles (Leitch 2009; Martin 2009). Its location thus gives *Parks and Recreation* particular resonance in an era when voters have lost confidence in the democratic process:

> 'When we were talking about this, we were in the middle of the election,' says *Parks and Recreation* co-creator (and one of [the] former writer-producers of *The Office*) Michael Schur. 'The economy hadn't collapsed yet, but we got the general sense that the government was going to be playing a more significant role in years to come. We had no idea how right we were.' Thus, the clueless bosses are no longer reporting back to the corporate home office: They're reporting back to Washington (Or, as the case may be, Pawnee City Hall.) On *The Office*, employees are shiftless, lazy, and uninspired by their work, so nothing gets done. On *Parks and Recreation*, it's the opposite: Idealistic wannabe politicians and concerned citizens strive to make the world a better place, and keep getting rebuffed by democracy (Leitch 2009)

Whereas *30 Rock* was cynically post-modern, exposing the selfish tendencies of its central characters, *Parks and Recreation* is remarkably positive about the behaviour of its public servants. Rural Indiana becomes a comedic space in which eccentric identities and relationships are embraced. Although the fictional Pawnee is shown to have a history of racism, misogyny and homophobia, it is also a location in which normative identities may be playfully subverted. There is no normal here. In this respect it plays out the complexities and queer possibilities of gender and sexuality in a rural setting:

> While gender codes may be somewhat more flexible in urban settings, this also means that people become more astute in urban contexts at reading gender. In the context of a small town where there are strict codes of normativity, there is also a greater potential for subverting the codes surreptitiously [...] the rural context allows for a different array of acts, practices, performances, and identifications (Halberstam 2005: 44)

This is played out in *Parks and Recreation*, as the show demonstrates the peculiarity of heteronormative behaviours and challenges the limits of homonormative models.

The show's protagonist, Leslie Knope (Amy Poehler), who tends to be the butt of jokes in the first season, is the moral pivot of the series by season two. In 'Pawnee Zoo' (2:1), Leslie officiates at the 'cute' wedding of two penguins to promote the local zoo, a storyline inspired by the same-sex romance of two penguins at San Francisco Zoo. Leslie becomes the focus of a media storm regarding the legalisation of gay marriage when it emerges that the penguins, shown having sex after the ceremony, are male. She is celebrated by Pawnee's gay bar, The Bulge, for supporting gay rights and attacked by Marcia Langman (Darlene Hunt) from Pawnee's Society for Family Stability Foundation (SFSF), who asserts: 'When gays marry it ruins marriage for the rest of us' (2:1). Leslie is a reluctant revolutionary. She was unaware that Tux and Flipper were both male but refuses to annul the marriage when the story breaks. Leslie's colleague and love interest, Mark Brendanawicz (Paul Schneider), congratulates her on being an activist but she insists she is mainstream; she is unwilling to accept a cake delivered to her office by the boys at The Bulge on the grounds that as a public official she cannot be seen to take a political stance. Leslie is no radical. When April Ludgate (Aubrey Plaza) introduces Leslie to her boyfriend, Derek (Blake Lee), and his boyfriend, Ben (Josh Duvendeck), Leslie is floored by their relationship:

> April: Hey! This is my boyfriend Derek, and this is Derek's boyfriend Ben.
> Derek: Hi.
> Leslie: Hey! Oh. Wait, sorry. What's the situation?
> April: What do you mean?
> Leslie: How does this work?
> April: Derek is gay but he's straight for me and he's gay for Ben and Ben's really gay for Derek. And I hate Ben.
> Derek: It's not that complicated.
> Ben: No.
> Leslie: Oh. Yeah. Sure.
> [Confessional to camera]
> Leslie: The thing about youth culture is I don't understand it.
> ('Pawnee Zoo', 2:1)

W654

HD-302157492

When Derek, April and Ben throw a party for Leslie at The Bulge, however, she is convinced to attend because they have made a poster of her based on Obama's famous 'Hope' poster designed by the street artist Shepard Fairey. Leslie is deeply flattered by the 'Knope We Can' poster, apparently unaware of its grammatical incongruity (Engstrom 2013: 10). For a woman whose stated ambition is to become president such an invitation is irresistible. Leslie literally becomes a poster girl for LGBTQ politics in this episode. Subsequent scenes at The Bulge satirise the enthusiasm of straight women for LGBTQ culture, showing Leslie dancing frenetically as she become increasingly inebriated. When Leslie appears on the local television talk show *Pawnee Today*, however, she is lambasted by the show's host, Joan Callamezzo (Mo Collins), by Marcia Langman from the SFSF, and by all the viewers who call in suggesting that she resign. By the close of the episode Leslie is driving Tux and Flipper to Iowa, where gay marriage is legal, having given her best friend, Ann Perkins (Rashida Jones), the go-ahead to date Leslie's ex-boyfriend, Mark Brandanowitz. As Leslie says to Ann: 'He may not be my gay penguin but he could be yours.' The debate about gay marriage is thus deployed to queer straight femininity *and* heterosexual romance. The pairing of two male penguins, said to 'mate for life', becomes a model for all relationships, contradicting the conservative mindset represented on *Pawnee Today*.

Echoing shows like *The West Wing* (NBC 1999–2006) and *Northern Exposure* (CBS 1990–5), *Parks and Recreation* offers its viewers an ideal America, in which liberal views are debated and queer identities validated. Its provincial setting appears to align *Parks and Recreation* with the retreatist narratives of postfeminist romantic comedies such as *Sweet Home Alabama* (Andy Tennant, 2002) and *Hart of Dixie* (The CW 2011–15):

> Typically tracing the reluctant movement of the independent, urban-dwelling professional woman to a rural, small-town setting, the retreatist ur-text exposes the heroine to a (hitherto unknown or forgotten) world in which personal relationships, the home and the community take priority over the ruthless commercial machinations of late-capitalist enterprise. While the protagonist initially experiences the remote environment into which she is jettisoned as alien, hostile and at odds with her usual tastes and

routines, she gradually acclimatizes to her new habitat and comes to appreciate the quaint, simple charms of small-town life – charms which are invariably enhanced by the presence of an attractive romantic prospect. Through the folksy wisdom and kind-hearted hospitality of the locals, the heroine undergoes a process of re-education, in which her urban 'feminist' individualism is reassessed alongside a home-and-community-oriented ethic of care (Munford and Waters 2014: 65–6)

Parks and Recreation offers a twist on the retreatist model, exploding the 'quaint, simple charms of small-town life'. Pawnee, Indiana – 'First in friendship, Fourth in obesity' – parodies the clichés of that postfeminist retreatist fantasy. The 'ruthless commercial machinations of late-capitalist enterprise' are just as evident here as in the big city. Sweetums, an influential local manufacturer, enlists the Parks and Recreation department's help to market their new 'nutritional' snack bar, Nutriyums. This alliance between a public body and a private corporation is stymied when Ann Perkins discovers that the bars are made primarily from high-fructose corn syrup ('Sweetums', 2:15). Pawnee is thus a warped mirror for national politics, and the series repeatedly addresses issues of identity.

Throughout *Parks and Recreation* Pawnee is shown to harbour historical and contemporary bigotry. In 'The Camel' (2:9), the Parks and Recreation department are involved in a City Hall competition to design a new mural to replace the current version of the 'Spirit of Pawnee':

> The artist, a delightful racist named Peter Thorbutte, was told to create an image that would express how [a proposed 1915 railway line] would better the town. In his mind, this meant showing a steam train blasting past Chinese stereotypes who are laughing at the Native Americans who are being mown down by the train while drunk on whiskey made by (naturally) the Irish, while the Irish folk (leprechauns, really) are yelled at by killjoy harpie suffragettes. Really, nobody looks good here (Knope 2011: 165)

Other City Hall murals include 'The Trial of Chief Wamapo', in which the chief of the indigenous Wamapoke tribe is shown tied to a tree as cavalrymen point a cannon at his chest, and 'Pawnee Zoo', in which Rabbi Heifetz is depicted in a cage alongside animal exhibits, as the

Pawneeans of 1935 mistook him for 'a new species' (Knope 2011: 168). At the end of this episode the town council decide they cannot afford to replace the offensive 'Spirit of Pawnee' mural and instead rename it 'The Diversity Express'. Racist aspects of American history are thus satirised. The murals in Pawnee City Hall are a visual reminder of the uncomfortable histories on which the United States is built. This is not a cosy vision of the authentic provinces as opposed to the tarnished inauthenticity of the metropolis; Pawnee plays out in microcosm issues that are at stake across America. As Emily Nussbaum observes in *The New Yorker*:

> *Parks* [*sic*] is not an overtly ideological show, but buried within it are thoughtful, complex political themes that extend into the larger world in a way that's rare for modern network shows [...] for all its warmth, *Parks* suggests the brutality of politics better than many dramas (2012a)

In season one, *Parks and Recreation* addresses the sexism and double-dealing of the political process as Leslie tries to become one of the boys ('Boys' Club' 1:4). In 'The Banquet' (1:5) she mistakenly gets a haircut at a barbers, of which she is very proud, despite the fact that people around her mistake her for a man or a lesbian as a result. Like Liz Lemon, Leslie's heterofemininity is mutable, making her an 'unruly woman' in postfeminist terms. In the same episode Leslie tries and fails to blackmail a fellow official in order to gain support for her project. Such storylines demonstrate the contradictions between Leslie's heteronormative desires and her inability to fully achieve hegemonic heterofemininity, just as her political ambition is confounded by her ethical refusal to play the 'boys' games by underhand means. Leslie embodies disordered femininity. Despite her predilection for paperwork and planning she is initially unable to manage her private life. In season two, she decides to hold a dinner party at her home to impress her current boyfriend, Justin Anderson (Justin Theroux), but Ann Perkins discovers that she is a hoarder, her house filled with newspapers and other detritus that she has been unable to throw out:

> Leslie: It's a little messy ...
> Ann: Your house is like a crazy person's garage! ('Leslie's House', 2:14)

When Leslie drafts tutors from the local college to help her de-clutter the house and staff her dinner party, she is accused of abusing her power. At the end of the episode it emerges that she has submitted to the subsequent investigation in order to ask Justin under oath whether he had enjoyed her party. In all these ways *Parks and Recreation* speaks back to postfeminist retreatism, just as *30 Rock* challenges the romantic scripts of Hollywood comedy. If there is any retreatist romantic re-education here it is a role reversal, with the appearance of Ben Wyatt (Adam Scott) at the end of the second season. Ben is a state auditor, who arrives in Pawnee with his boss, Chris Traeger (Rob Lowe), to investigate the town's finances. During season three, Ben develops a romance with Leslie and settles in Pawnee, convinced of its charms by her undimmable enthusiasm.

Parks and Recreation's surreal take on local politics extends to municipal functionaries, so that the librarian is a Machiavellian villain:

Leslie: Pawnee's Library Department is the most diabolical, ruthless bunch of bureaucrats I've ever seen. They're like a biker gang, but instead of shotguns and crystal meth they use political savvy, and shushing [...]
Tom: Punk-ass book jockeys. ('Ron and Tammy', 2:8)

This conversation introduces Tammy Swanson (Megan Mullally), the second ex-wife of Leslie Knope's boss, Ron Swanson (Nick Offerman). Tammy first appears when Pawnee Library vies with the Parks and Recreation department for Leslie's beloved Lot 48, a site on which she dreams of building a new park. Mullally's award-winning performance as Karen Walker in *Will and Grace* (NBC 1998–2006) informs her roles on *30 Rock*, where she plays Liz Lemon's adoption agent, and *Parks and Recreation*. Danielle Mitchell argues that, in *Will and Grace*, Karen Walker 'symbolizes the programme's most progressive political work [...] by challenging the binary construction of sexuality and working to queer marriage' (2006: 86). This queer dynamic is carried through to *Parks and Recreation* as, in the skewed world of Pawnee, Indiana, Ron and Tammy are a particularly skewed couple. When they first meet, Tammy tells Leslie, 'He's my man and we have something twisted and beautiful' ('Ron and Tammy', 2:8).

Mullally and Offerman are a married couple and stage comedy shows together, often appearing on chat shows such as *Conan* (TBS 2010–), *Today* (NBC 1952–) and *The Tonight Show Starring Jimmy Fallon* (NBC 2014–) to promote their work. In 2016 they undertook an intensive tour of the United States and UK with a comedy revue, *The Summer of 69: No Apostrophe*. Their work on *Parks and Recreation* is thus informed by their extradiegetic celebrity – and vice versa. Mullally and Offerman represent their relationship as an eccentric heterosexual partnership. The Ron and Tammy relationship on *Parks and Recreation* plays upon and amplifies aspects of their celebrity personae.

When Leslie approaches Tammy to discuss Lot 48 in season two, she is unnerved by Tammy's conciliatory approach, but it emerges that this conceals a different agenda, as Tammy uses Leslie to get to Ron. Although Ron initially describes Tammy as 'programmed by someone from the future to come back and destroy all happiness' (2:8) – a feminine Terminator – he is ambushed by Leslie's attempt to reconcile the divorced couple. The subsequent sequence shows Tammy and Ron having coffee in a diner, screaming at each other, eating in separate booths, eating each other, trying to have sex on a table, then running from the diner and into a motel room while stripping their clothes off. Ron later disturbs Leslie by describing the experience as 'so intense I didn't know where my flesh stopped and hers began [. . .] that woman really knows her way around a penis' ('Ron and Tammy', 2:8). This hyperbolic depiction makes heterosexual 'passion' strange, marking it as deviant. It transpires that Tammy is using Ron to acquire Lot 48 for the Library Department and Ron, a broken man, asks Leslie to help him break up with Tammy again. Their final encounter shows Ron emerging from Tammy's office with part of his moustache missing and a drawing pin stuck in his forehead. Lot 48 is safe but he and Leslie flee the Library Department. This satire on desire and the trope of the femme fatale queers heterosexuality, building on Mullally's role in *Will and Grace* and on Offerman and Mullally's extradiegetic celebrity. Ron and Tammy's passion is transgressive, destructive and aberrant.

In later episodes Tammy comes back to 'mess with' Ron again, and Leslie and her team have to stage an intervention to return an addled Ron, dressed in a silk kimono with his hair corn-rowed, to his senses ('Ron and Tammy 2', 3:4; Figure 2.3). Tammy is aggressive, scheming and evil, a femme fatale who works against the stereotype of the spinsterish female librarian. Her role is significant within the sitcom because she violently disturbs the monolithic Ron Swanson, a comic embodiment of American retromasculinity.

Parks and Recreation's rescripting of heteronormative romance only goes so far, however. Despite its characters' eccentricities, the sitcom eventually accedes to a 'happy ending' by ushering them into heteronormative relationships, thus eliding the queer potential of friendships between Donna Meagle (Retta) and Tom Haverford (Aziz Ansari) or Leslie and Ann. This is a dominant feature of contemporary American sitcom. While such comedies address and deconstruct heteronormativity, they often fail to follow through the queer possibilities that are evoked. These comedies are marked by their 'contradictory nature and [. . .] sophisticated use of narrative devices', but those contradictions do not produce queer alternatives to the heteronormative script (Lotz 2006: 98–9). The 13-episode finale shoots *Parks and Recreation* into a future '2017', principally signified by holographic tablets provided free to the inhabitants of Pawnee by the ICT corporation Gryzzl. Leslie and Ben have triplets at the end of season six; the children rarely appear on screen in season seven but are depicted as exhausting their parents. Ron Swanson leaves the Parks and Rec department to set up a private business, The Very Good Building and Development Company, marries Diane Lewis (Lucy

Figure 2.3 Ron under his ex-wife Tammy's spell in 'Ron and Tammy 2' (*Parks and Recreation*, 3:4, NBC, 2009–15).

Lawless) and quietly has a son with her. Ann Perkins and Chris Traeger agree to have a child together and then become a couple. April Ludgate and Andy Dwyer (Chris Pratt) settle down and become parents. The model is much the same throughout. Tom Haverford and Donna Meagle both find ideal partners and pair off. This is an entirely Hollywood ending for *Parks and Recreation*'s small-town eccentrics.

This heteronormative conclusion works against the queer community that *Parks and Recreation* created. As one reviewer noted:

> it's a celebration of beginnings in addition to endings, of the idea that there are always possibilities, even if those end up leading you back to the same people (kind of like a wedding!). [...] All the show needed to end on a high note was to allow all of its characters the chance to renew their vows. (Thurm 2015)

Such hyperbole inadvertently describes the heteronormative narrative trajectory to which *Parks and Recreation* eventually accedes. While the show has an impressive track record in addressing feminist and queer identities, it cannot resist the gravitational pull of a Hollywood ending (Engstrom 2013). In season six, Billy Eichner is introduced as the campily petulant government employee Craig Middleman when Pawnee merges with the rival town Eagleton, but he only becomes a permanent character in the final season and is then married to Donna and Tom's hairdresser, Typhoon (Rodney To), in the penultimate episode ('One Last Ride – 1', 7:12). Happiness here means residing within a married couple; the 'gay penguin' scenario that opened the second season is here recapitulated as a straighter model where relationships are endorsed by heteronormative legislation. The circular inevitability which 'leads you back to the same people' is not just 'kind of like a wedding', it *is* a wedding, with the sexual politics that weddings entail: 'Marriage flattens out the varied terrain of queer social life and reduces the differences that make queers, well, queer, to legal distinctions that can be ironed out by the strong hand of the law' (Halberstam 2012: 114). *Parks and Recreation*'s finale exposes the tension between the visibility of queer identities on television and television's tendency to queer identity:

> At the same time that more queers are making it to television, television itself is being remade, some might say, as more queer:

more eccentric and playful, more connective and transformative, with more stand-out strangeness than just stand-up straightness. Yet those textualities and sexualities need not – in fact, often do not – go together in quite that way. That is, the point that some television forms may be becoming, in a sense, more queered doesn't necessarily mean that more queers appear in them [...] (Joyrich 2014: 135)

There appears to be a law of diminishing returns where contemporary sitcom queers heterosexual hegemony. Nevertheless, the rackety and slapdash final season of *Parks and Recreation* offers some food for thought.

Parks and Recreation largely ignores LGBTQ identities as its narrative progresses, yet – perhaps, as Joyrich suggests, *because* it does so – it produces a complex and contradictory rendering of heterosexuality even as it ushers its main cast into heteronormative units. In the two-part finale the temporal juxtapositions between the diegetic narrative and the futures it depicts cut through linear time in a manner which gestures towards other possibilities. Ron, Leslie and Ben in particular are afforded projected futures that are introduced initially through a split screen; the time frame is so confusing (2017? 2012? 2025?) that the year is constantly reiterated in a subtitle. As each cast member is given a happy ending the shifting temporality of the finale mitigates against the notion of *ending* at all. Ron, happily married (we assume) to Diane, is last seen returning to the wilderness, gleefully paddling a canoe alone across a spectacular lake after Leslie has secured him the job of managing a National Park. Tom Haverford has paradoxically found success by writing bestselling books about failure. In 2025 Leslie and Ben are both invited to run for Governor of Indiana and Ben steps aside. We then see Leslie's address at Indiana University in 2035 where she refers to new challenges, and some years later she and Ben attend Jerry/Larry/Garry Gergich (Jim O'Heir)'s funeral with a secret service detail. Could Leslie have achieved her goal of becoming president? The showrunner Michael Schur, who co-wrote the finale with Amy Poehler, says that they deliberately left that question hanging (Berkshire 2015).

This refusal to provide a final resolution is signalled through one of *Parks and Recreation*'s most bizarre characters. Tom Haverford's sometime friend and business partner, Jean-Ralphio (Ben Schwarz), fakes his own death to run off to Tajikistan and set up a casino (Berkshire 2015). Death really does have no dominion here. The refusal of a conclusive ending, to finitely stop the narrative, is a reminder of *Parks and Recreation*'s queered aesthetic. Just as the gender politics of the show offer a taste of prime-time liberal feminism (Engstrom 2013; Galo 2015), so heteromasculinity within *Parks and Recreation* is constantly undercut. The performativity of straight, white masculinity is foregrounded through male characters' alter egos: Ron Swanson as heartthrob jazz saxophonist 'Duke Silver', Andy Dwyer as 'Burt Macklin' or 'Jonny Karate', and Ben Wyatt's predilection for cosplay. Heterosexual hegemony is disturbed in *Parks and Recreation* even though the show does not fully commit to a queer politics.

Postscript

The feminist praxis of *30 Rock* and *Parks and Recreation* has been played out in the activities of its stars. Both Tina Fey and Amy Poehler have been instrumental in supporting younger women in television comedy, while Poehler's Smart Girls website advocates 'there's power in looking silly and not caring that you do' (Shuttleworth 2015). This is significant at a moment when organisational structures frequently militate against women gathering together or working collectively (Negra in Gill et al. 2016: 727). Fey wrote and produced *Unbreakable Kimmy Schmidt* (Netflix 2015–), starring Ellie Kemper as an innocent 20-something adjusting to life in New York after being rescued from a cult. Poehler backed Ilana Glazer and Abby Jacobson's independent web series *Broad City*, becoming the show's executive producer when it moved to television (Comedy Central 2014–). Such intergenerational alliances are reiterated in Comedy Central's 'Sisters' sketch, in which Glazer and Jacobson play delinquents 'rescued' by Fey and Poehler's nuns (Spanos 2015). The skit promotes Fey and Poehler's film *Sisters* (Jason Moore 2016), deconstructing the visual narrative by mocking the voice-over – 'Typical male narrator . . .' – and commenting sardonically that nobody wants to see a film where lots of women talk to each other.

Another sketch for *Inside Amy Schumer* (Comedy Central 2013–), 'Last fuckable day', parodies the sexism and ageism of Western media, as Schumer stumbles upon Fey, Julia Louis-Dreyfus and Patricia Arquette celebrating 'the day when the media decides you're not believably fuckable any more'. The older women confirm that this only applies to women, as 'men are fuckable forever' (Handy 2016). Rather than being angry or upset, however, Fey, Louis-Dreyfus and Arquette are delighted, as this means they no longer have to maintain 'this' – a groomed, svelte appearance. To underline the point Louis-Dreyfus chugs a carton of melted ice cream, burps and farts loudly to applause around the table, and is cast off in a rowing boat smoking a cigar as Fey goes home to 'wax her beard'. This intergenerational party, echoing the eccentric, queered community of *Parks and Recreation*, indicates a feminist dialogue that was impossible between Liz Lemon and Cerie Xerox on *30 Rock*. One can only hope that television comedies which show women working, laughing and celebrating together may afford a more feminist environment for generations to come.

This chapter has mapped some of the strategies evident in two primetime comedies that address heterosexual hegemony. *30 Rock* and *Parks and Recreation* expose the exigencies of postfeminist heterofemininity, Hollywood romance and the intersectional politics of twenty-firstcentury popular culture. Neither offers an ideal heroine or a perfect community; rather these shows render identity and community as problematic and always already compromised. These are not fantasy solutions but surprisingly realist commentaries on gender and sexual identity. The failure of characters in these shows to fully inhabit heteronormative fantasies opens up other possibilities, queering heterofemininity and exposing the performativity of hegemonic masculinity. The next chapter expands the discussion of hegemonic masculinity and its effects by examining one of the most successful contemporary American sitcoms, *The Big Bang Theory*.

CHAPTER 3

THE BIG BANG THEORY: QUEERING MASCULINITY IN AMERICAN SITCOM

This chapter examines what happens when non-hegemonic masculinities are at the centre of a mainstream American sitcom; how the queer potential of eccentric masculinities is curtailed and how that dynamic affects female characters within the show. *The Big Bang Theory* (CBS 2007–) is an internationally successful American sitcom which appears to play against hegemonic masculinity. Following the original broadcast of the second season, when CBS aired repeat episodes after its 2009 ratings winner *Two and a Half Men* (2003–15), viewing figures for *The Big Bang Theory* exploded (Wyatt 2009):

> In 2013/2014 primetime on CBS, according to Warner Brothers, *The Big Bang Theory* averaged 'over 23 Million viewers per original telecast, making it the #1 sitcom and the #2 programme in all of Prime' [...]. Likewise, in syndication, it ranked as the number one programme in 2013/2014. Internationally, the viewership counts also remain impressive: for 2013/2014, *The Big Bang Theory* garnered, per telecast, 1.9 million viewers in Germany (PRO7), 1.5 million viewers in Canada (CTV), 875,000 in Australia (NINE), 800,000 in Italy (ITALIA1) and 590,000 in the United Kingdom (E4/CHN4). (Weitekamp 2015: 76, citing direct email communication from Scott Rowe, Senior Vice President, Worldwide Television Communications, Warner Brothers, 18 July 2014)

Margaret Weitekamp notes that this may just be the tip of the iceberg as the multi-platform consumption of television is now impossible to track, although she cites evidence that '"*The Big Bang Theory* was the single most illicitly shared CBS programme and the second most shared overall", behind only HBO's *Game of Thrones*' (2015: 77). As I write, *The Big Bang Theory* is in its tenth season, having celebrated its 200th episode in February 2016, and on 8 November 2016 CBS announced that a spin-off based on Sheldon Cooper's early life was in development. David Lavery memorably described the series as: 'Chuck Lorre and Bill Prady's nerdapalooza, a cultish from the get-go friends sitcom which follows the hilariously pitiful lives of four Caltech scientists and comic book geeks' (2012). In its central cast of characters – Leonard Hofstadter (Johnny Galecki), Sheldon Cooper (Jim Parsons), Howard Wolowitz (Simon Helberg) and Rajesh Koothrappali (Kunal Nayyar) – *The Big Bang Theory* addresses non-hegemonic masculinities, deploying established cinematic and televisual tropes such as the nerd, the bromance, the camp straight man and the socially dysfunctional academic.

The Big Bang Theory has circumnavigated the fiction of hegemonic masculinity, offering a comedic space in which eccentric gender identities may be rehearsed without apparent censure. Judith Halberstam argues that:

> Masculinity [...] becomes legible as masculinity where and when it leaves the white male middle-class body. Arguments about excessive masculinity tend to focus on black bodies (male and female), latino/a bodies, or working-class bodies, and insufficient masculinity is all too often figured by Asian bodies or upper-class bodies; these stereotypical constructions of variable masculinity mark the process by which masculinity becomes dominant in the sphere of white middle-class maleness. (1998: 2)

The male protagonists in *The Big Bang Theory* are certainly marked by race and ethnicity yet they also represent a middle-class community of male academics. Their masculinity is mitigated by their nascent status; they are not yet fully established as professionals or as fully masculine. As overeducated young geeks they are neither fully adult nor fully sexual. Leonard and Raj's ambitions to gain a permanent girlfriend and

Wolowitz's desire for any (female) sexual partner indicate their transitional status during the first five series. Leonard, Sheldon, Raj and Wolowitz are 'insufficiently masculine' but they aspire to hegemonic masculinity. They are fan*boys*, caught in an adolescent time warp of comics and gaming. The 'insufficient masculinity' of the group constitutes the comedy of the early seasons, as they attempt to perform hegemonic masculinity and fail. It is this failure which opens up a queer reading of *The Big Bang Theory*, following Halberstam's concept of failure as a queer narrative strategy in the face of the big bang of early twenty-first-century capitalism:

> I tell it here as a tale of anticapitalist, queer struggle. I tell it also as a narrative about anticolonial struggle, the refusal of legibility, and an art of unbecoming. This is a story of art without markets, drama without a script, narrative without progress. The queer art of failure turns on the impossible, the improbable, the unlikely, and the unremarkable. It quietly loses, and in losing it imagines other goals for life, for love, for art, and for being. (2011: 88)

The male characters in *The Big Bang Theory* offer a prescient example of queer straight masculinity: a masculinity mined for its comic potential but ultimately resolved and contained through the series' gravitational shift in the latter seasons toward a heteronormative destination. As the four friends are paired off, their queer potential is curtailed. They are made legible and 'win' a legitimate place in neoliberal Western society through the progressive script of Hollywood romance. In short, the geeks become 'proper' men, gaining access to hegemonic masculinity through heteronormativity.

The homosocial friendship group is often represented in television sitcom as a safe space in which men can rehearse insecurities and desires beyond the narrative of heterosexual romance (Spangler 1992; Miller 2006; Feasey 2008; Becker 2009). Much of the comedy in the first five seasons of *The Big Bang Theory* addresses the group's inability to secure girlfriends. Leonard's unfulfilled desire for his neighbour Penny (Kaley Cuoco) began as a central storyline and they became an established couple in the fifth season. While heterosexuality provides comic scaffolding within the show, the homosocial friendship group is its narrative focus, detailing the affectionate irritations of men who live, work and play together. *The Big Bang Theory* centres on young men who represent eccentric accounts of gender and sexual identity and are consequently liable to queer readings, yet the series has been unable to resist the gravitational pull of heteronormativity. By the sixth season the central characters are all paired off, their queer 'failures' narratively resolved into the endgame of a heterosexual romance plot. Even Sheldon, the most eccentric figure within the group, is aligned with the dominant norm. Hence, although *The Big Bang Theory* offers a range of appeals to its audience via an array of gender and sexual identities, it refuses to imagine any destination other than that of the straight couple. In these terms it is one of the most interesting sitcoms on American television, rehearsing the potential of queer identities, and addressing homophobic and racist traditions in popular television even as it accedes to them.

Queer Masculinities in Contemporary American Sitcom

In the late twentieth and early twenty-first centuries, American sitcom developed a track record for presenting queer masculinities. Series such as *Frasier* (NBC 1993–2004), *Dharma and Greg* (ABC 1997–2002) and *Malcolm in the Middle* (Fox 2000–6) offer glimpses of men who perform outside the dominant fiction of hegemonic masculinity: the effete bourgeois intellectual, the 'new' man, the camp heterosexual. Much of the comedy in these shows depends upon the nuances of such 'peculiar' figures but they may also be understood as contemporary responses to anxieties about Western heteromasculinity. While male characters in television comedy have historically offered ambivalent accounts of masculinity as asexual, sexually frustrated or childlike, they also address concerns about how gender is inscribed and understood. Carlen Lavigne charts hybrid masculinities in the 2010 Fox police comedy series *The Good Guys*, reading it as a self-consciously ironic response to cinematic tropes of the 'Retributive Man' and the 'New Man' in the 1980s, and proposing that 'The series thus both explores and subverts "typical" masculinities' (2013: 74). The parodic tone of *The Good Guys*, while appropriate for comedy, aligns complex accounts of masculinity with the problematic politics of a neoliberal aesthetic, where sexism and sexual harassment may be depicted within the narrative as if the 'safe' space of television inoculates the perpetrator from any consequences for his actions. Such narrative strategies do have an impact, however: 'Sexual harassment and the objectifications of women thus become an ongoing comedic theme, while the women themselves have little agency within the series' (Lavigne 2013: 76). Where there is a liberal account of masculinity, female characters are often marginalised or underdeveloped.

The Good Guys 'ironically' references hegemonic masculinity, a fictional construct understood as 'white, heterosexual, competitive, individualist and aggressive' (Feasey 2008: 2). Robert Hanke usefully summarises hegemonic masculinity as

> express[ing] the general idea of assumptions and beliefs about masculinity that have become common sense, that may be uncritically absorbed or spontaneously consented to, but that are presumed to have an imperative character in shaping consciousness, norms of conduct, affect, or desire. (1998: 185)

Hegemonic masculinity is thus an elusive, illusive and allusive structure of feeling, an ephemeral discourse with material effects. Although the fiction of hegemonic masculinity may seem to be undermined in television comedies such as *The Good Guys*, its authority is 'ironically' endorsed, as the power inherent in this gender discourse is predicated on the evacuation of an equally fictive 'other'. Michael Kimmel argues that this dominant cultural fantasy of masculinity is dependent on absence rather than presence: 'that being a man means "not being like a woman" irrespective of the age, ethnicity, class, race, or sexual orientation of the male in question' (Kimmel 2004, cited in Feasey 2008: 3).

Kimberly R. Walsh, Elfriede Fürsich and Bonnie S. Jefferson examine this dynamic in *The King of Queens* (CBS 1998–2007) and *According to Jim* (ABC 2001–9). These sitcoms feature 'mismatched couples': male protagonists married to women who are more attractive and intelligent than they are. In such series the longstanding dynamic of the married couple in American sitcom is rewritten only slightly, the comic focus remaining on the 'dumb', slovenly husband who dominates the narrative at the expense of his smarter, prettier wife. Walsh, Fürsich and Jefferson argue that such sitcoms deploy 'traditional masculinity as a branding device. Sexist storylines, then, become commodified nostalgic packages connecting viewers to "better" (television) times' (2008: 131). Masculinity is thus directly addressed in popular television comedy, presented ironically, nostalgically and with reference to the broad array of televisual and cinematic tropes that hegemonic masculinity entails. Even as dominant forms of masculinity are questioned and parodied, their narrative authority and centrality continues. Figures who represent non-normative gender roles are placed in the margins of the mismatched couple sitcom, as 'secondary characters who are close friends or extended family members [...] they are depicted as childlike, weak, dissatisfied with their lives, and ultimately unhappy – and they are consistently laughed at' (Walsh, Fürsich and Jefferson 2008: 130).

Such queer marginal characters take centre stage in the friends-as-family sitcom which emerged in the 1990s (Feasey 2008: 22). These sitcoms updated the traditional nuclear family sitcom, ushered in by the success of ABC's *Roseanne* (1988–97) and NBC's identification of a new target audience as it lagged behind in the ratings:

> As more families owned two or more television sets, it was becoming more common for family members to watch separately, and thus designing shows aimed at particular audience segments became even more pragmatic. NBC began to aggressively pursue the young, hip, urban, professional audience so successfully courted by Fox. Beginning with the hit *Seinfeld* (1990–98), NBC aired a slew of sitcoms featuring young, white, unmarried, urban and upscale characters: *Mad About You* (1992–99), *Frasier* (1993–), *Friends* (1994–), *Caroline in the City* (1995–99), *Suddenly Susan* (1996–2000), and *Veronica's Closet* (1997–2000), propelled NBC to number one in the ratings. (Morreale 2003b: 248)

Such friendship-group sitcoms offered a queer potential that indicated alternatives to the nuclear family, although many shows were founded on the narrative arc of privileged white urban youth in search of (straight) romance. The end of these shows often featured the pairing up of central protagonists – Niles and Daphne, Ross and Rachel – thus confirming the centrality of the heterosexual couple. Nevertheless, friendship-group comedies offered a space in which homosocial and homoerotic identities could be rehearsed even as they were superseded by the narrative of heteronormativity.

Homosocial and homoerotic comedy has a masculine genealogy visible in double acts stretching back beyond Laurel and Hardy to vaudeville and variety. Mark Simpson cites Jerry Lewis and Dean Martin, and Morecambe and Wise as examples of the ostensibly 'straight' men of comedy who 'play with queerness because they exist in a space which pretends not to know what "homosexuality" is' (1998: 144). This ostensible innocence does not elide the queer potential of such partnerships, but censorship and social mores keep it strictly under wraps, even when the double act share a bed. The homoerotic script of male double acts has remained carefully coded and in the closet. By the 1990s, however, sexuality politics were out on screen. Kelly Kessler notes the 'onslaught of gay and lesbian characters' in American prime-time network shows, particularly sitcoms, but questions the popular understanding of this as a 'gay renaissance' (2006: 130). Queer representation is not only about the visibility of LGBTQ characters but also about the terms within which they are framed (Avila-Saavedra 2009).

As the homoerotic potential of male friendships came out of the closet, American sitcoms began to foreground their dynamics as part of the cultural script. In the comedic juggernaut that was NBC's *Friends* (1994–2004), the 'gay' aspects of Joey Tribbiani (Matt LeBlanc) and Chandler Bing (Matthew Perry)'s bromance were frequently acknowledged, indicating their urban liberal metrosexual *habitus*. Rebecca Feasey reads Chandler and Joey as extending the terms of homosocial friendship between straight men despite the humour often relying on homophobic jokes: 'In this way, *Friends* can be seen to present a potentially positive representation of male bonding because these men do not let societal fears of being labelled interrupt or destroy their intimate relationships' (2008: 27). By verbally confronting the 'gay' aspects of their characters or relationships, *Friends* gives Chandler and Joey permission to be intimate, in a doublethink strategy where they cannot *be* gay because they *speak* of it. Margo Miller calls this manoeuvre 'ironic dismissal' and conversely argues that it signifies a 'new hostility toward queerness in straight male characters' (2006: 148), where gender and sexuality are carefully policed within ostensibly liberal regimes of representation.

Miller proposes *Seinfeld* (NBC 1989–98) as a more positive example of queer representation, as the characters speak queerly but do not employ 'ironic dismissal' to disavow queer identities:

> *Seinfeld* explores alternative forms of masculinity without linking effeminacy and homosexuality in an ironic dismissal. Although

Seinfeld's characters reject traditional aspects of masculinity and embrace activities like cooking, cleaning, and singing, they never approach the 'sensitive guy' characters of other sitcoms. *Seinfeld* does not find it contradictory for men to act feminine or straight men to act gay. Instead, its characters mock masculine conventions and highlight the humour intrinsic to performing heteronormally. (2006: 149)

One explanation for *Seinfeld*'s more eccentric, less hegemonic depiction of masculinity may be its ethnic heritage in a specifically Jewish tradition of comic discourse. While Chandler and Joey are, respectively, WASP and Italian American – and *Friends* is situated in a remarkably WASPy New York – Jerry Seinfeld and his friends are always already other to the perceived 'norm'. The head of programming at NBC initially rejected *Seinfeld* as 'too New York, too Jewish' (Morreale 2003a: 275). While Jerry is the only explicitly Jewish character in the show, the 'cultural Jewishness' of *Seinfeld* has been widely recognised (Johnson 1994; Auster 1998).

Where a sitcom focusses on an openly gay male character, the dismissal of sexuality is less ironic and ironically more evident. Several critical accounts of NBC's *Will and Grace* (1998–2006) remark on the desexualisation or heterosexualisation of Will Truman (Eric McCormack) and the manner in which hegemonic masculinity is defined against the camp gay man (Conway 2006; Feasey 2008; Avila-Saavedra 2009; Needham 2009). Lynn Joyrich argues that 'Will is, in effect, placed in a male/female couple, as the show is centred on his relationship with his female roommate/soulmate', while his best friend, the hysterically camp Jack (Sean Hayes), combines all the historical televisual strategies for dealing with 'funny' gay men: 'the knowing secondary character whose life doesn't get the attention, the obvious stereotype turned into camp, the object of jokes based on hints and innuendos, and so on' (2009: 39). The 'epistemology of the console' has commodified the closet, making gay characters a stock feature of sitcom while erasing their sexuality or making them the joke (Joyrich 2009). Guillermo Avila-Saavedra observes that, for most of *Will and Grace*'s run, 'Will Truman was sitting by himself in America's prime-time network television gay bar' (2009: 5). Even without an openly gay character, contemporary American sitcom still anxiously patrols the borders of hegemonic masculinity, deploying queer straight men to demonstrate how *not* to do masculinity. One prescient example of this is *The Big Bang Theory*'s stablemate, *Two and a Half Men*.

Two and a Half Men

Chuck Lorre, who with Bill Prady is the producer, writer and creator – 'showrunner' – of *The Big Bang Theory*, has a track record in sitcom with a gender theme. He also worked on *Roseanne* (CBS 1988–97), *Grace Under Fire* (ABC 1993–8) and *Cybill* (CBS 1995–8), all sitcoms featuring strong female leads which engage with feminist issues. *Two and a Half Men* and *The Big Bang Theory* 'were co-created by Chuck Lorre, they tape on adjacent stages on the Warner Brothers lot, and they share several writers and much of their technical crews' (Wyatt 2009). Yet *Two and a Half Men* seems to pre-date second-wave feminism, offering unreconstructed white men whose jokes are frequently at the expense of female characters.

Lorre is one of the most successful showrunners in contemporary American sitcom. By 2010 he was producing two hit shows (*Two and a Half Men* and *The Big Bang Theory*) and nurturing a third sitcom, *Mike and Molly* (CBS 2010–16), which was the highest-rated new comedy that year (Hibberd 2010). All his CBS shows are based on the traditional three-camera American sitcom format. His work – particularly on *Two and a Half Men* – has tended to garner widespread criticism and few awards but the profit margins are impressive:

> [*Two and a Half*] *Men* and *Big Bang* rank near the top of the chart for advertising rates on broadcast – pulling $207,000 and $195,000, respectively, per 30-second spot [in 2010]. Plus, there are lucrative syndication dollars that Lorre enjoys along with the studio – *Big Bang* sold for about $1.5 million per episode this year, and *Men* just resold for another seven years into syndication after initially going for a record $2 million per episode. (Hibberd 2010)

Two and a Half Men is situated in the homosocial space of a beach house shared (for the first eight seasons) by two brothers, Charlie Harper (Charlie Sheen) and Alan Harper (Jon Cryer), in which Charlie is the (butch) feckless lothario and Alan the (camp) geek. The characters are based on the actors' star personae: Sheen's hypermasculine early roles in films such as *Platoon* (Oliver Stone, 1986) and *Eight Men Out*

(John Sayles, 1988), which he later parodied in *Hot Shots* (Jim Abrahams, 1991); and Cryer's early role as Duckie in *Pretty in Pink* (Howard Deutsch, 1986), which has inflected many of his subsequent roles in television and film, such as Jim 'Wash Out' Pfaffenbach, also in *Hot Shots*. Charlie Harper's character is also informed by the celebrity discourse surrounding Sheen's notoriously chaotic personal life.

Charlie and Alan, together with Alan's son, Jake Harper (Angus T. Jones), form an ersatz family unit, with Charlie the irresponsible parent and Alan the anxious carer. The presentation of Charlie and Alan as archetypal odd couple is played up throughout the show, performed as unarguably heterosexual despite Alan's 'feminine' attributes. This structure would seem to provide potential for a complex examination of heteromasculinity, yet the sitcom depends heavily on stereotypical storylines in which women are frequently positioned as irretrievably 'other'. The brothers' relationships with women are dysfunctional. Charlie beds a series of what he refers to as 'hotties' and Alan's ex-wife is vilified as heartlessly manipulative, while Charlie and Alan's mother is dominating and cold. *Two and a Half Men*'s disturbing sexual politics have been noted in popular reviews of the show. Graeme Blundell in *The Australian* described it as a 'sometimes creepy, misogynistic comedy' (2010), while Catherine Deveny in *The Age* called it 'a morally bankrupt orgy of chauvinism and media-sanctioned misogyny' (2009). Such reactionary politics are also played out in Sheen's star persona. Jon Hozier-Byrne notes the array of celebrities convicted of domestic abuse (including Sheen himself) who appeared on stage at the *Comedy Central Roast of Charlie Sheen* (Comedy Central 2011), arguing that Sheen's Latino ethnicity is played down in his performance of a 'maverick' white masculinity (2013). Examples of the aggressive misogyny on show at Sheen's Roast include 'jokes' such as: 'You are just like Bruce Willis. You were big in the eighties and now your old slot is being filled by Ashton Kutcher.' Sheen's public breakdown in February 2011, which resulted in his sacking from the cast of *Two and a Half Men* during its eighth season and the substitution of Ashton Kutcher as both a new character and a slightly different version of masculinity, may have changed the dynamic of the show but also led to its demise in 2015 (Pilkington 2011). My account refers to the first eight seasons, when *Two and a Half Men* topped the ratings. Those shows continue to circulate as reruns, box sets and online via sites such as YouTube.

Two and a Half Men privileges Charlie Harper's hypermasculinity and disavows femininity, queer sexuality or 'aberrant' masculinity, shoring up hegemonic masculinity by counterpointing it with such derogated 'others'. Alan Harper's queer heteromasculinity is constituted as inadequate in relation to Charlie's predatory sexual pathology. While the young Jake Harper implied a future for this long-running and highly successful format, it is hard to see where it could have gone even after Kutcher's arrival, as the show's success was founded on a formulaic comedy built around Sheen's performance and his celebrity persona. *Two and a Half Men* can be understood as a hysterical response to the shifting ground of gender and sexual identity in the early twenty-first century. Charlie Harper is an overdetermined, hyperbolic fantasy of heteromasculinity; a permanent adolescent, he performs a masculinity at the service of its drives and hormones, unable to sustain any relationship apart from the one he has with his brother. As the theme tune states, this series is about 'Men, men, men, men, manly men, men, men – ME-E-E-N' but it has little imagination in its account of the masculinities on offer. Disturbingly, it has been one of the most successful sitcoms ever broadcast on American network television (Mills 2009: 127; Lawson 2011). Charlie Harper's hyperbolic masculinity is diametrically opposed to the array of queer masculinities at the centre of *The Big Bang Theory*. Where *Two and a Half Men* offers a reactionary and regressive account of gender, *The Big Bang Theory* presents a range of masculinities via a cast of eccentric geeks.

The Big Bang Theory

The white middle-class geek, once a derogated, marginal figure in American popular culture, has become a mainstream hero in the twenty-first century. James Bray maps the rise of the geek from John Hughes movies in the 1980s, through geek directors such as Quentin Tarantino and Kevin Smith in the 1990s, to the success of actors and writers such as Simon Pegg and Edgar Wright (2010). Geeks are now recognised as a consumer group (Blobel 2012), with the term 'geek chic' in the *Oxford English Dictionary*: 'Geek hasn't beaten the mainstream, it's the new iteration *of* the mainstream' (Warren Ellis, cited in Harrison 2013: 8). The geek thus represents a particular kind of hegemonic masculinity. While conforming to dominant categories of race, class and gender – they tend to be white, educated, middle-class boys – geeks are stereotypically weak, ill-groomed and uncomfortable with women.

The geek thus intersects with the category of the queer straight man, a figure increasingly apparent on American television in the early 2000s:

> TV's queer straight guys reveal a post-closet culture working through the fact that gender and sexual identity categories don't easily map onto the diversity of people's experiences and remind us that heteronormative alignments of sex, gender, behaviour and desire are not natural or inevitable. (Becker 2009: 136)

The Big Bang Theory can be understood in these terms, as evincing a queer masculinity that challenges binary accounts of gender and sexuality. Leonard Hofstadter and Sheldon Cooper share the apartment across the hall from Penny (Kaley Cuoco) but are not fashioned as a butch/femme couple like Charlie and Alan in *Two and a Half Men*. Leonard is camp and heterosexual, while Sheldon evades binary understandings of gender or sexuality. Both are eccentrically queered. Largely asexual, Sheldon is implicated in a relationship with Leonard's mother during the second season and acquires a girlfriend in the fifth. When Beverly Hofstadter (Christine Baranski) visits her son Leonard, she deploys her psychiatric expertise to offer an acute account of each character's traits and weaknesses. Having lunch with Leonard and his friends at his workplace, her explanation of the relationship between Howard Wolowitz and Raj Koothrappali is apposite:

Howard: [of Leonard's achievements] You must be very proud.
Beverly: Why? They're not my accomplishments? I must urinate. [exits]
[while Leonard's mother is gone, his friends tease him]
Raj: Yeah, you're like the Jar-Jar Binks of the Hofstadter family.
Howard: Oh, meesa thinking you look so-so sad! Next time, don't bring yousa mama to work.
[Leonard is piqued and responds as his mother returns to the table]
Leonard: Howard lives with his mother and Raj can't talk to women unless he's drunk. Go!

Beverly: That's fascinating. Selective mutism is quite rare. On the other hand, a Jewish male living with his mother is so common, it borders on sociological cliché. You know, both selective mutism and an inability to separate from one's mother could be due to a pathological fear of women. That would explain why the two of you have created an ersatz homosexual marriage to satisfy your need for intimacy. ('The Maternal Capacitance', 2:15)

Wolowitz and Raj, shocked by Beverly's analysis, bicker like an old married couple and immediately prove her point. Where Charlie Harper's pursuit of women in *Two and a Half Men* is often performed at the expense of women, with female characters either evacuated of personality as 'babes' or demonised as bad mothers/wives/girlfriends, Wolowitz and Raj's pursuit of women is performed at their own expense, exposing their fears and desires. The male protagonists in *The Big Bang Theory* represent what Robert Heasley classifies as 'queer straight':

> Males living in the shadow of masculinity are sweet guys perhaps, but they can also be pretty shut down emotionally, in part because straight male emotions such as anger do not fit them and they do not allow themselves 'female emotions' such as sadness or fear. It is safer not to say anything, not show anything, and attempt to get by. The body of these men is not represented in the image of straight or gay masculinities; there is no appearance of an image of 'self' – no public voice, only quiet knowing of being 'different', a self-identity of being 'non'. They may live inside the space of computers, musical instruments, books, or other such places that provide safety from the storm of hetero-normative masculinity. Almost by the nature of living in the shadow, they seek each other out and 'play' most of their lives with other men who quietly 'go along' with the mainstream but are never fully engaged in the dominant hetero-masculine world. (2005: 318–19)

This categorisation of 'queer straight masculinity' is part of Heasley's wider project to map a range of queer straight male identities. While aspects of it neatly fit with the male characters in *The Big Bang*

Theory – they are 'in the shadow' of hegemonic masculinity and they 'live inside the space of computers' – it would be misleading to align them with Heasley's typology of queer masculinities as identity project: 'to begin to give voice and legitimacy to the queerness that exists within the straight world' (2005: 319). *The Big Bang Theory* offers a complex and polysemic account of queer straight masculinities. Leonard, Sheldon, Raj and Wolowitz are humorous characters so the show by no means simply endorses the identity of 'queer-straight' as desirable or comfortable. As Ron Becker notes in his discussion of the 'guy love' in NBC's medical comedy *Scrubs* (2001–8): 'That most queer straight guys are found safely wrapped in comedic irony reveals a culture nervously processing its changing politics of gender and sexuality rather than one fully confident in a vision of some queer future' (2009: 135).

Nevertheless, like *Scrubs*, *The Big Bang Theory* makes the relationships between its male protagonists central to the narrative and, over several seasons, depicts the close emotional bonds they develop. Raj Koothrappali and Howard Wolowitz's 'ersatz marriage' is emblematic of this: their friendship is represented as funny and peculiar but it is not dismissed. Their relationship becomes part of the sitcom's storyline, so much so that there are tensions between the two friends when Howard begins to date his future wife, Bernadette Rostenkowski (Melissa Rauch). Their 'ersatz marriage' has received widespread fan attention, including fanfiction which brings the homoerotic potential of their relationship to the fore (see, for example, Jenni_Snake 2013). Heasley's definition argues that such queer straight men 'do not allow themselves "female emotions" such as sadness or fear' (2005: 318), yet Leonard, Raj and Howard are able to express such emotions. Part of the sitcom's appeal is its ability to address complex emotional relationships while maintaining the necessary comedy. The Apple co-founder Steve Wozniak has asserted that *The Big Bang Theory* regularly moves him to tears through its poignant representation of the friends' emotional lives, saying that he identifies with their social awkwardness and relationship troubles (cited in Miller 2013).

The complex articulations of masculinity in the show are facilitated by the characters' age – their extended adolescence – their class identities and their ethnicities. The privileged environment of the university clearly places Leonard, Sheldon, Howard and Raj as overeducated geeks. Because they are the central focus of the show, these characters make nerdish obsessions with comic books and science fiction the norm, effectively presenting hegemonic masculinity as 'other' to their queerly various masculinities. *The Big Bang Theory* is built upon this endorsement, deploying set dressing, dialogue and storylines which reference fan subcultures that stretch far beyond the sitcom:

> Models, action figures and posters decorate the apartments depicted throughout the show. More so, the characters themselves have conversations, arguments, and debates rooted in science fiction, table-top gaming, online or console games, cosplay and comic books. Getting the details right becomes an inside joke for fans who enjoyed seeing their hobbies portrayed accurately on-screen. (Weitekamp 2015: 82)

There is no 'ironic dismissal' here, nor is there a Charlie Harper character against which the group can be judged. When a male character appears who successfully performs hegemonic masculinity he is quickly disposed of or undermined. Several of Penny's boyfriends are dealt with in this manner in the first five series: Zack (Brian Thomas Smith) is lampooned for his lack of intelligence, and Kurt (Brian Patrick Wade) is shown from the pilot to be a violent and unpleasant character. When Kurt turns up at Penny's party in 'The Middle Earth Paradigm' (1:6), he represents the epitome of her bad choices in men and inadvertently brings Leonard and Penny together for the first time.

In 'The Financial Permeability' (2:14), Leonard is once again pitted against Kurt when he tries to retrieve money Penny has lent her ex-boyfriend (Figure 3.1). In this sense *The Big Bang Theory* offers queer masculinities that are central to the storyline: they are 'in the shadow of masculinity' (Heasley 2005: 317–19) but the comedy privileges their 'insufficient masculinity' (Halberstam 1998: 2) as desirable. To be a geek in the twenty-first century has cultural capital: 'Since the 1980s and 1990s [...] the geek or nerd stereotype changed as the business of networked computers made millionaires and billionaires of its pioneers. After the late 1990s dot-com boom, geek became chic' (Weitekamp 2015: 80). The men (and it was once again mostly men) who emerged from the early ICT industry, such as Bill Gates and Mark Zuckerberg, now represent wealth and power but also idiosyncratic

Figure 3.1 Sheldon, Howard, Raj and Leonard confront Kurt in 'The Financial Permeability' (*The Big Bang Theory*, 2:14, Chuck Lorre Productions/Warner Bros Television, 2007–).

genius: 'Thick glasses and a cardigan thus become the red braces and power shoulders of the twenty-first century. Enticingly, you become both an outlaw and a member of an elite' (Harrison 2013: 8). The geek has gained cultural approval and *The Big Bang Theory* rides this wave of social endorsement.

Nevertheless, Leonard, Sheldon, Howard and Raj make masculinity visible *because* it differs from the hegemonic fantasy. As career academics they are already positioned as outside the 'normal': 'In the mediated world, "real" masculinities are often working-class, rural and anti-intellectual. Even straight male characters that do not adhere to some of these characteristics are not "real" men' (Avila-Saavedra 2009: 17). Those 'real' masculinities are represented in *The Big Bang Theory* by Zack and Kurt, whose onomatopoeic single-syllable names denote their authentic, anti-intellectual credentials. Leonard, Sheldon, Howard and Raj represent a boyish alternative to hegemonic masculinity but their status within *The Big Bang Theory* is transient and unsustainable. Such Peter Pan lifestyles cannot be infinitely extended. Over the ten seasons of *The Big Bang Theory* its cast has visibly matured and the characters' boyish 'nerdapalooza' is discomfiting for a corporate culture that ultimately endorses dominant hegemonies. This may explain why a romantic narrative has gradually scooped up each character and carried them to the safer shores of heteronormativity.

Race and Ethnicity in *The Big Bang Theory*

The queer masculinities of Leonard, Sheldon, Howard and Raj are inflected by discourses of race and ethnicity in complex and problematic ways, most overtly through the Jewish American identities of Leonard Hofstadter and Howard Wolowitz and the immigrant Indian identity of Raj Koothrappali. Leonard and Howard's characters follow the Jewish tradition of the schlemiel, a figure who 'subverts traditional versions of masculinity' (Gillota 2010: 161):

> The schlemiel [...] is a sort of cosmic fool combined with cosmic victim. Accident-prone and ineffectual, he is the universe's unfortunate passive bystander, to whom life happens, especially as embarrassing circumstance, and for whom taking the initiative and seeking active agency ends almost invariably in frustration and humiliation. (Buchbinder 2008: 229)

This effectively describes Leonard's relationship with Penny in the first five seasons and Howard's many attempts to 'seduce' women before meeting Bernadette. David Buchbinder proposes the schlemiel as a version of inadequate or incompetent masculinity that may be 'understood as enacting *a resistance to or even a refusal of* the coercive pressure of the gender system' (2008: 235, emphasis in original). While the schlemiel troubles hegemonic masculinity, however, he is situated in relation to it. As a comic type he can be read as reinstating the dominant norm precisely because of his deviant performance of masculinity.

This tension produces some problematic gender dynamics in *The Big Bang Theory*. For example, Howard's schlemiel persona is constituted in relation to his overbearing Jewish mother, an ethnic stereotype without potential for recuperation as Mrs Wolowitz is heard but never seen. An invisible grotesque, Mrs Wolowitz's screeching narration of bodily functions, together with Howard's references to her obese, hairy, ageing body, confirm her abject role in the comedy as the epitome of monstrous femininity (Russo 1986; Creed 1993). In literary fiction the Jewish mother is a standard trope:

> Too well we know the Jewish mother our male writers have given us, the all-engulfing nurturer who devours the very soul with every

spoonful of hot chicken soup she gives, whose every shakerful of salt contains a curse. Too well we know the feeder whose hard-wrung offerings are imbibed as poisons. [...] Thus our Portnoys, knowing on some level that they have been thieves, eliminate their debt by making their tormented mothers into cardboard demons [...] Thus is the Jewish mother shrunk and manhood reached. (Duncan 1983: 27–8)

This dynamic is realised in *The Big Bang Theory* by the two-dimensional characterisation and literal invisibility of Mrs Wolowitz. Howard's transition from boy to man is enabled via his marriage to Bernadette at the end of season five but his new wife already shows signs of oedipally replacing his mother, as Bernadette replicates Mrs Wolowitz's voice and competes with her to become Howard's primary carer. The demise of Mrs Wolowitz in 'The Comic Book Store Regeneration' (8:15), following the death in 2014 of Carole Ann Susi, the actor who voiced her, is memorialised in 'The Leftover Thermalization' (8:18), where the cast sit down to a massive dinner of food from Mrs Wolowitz's defrosted freezer, including two of her infamous briskets. The episode is elegiac, yet still represents the Jewish mother as a grotesque 'feeder'. Although Mrs Wolowitz's character is developed in seasons seven and eight through her relationship with Stuart Bloom (Kevin Sussman) – we finally discover her name when he calls her 'Debbie' in the season 7 finale – she remains a running joke in the show. This grotesquely misogynist stereotype gives some indication of the skewed gender dynamics that underpin queered masculinity in *The Big Bang Theory*.

One can also question how non-normative Jewish masculinity is in the genealogy of American sitcom. Several critics have acknowledged the centrality of schlemiel masculinity in American film and television comedy (see, for example, Johnson 1994; Gillota 2010). The 'insufficient masculinity' of figures like the schlemiel is so much a part of the comedy landscape that it is hard to see how they can be read as resistant to hegemonic masculinity when they are so reliant upon it as a cultural given. David Gillota argues that Larry David's schlemiel persona in *Curb Your Enthusiasm* (HBO 2000–11) enacts the 'ethnic anxiety felt by so many successful American Jews' (2010: 156) in his ambivalence towards both Jewishness and WASP America. The contemporary schlemiel in American sitcom is thus both white and ethnically marked. Gillota proposes that this ambiguous ethnicity enables David to critique both privileged middle-class Jewish culture and mainstream white America by refusing to fully identify with either. Ron Eglash goes so far as to argue that 'Leonard Nimoy's Jewish identity readily orientalized Spock' (2002: 55). Leonard Hofstadter and Howard Wolowitz, however, represent a more traditional depiction of Jewish masculinity, their neuroses and mother-issues conforming to a stereotype of Jewish American masculinity which is reliant on a derogated feminine other. The rejection or death of the mother thus becomes symbolic of achieving adulthood. Leonard and Howard cannot remain boyish geeks forever and, following the narrative trajectory that the show established from season five, growing up means leaving their mothers behind and acquiring wives. *The Big Bang Theory* is now entirely predicated on a heteronormative arc. Leonard and Howard's interesting 'failures' are thus ironed out as the show develops, their queer masculinities recuperated at the expense of the women that surround them.

Raj's 'otherness' is even more problematic. Rajesh Koothrappali's Indian identity has always been a source of comedy within *The Big Bang Theory*, often dependent on a range of Orientalist stereotypes that position Indian masculinity as feminised. In Raj's 'ersatz marriage' with Howard he is repeatedly characterised as the 'wife' and there is much dialogue about his metrosexual penchant for 'women's' media such as chick-flicks and *Grey's Anatomy* (ABC 2005–), or female pop stars like Taylor Swift and Beyoncé. Raj's non-normative gender identity is frequently examined within the sitcom as a problem. If the other three male leads have been secured within heterosexual partnerships, Raj remains queerly intransigent, unable to sustain a long-term relationship outside his bromance with Howard. Raj's camp straight persona thus conforms to a standard dynamic in contemporary American television: 'it is not unusual for television programmes to establish characters who, diegetically, are "really" gay in order to establish (not always successfully) that the others are not' (Joyrich 2009: 24–5). Just as Jack's queenily camp performance straightens out Will's gay identity in *Will and Grace*, so Raj's metrosexual queerness confirms Leonard, Howard and Sheldon's heteromasculinity. That this dynamic is delivered by the only non-white character compounds its dubious provenance.

Episodes which address the 'problem' of Raj's gender and sexual identity often feature storylines concluded by homophobic or racist punchlines. 'The Transporter Malfunction' (5:20) addresses Raj's sexuality. In desperation at being the only one of the group still single, Raj asks his parents to find him a potential bride. His first dates with Lakshmi (Chriselle Almeida) go so well that he considers marrying her, only to discover that she is a lesbian who assumes he is gay. She proposes that they have a faux marriage to placate their respective parents. Raj seriously considers this but is dissuaded by Howard and Bernadette, who then buy a Yorkshire terrier to console him. He is delighted with this miniature pet, wondering if the tiny dog will fit in his 'man purse'. Bernadette gets the final word, saying: 'Heterosexual my ass'. In season six Raj finally finds a girlfriend, Lucy (Kate Miccuci), who is as socially dysfunctional as he is: 'You have bigger emotional problems than I do and I find that very attractive in a woman. I think you're wonderful' ('The Love Spell Potential', 6:23). This relationship ends at the season six finale and, while Raj later develops relationships with Emily Sweeney (Laura Spencer) and Claire (Alessandra Torresani), they do not last.

As the only one of the four men in the show who does not sustain a long-term relationship, Raj offers some potential for a positive account of non-normative heteromasculinity but this is problematised by the intersectionality of his race and gender. Much of the humour around his inability to conform to normative Western heteromasculinity is dependent on Orientalist tropes. *The Big Bang Theory* appears to acknowledge this in Raj's occasional comments that other characters are being 'racist', but inserting this word into the script does not prevent it from being so. As with the use of 'ironic dismissal' as a means of denying the homoerotic potential of homosocial relationships between men in sitcom, this 'ironic dismissal' of racist humour engages both homophobic and racist tropes as it links Raj's aberrant heteromasculinity to effeminacy and his Indian identity (Miller 2006). The queered masculinities which Leonard, Howard and Raj present in *The Big Bang Theory* are thus complex iterations of gender, race, ethnicity and class identities. The show offers a knowing account of sexual and racial stereotypes, addressing offensive issues and appearing to pre-empt critical responses, yet that does not inoculate *The Big Bang Theory* against homophobia, sexism and racism (Peterson 2009; Zakos 2013).

Sheldon Cooper: A Third Gender?

Sheldon Cooper is the sole WASP male character in the principle cast and his masculinity is the most overtly aligned with queer possibilities. He comes from a Texan Christian family and is initially figured as asexual, eschewing sexual or physical contact of any kind. He is the ubergeek, recognised by his peers as surpassing their social dysfunction but, unlike Leonard, Howard and Raj, Sheldon does not care about being different. When Penny asks Leonard about Sheldon's sexual preference in season two, it is suggested that he has none:

Penny: I know this is none of my business, but I just ... I have to ask – what's Sheldon's deal?
Leonard: What do you mean, 'deal'?
Penny: You know, like, what's his deal? Is it girls? Guys? Sock puppets?
Leonard: Honestly, we've been operating under the assumption that he has no deal.
Penny: Come on, everybody has a deal.
Howard: Not Sheldon. Over the years, we've formulated many theories about how he might reproduce. I'm an advocate of mitosis.
Penny: I'm sorry?
Howard: I believe one day Sheldon will eat an enormous amount of Thai food and split into two Sheldons.
Leonard: On the other hand, I think Sheldon might be the larval form of his species. Someday he'll spin a cocoon and emerge two months later with moth wings and an exoskeleton.
Penny: Okay, well, thanks for the nightmares. ('The Cooper–Nowitzki Theorem', 2:6)

Marking Sheldon as a different species, as not-human, serves to confirm the extent to which he is the queerest component of an outsider cast and also demonstrates how the sitcom struggles to accommodate difference. Sheldon is never explicitly categorised in *The Big Bang Theory*, asserting 'I'm not crazy, my mother had me tested', but many critics place him on the autistic spectrum, as 'the poster boy for high-functioning OCD'

(Harrison 2013: 7). When directly asked about Sheldon's sexual orientation in 2010, Chuck Lorre refused to name his 'deal', proposing the character as 'other':

> 'Why would we have to [define him] if the character is so thoroughly focused on his work?' he argues. 'If touching other human beings of *any* gender is irrelevant to him, why label the thing? Why can't there be a *third* gender – male, female and *Sheldon*?' (cited in Ausiello and Patrick 2010)

Lorre's evident confusion of gender and sexuality is telling. In the early seasons, Sheldon rarely allows physical contact with other characters and where he does it is depicted as a significant moment in the comedy's situation. His awkward but sustained hug with Penny when she gives him a napkin used by Leonard Nimoy for Christmas produced a huge response from the studio audience ('The Bath Item Gift Hypothesis', 2:11; Figure 3.2). Sheldon describes sex as 'coitus', a scientific-medical term which strips sexuality of its romantic and cultural affiliations; unlike Leonard, Howard or Raj, he did not seek a romantic or sexual partner. His relationship with Amy Farrah-Fowler (Mayim Bialik) comes about at the end of season three as a result of Howard and Raj setting up

Figure 3.2 Sheldon hugs Penny in 'The Bath Item Gift Hypothesis' (*The Big Bang Theory*, 2:11, Chuck Lorre Productions/Warner Bros Television, 2007–).

an online dating account for him without his knowledge ('The Lunar Excitation', 3:23). Like Raj, Sheldon has been a useful plot device within the show's narrative. He is a major source of comedy as the sitcom tracks his makeover-style journey from asexual to heterosexual.

Ela Przybylo proposes asexuality as a radical identity because it calls attention to the performance of all sexual behaviours: 'alternative repetitions are powerful because they suggest to other actors that repeating differently is *possible*, and most importantly, that the most frequently repeated sequences are not by any means "natural" or "innate"' (2011: 456). Following Judith Butler, she argues that 'Repeating differently, alternatively, plurally, asexuality will create spaces of sexual complication, and of sexusocial rupture' (2011: 457). Sheldon's asexuality has certainly caught public attention. He is the breakout character of *The Big Bang Theory*, featuring prominently on official merchandise and fan sites, and now the subject of a spin-off series. A Google search for 'Sheldon Cooper' on 23 March 2012 yielded 'about 29,400,000' results, while a search for 'Leonard Hofstadter' at the same time yielded just 802,000 hits. Jim Parsons has won several awards for this role. Sheldon embodies the potential for television comedy to offer a wider range of performative identities through which debates about gender and sexuality may be addressed. Such identities work against the hegemonic stereotypes of 'manly men' visible in series such as *Two and a Half Men* and gesture toward more variable and unclassifiable accounts of gender and sexuality. Yet there are significant conditions which enable these performances of queer masculinity, namely a white middle-class aesthetic which often stereotypes female characters.

The Big Bang Theory does not have a gay or lesbian character, even though its central male cast may be read as camp, queer, feminised, closeted or of indefinable sexuality. That there is not yet room for an out LGBTQ character even in a minor role on *The Big Bang Theory* speaks to the limitations of American network television per se and the poor record of CBS in particular. In the annual GLAAD analysis of LGBTQ representation on television CBS has often featured as the lowest-ranking broadcast network. For the 2016–17 season GLAAD recorded the following statistics:

- ABC posts the highest percentage of LGBTQ regular characters of all five broadcast networks with 7.3 per cent.

- FOX has the second highest percentage of LGBTQ regulars (6.4 per cent), which is still above the percentage of LGBTQ regulars on broadcast as a whole.
- The CW is third with 4.3 per cent of its series regulars counted as LGBTQ, and NBC follows at 3.9 per cent. CBS comes in last at 2.2 per cent. (2016: 6)

This does not of course register the sexuality of the actors who play the characters. Jim Parsons's ten-year relationship with Todd Spiewak was casually mentioned in a 2012 profile for *The New York Times* about his performance in the title role of *Harvey* on Broadway (Healy 2012); they were married in 2017. Parsons also played the AIDS activist Tommy Boatwright in Larry Kramer's *The Normal Heart* on Broadway in 2011 and reprised that award-winning role in the 2014 HBO film, for which he was once more nominated for an Emmy. The annual GLAAD index is thus a useful measure but something of a blunt instrument; it does not for example account for the implications of an openly gay actor representing straight masculinity. Neil Patrick Harris's performance as the hypermasculine Barney Stinson in *How I Met Your Mother* (CBS 2005–14) is distinctly inflected by his gay star persona:

> The characterisation and performance of Barney embraces both artifice, because the audience is aware that he is a gay man playing (excessively) straight, and stylisation through his polished and scrupulously maintained appearance. Barney's camp masculinity intentionally marks the performance, and, therefore the bachelor archetype itself, as excessive and performative. [...] In this way, *How I Met Your Mother* deliberately and playfully uses the character of Barney to expose cultural images of masculinity and outmoded ideas of masculinity as the 'natural' form of man, to unpick the construction of the 'invisible gender'. (Thompson 2015: 24)

While Harris's performance may deploy camp to unpick the normative construction of masculinity in *How I Met Your Mother*, Parsons's performance as Sheldon in *The Big Bang Theory* is unmarked within the context of his geekish group. Although Sheldon's social dysfunction is extreme – and extremely comic – it is above all genuine. As Parsons notes, Sheldon's central characteristic is his blunt honesty (cited in Huver 2016). Sheldon is childlike rather than camp. That appellation could more meaningfully be applied to Leonard, Howard or Raj. Sheldon's asexual, childlike masculinity thus does not signify an unpicking of the 'invisible gender'. His queerness is situated in a preadolescent indeterminacy which *The Big Bang Theory* carefully repositions from season six on. It is as if Sheldon's difference cannot be tolerated even as comedy.

This shift within the sitcom toward a more conventional heterosexual future for all its central cast is a notable refusal to follow the queer trajectory of alternative kinship models:

> As [Lee] Edelman argues in *No Future* and as Kathryn Bond Stockton demonstrates in her book on the queer child, *Growing Sideways*, the child is always already queer and must therefore be quickly converted to a proto-heterosexual by being pushed through a series of maturational models of growth that project the child as the future and the future as heterosexual. [. . .] Obviously heterosexual relations are not essentially bound to 'regularity and repetitiveness', yet the bourgeois family matrix, with its emphasis on lineage, inheritance, and generation, does tend to cast temporal flux in terms of either seamless continuity or total rupture. (Halberstam 2011: 73–4)

Queer temporality as a mode which challenges the linearity and lineage of heteronormative identities offers a useful way of understanding Sheldon Cooper and his 'development' within the sitcom narrative. Just as traditional American studio-based sitcoms like *The Big Bang Theory* tend towards 'regularity and repetitiveness' as a formulaic television format constituted of familiar characters and tropes, they also accede to heteronormative models of growing up and growing old. Sheldon's and his friends' queer potentials are thus hoovered into a heterosexual future which can only be imagined within the bounds of Hollywood romance and the monogamous heterosexual couple. Sheldon's childlike qualities continue as the series progresses beyond season six, but they are framed in relation to the central romance between Leonard and Penny, who frequently behave as if he is *their* child, and the developing relationship between Sheldon and Amy, or 'ShAmy'.

Resolving Queer Masculinities

The Big Bang Theory demonstrates how comedic representations of masculinity can challenge heteronormative gender scripts, yet the manner in which those challenges are contained exposes cultural anxieties which continue to adhere to any form of non-normative identity, even in the most apparently 'liberal' environment. Just as in the late 1990s and early 2000s there was a focus on comedies about single white professional women, the millennium has marked an 'intensification of interest in the lifestyles and morals of single white men, too' (Thompson 2015: 33). *The Big Bang Theory* reveals how challenges to traditional masculinity (and femininity) are often shut down or curtailed. By season six the show began to eschew its queer indeterminacies and work towards a more clearly heterosexual destination by pairing off its protagonists. Leonard and Penny became an established couple and Howard and Bernadette got married. Sheldon's relationship with Amy Farrah-Fowler was part of the central narrative by season four and Raj began seeing the equally dysfunctional Lucy in season six. Storylines began to focus on Sheldon and Raj in particular as a means of resolving their queer potential and securing them more firmly within a heterosexual matrix. In the penultimate episode of season six, Raj and Lucy kiss through a wire fence; she has run out on their date, climbing through a toilet window and becoming trapped in the restaurant's back alley. Raj declares his feelings for her and they kiss through the fence as the studio audience voices an approving 'Aaaaaah' ('The Love Spell Potential', 6:23). This sentimental moment works to confirm that heterosexual romance overcomes all odds, bringing two misfits together to make a 'proper' unit.

In the same episode, the question of Sheldon and Amy's relationship is raised during a game of Dungeons and Dragons. Within the game Bernadette casts a love spell on Sheldon and Amy, suggesting that their avatars have sex, and this upsets Amy because she sees it as underlining the impossibility of their having a physical relationship in real life. She leaves the game and goes to Sheldon's bedroom, where he is sent by the others to comfort her:

Amy: They think our relationship is a joke.... Sheldon, are we ever going to have an intimate relationship?
Sheldon: Before I met you, I never had any interest in being intimate with anyone.

Amy:	And now?
Sheldon:	And now what?
Amy:	Do you have any interest now?
Sheldon:	I have not ruled it out.
Amy:	[with irony] Wow, talk dirty to me.
Sheldon:	I know it doesn't seem like it to you, but for me what we have is extremely intimate.
Amy:	I know that, it's just that part of me wants more.
Sheldon:	More? Look at us! It's only been three years and here we are in bed together! ('The Love Spell Potential', 6:23)

Sheldon and Amy then consummate their relationship in virtual terms, through their Dungeons and Dragons avatars, by *talking* through removing each other's clothing and becoming physically intimate. This offers a remarkable solution to the Sheldon 'problem', constituting him as heterosexual in theory if not in practice. One could argue that this sequence represents a queer romance in its careful negotiation of Sheldon's particular needs, but it works very hard to resolve the situation via a heterosexual conclusion.

By season nine Sheldon and Amy finally have 'coitus', both saying that they enjoyed it more than they thought they would ('The Opening Night Excitation', 9:11; Figure 3.3). It is Amy's birthday and Sheldon

Figure 3.3 Sheldon and Amy in bed after their first experience of 'coitus' in 'The Opening Night Excitation' (*The Big Bang Theory*, 9:11, Chuck Lorre Productions/Warner Bros Television, 2007–).

'gives it to her' as her present. While this phrase is treated as a joke there is no ambiguity about the sexual and gender dynamic of their relationship. Likewise, there is no consideration of any other possibility for Raj or Sheldon: that they might be gay, bisexual or asexual. In this manner *The Big Bang Theory* marshals its misfits toward the only desirable destination: a heterosexual ending. Howard and Bernadette's wedding at the end of season five is emblematic of this shift. With the bride in white, Amy as an over-enthusiastic bridesmaid and Sheldon as Justice of the Peace, the ceremony combines eccentric individualism with wholly conventional Hollywood romance in a style familiar from teen movies (Best 2005). Within the ShAmy pairing the conventional gender dynamic is increasingly marked. While Amy was initially introduced to the show as a female version of Sheldon, with no interest in romance, she subsequently becomes maniacal in her pursuit of heteronormative femininity. It is Amy who is distressed by their lack of intimacy in 'The Love Spell Potential' and she is constituted as a civilising influence on Sheldon, teaching him how to behave in social situations. In short, Amy does all the emotional labour. Sheldon and Amy thus conform to stereotypical gender roles: Amy is an emotional woman to Sheldon's rational man. Like Sheldon, Amy's transformation is a comedic makeover. She has a queer 'girl-crush' on Penny in seasons four to six but by season seven Amy has become more conventionally socialised. She has learnt her heterofemininity, with help from Penny and Bernadette, in a manner familiar from popular Hollywood romcoms. The combination of romance with Sheldon and a newly 'feminine' persona puts Amy back in place as a *proper* woman.

Amy L. Best notes the function of romance as a means of herding irregular subjects back to more normative gender and sexual roles:

> It is the repeated invocation of romance without an interrogation of its cultural and political foundations that works to obscure the normative dimensions of heterosexuality while also stabilizing them. Largely relegated to the realm of feeling, romance is thought to be private, intimate, and above all else, outside the contested terrain of politics; in this way, it conceals the very political workings of domination it serves. Romance carries tremendous ideological force; it naturalizes and normalizes heterosexual and gender controls and shapes and organizes modern constructions of self. (2005: 195)

This is very evident in later seasons of *The Big Bang Theory*. When the writer Steve Molaro took over as showrunner from Bill Prady in season six there was a shift in focus from the homosocial friendship group towards the heterosexual couple, making it 'a traditional family comedy' (Goldberg 2016). Although the original friendship group remains intact, any unconventional sexual or social affiliations have been carefully shepherded into more legitimate pairings. It is indeed 'a *traditional* family comedy' (Goldberg 2016, my emphasis). In a polemical piece which celebrates the rise of gender and sexual variance, Halberstam argues against gay marriage as an institution which 'flattens out the varied terrain of queer social life and reduces the differences that make queers, well, queer' (2012: 114). This certainly seems to be the case in *The Big Bang Theory*, as the show has 'flattened out' queerly interesting aspects of its central male characters. Romantic and marital trajectories within the show have been developed at the expense of its female cast, pushing Penny, Bernadette and Amy into increasingly stereotypical roles.

From the outset *The Big Bang Theory* was not going to be a feminist comedy. Penny's surname has never been revealed, indicating her original characterisation as a fantasy girl in the flat across the hall. She conforms to Hollywood stereotype as blonde, white, slim and 'not too bright' (Zakos 2013). Although her character has been developed and she often gets the punchline, she is largely there to be the 'straight' woman for the male cast's comedic interactions. Kaley Cuoco has described the role as like 'being "Wendy to the Lost Boys"' (cited in Weitekamp 2015: 81). This fantasy of femininity – as girl/mother to a group of errant youths – neatly encapsulates a problem that the show has signally failed to resolve. *The Big Bang Theory*'s writers and directors are almost entirely male, as are its executive producers, Lorre, Prady and Molaro (Zakos 2013). This gender imbalance may explain the lack of imagination as the series ploughs onwards with an increasing dependence on stereotypical tropes. Just as Penny's character has limited potential for development, so Bernadette and Amy are restricted by their position on the margins of the central dynamic between the four male leads following their arrival in season three (McIntosh 2014: 203): 'Written primarily as supporting characters, the female scientists serve primarily to support the character development experienced by the core male actors over six seasons' (Weitekamp 2015: 86).

As I noted in Chapter 1, the 'sidekick' role can be understood as a queered position, but here it works to make Bernadette and Amy progressively more stereotypical (Roof 2002). Amy's emotional labour in her relationship with Sheldon is mirrored by Bernadette's role as Howard's wife and primary carer following the death of his mother. Although Bernadette earns more than Howard, and is more intellectually gifted than he is, she is careful to disguise these aberrant aspects of their relationship, in order 'to protect his manhood':

> Overall, neither Amy or Bernadette are accepted just as intelligent, successful women by the group. Instead, their intelligence is not a feature that defines these characters for themselves, but instead functions as a means to attract and maintain the attention of their men. (McIntosh 2014: 203)

This is played out within the show as comedy, with Sheldon often belittling Amy's work in neurobiology, regarding that field as less important than his own.

As *The Big Bang Theory* rolls toward the end of its tenth season there are once more rumours that the show may be nearing the end of its life. Several of the cast have allegedly hinted that ten seasons might be enough; its predecessor, *Friends*, ended at that point. Part of the debate is financial, as the cast are now out of contract and renegotiating their fees:

> The show's three stars – Johnny Galecki (Leonard), Kaley Cuoco (Penny) and [Jim] Parsons are among the highest paid in TV, earning $1 million per episode. (This is said to have caused some dissent in the cast – Mayim Bialik (Amy) and Melissa Rauch (Bernadette) struggle along on $100,000 per installment). However, the show is a big earner for CBS – its ninth season was the highest-rated non-sports broadcast of the year, averaging 20 million viewers per episode – meaning that its cast can extract a high fee. (Martin 2016)

Such statements are a useful reminder of how gender and sexual behaviours are tied to economic realities. As the gender pay gap continues to disadvantage women, *The Big Bang Theory* offers a salutary account of the literal and figurative costs of queering masculinity in television comedy.

Comedy has historically represented an arena in which hegemonic masculinity can be challenged and queer masculinities can be performed, primarily through a comic focus on individuals who fail. *The Big Bang Theory*'s depiction of queer straight masculinities offers a tantalizing glimpse of what might be possible even as it firmly shuts the door on non-normative gender and sexual identities. One explanation for this may be the economies of a prime-time ratings success. Halberstam's proposal of failure as a radical strategy which resists late Western capitalism argues for 'a story of art without markets, drama without a script, narrative without progress' (2011: 88). *The Big Bang Theory* at first appears to depict such a story/drama/narrative through the idiosyncratic community which Penny, Sheldon, Leonard, Howard and Raj form in the early seasons. However, as the show gained awards and climbed the ratings, making enormous profits for its production company, it was ineluctably drawn back to the aesthetic economy of the market and now follows the statutory Hollywood script. In the end, *The Big Bang Theory* evinces a narrative which falls in line with the progressive temporality of heteronormativity. In the next chapter I examine a format which may be less wedded to the temporal economies of heteronormativity: British sketch comedy.

CHAPTER 4

SMACK THE PONY: FEMINIST NEGOTIATIONS IN BRITISH SKETCH COMEDY

Whereas sitcoms which feature queer possibilities may be reincorporated into heterosexual hegemony, as with *The Big Bang Theory*, sketch comedy offers a more liberal potential. As I argued in Chapter 1, the fluid format of early American television comedy harboured playful and eccentric representations of gender and sexuality. *The Burns and Allen Show* and *I Love Lucy* drew on vaudeville traditions, blurring the lines between television sitcom and variety formats. Here I examine those possibilities in a very different context: millennial British television sketch comedy. My example emerged at a crucial moment in British popular culture, when feminism was allegedly being subsumed by postfeminist popular culture and women's bodies were centre stage as both subject and object. Running for only three seven-episode series on Channel 4 (1999–2001), followed by two Christmas special episodes in December 2002 and January 2003, the British sketch show *Smack the Pony* continues to generate discussion among fans and critics (Lewisohn 2003: 705–6). It featured in the 2001 and 2003 line-up for the fundraising gala *Comic Relief* (BBC) and was revived for *Comic Relief* 2017. In 2012, episodes of *Smack the Pony* were screened as part of a British Film Institute season on 'Trailblazers: queens of comedy' during the festival which heralded the London Olympics (BFI 2012b). Other screenings in the 'Trailblazers' season included work by Joyce Grenfell, Beryl Reid, Victoria Wood and Barbara Windsor, tracing a genealogy of women in British comedy.

Victoria Pile, the show's producer, and its three stars, Fiona Allen, Sally Phillips and Doon Mackichan, took part in a post-screening question-and-answer session as part of the BFI event (BFI 2012a). The show continues to circulate via YouTube clips and fan sites; it is still available in full for free in the UK via Channel 4's on-demand All 4 site.

Smack the Pony's stars have significant careers in British television comedy and the show gave some of its guest performers – such as Sarah Alexander, Darren Boyd, Miranda Hart, Kevin Eldon and Peter Serafinowitz – early television roles. Doon Mackichan began her career on television in the 1980s, working with Harry Enfield, Steve Coogan and Chris Morris in character and sketch-based comedy. Fiona Allen also began working in comedy and television drama in the 1980s, including a substantial role on *Coronation Street* in 1999. Sally Phillips is slightly younger than her co-stars, emerging in the short-lived Channel 4 sketch show *Six Pairs of Pants* in 1995, alongside Simon Pegg and Jessica Hynes (née Stevenson). Based around a core cast (the three leads were often joined by Sarah Alexander) who are uniformly young, white, pretty, slim and apparently middle-class and heterosexual, *Smack the Pony* does not directly address 'othered' identities such as black, working-class or LGBTQ women. Yet this millennial sketch series offers a clownish and queered vision of hegemonic femininity caught in the glare of postfeminist popular culture.

From the outset the show presented itself as apolitical, as Doon Mackichan noted in a 2015 interview:

> *Smack the Pony* was different to anything I'd seen before. We didn't do anything about diets or sexual politics. 'Let's just let women be clowns', we said. I'd been doing standup for ages and had become thoroughly disheartened by the fact that other female comics all tended to tackle the same subjects. People would say, 'Do you do any period jokes?' and I'd go, 'Well, no, I don't.' (cited in Barnett 2015)

Such statements stereotype 'feminist' comedy as confined to addressing narrowly defined gender issues but Mackichan's comment is also symptomatic of postfeminist discourse in its refusal to be politically identified. *Smack the Pony* is shaped by the postfeminist context of its commissioning and production in the late 1990s and early 2000s, yet the sketches demonstrate an awareness of this context in their relation to feminism and gender politics. As Sally Phillips asserts in the same interview:

> It was the late 1990s. The Spice Girls had happened and Caroline Leddy – then the comedy commissioner at Channel 4 – felt that a sketch show by a trio of girls could finally work. There'd been a few around before, but people hadn't been that interested. (cited in Barnett 2015)

Smack the Pony was thus commissioned as a response to popular interest in 'girl power' and the emergent phenomenon of postfeminism. The show consequently navigates two different imperatives: the history (and alleged failure) of comedy sketch shows led by a female cast, and the contradictory agendas that emerged with the neoliberal emphasis on postfeminism in popular culture.

Contexts: Not a Feminist Sketch Show

Victoria Pile's career trajectory situates *Smack the Pony* within a distinct history of women in television comedy. Pile writes, produces and directs, playing a key creative role in the production of *Smack the Pony*, *Green Wing* (Channel 4 2004–6), and *Campus* (Channel 4 2011). A 2006 interview in *The Telegraph* depicted her as a rising star and Pile was cited as 'a huge talent' in *The Guardian*'s Media Top 100 of 2006, yet her career began almost 30 years earlier (Raphael 2006). She began writing material for the BBC sketch show *Not the Nine O'Clock News* (1979–82) in 1980 (Banks and Swift 1987: 208). Its stars, Rowan Atkinson, Griff Rhys Jones, Mel Smith and Pamela Anderson, represented the 'alternative' comedy that was beginning to appear on British television in the '80s. *Not the Nine O'Clock News* parodied political figures and contemporary news stories but also satirised television formats and the new phenomenon of the music video. Episodes often ended with a musical number, such as 'Nice video, shame about the song', a spoof video which parodied the burgeoning MTV culture of style over substance. The show's 'open-door' policy for new writing – allowing anyone to send in material – made it 'a fertile training ground for new talent' (Lewisohn 2003: 580).

The popular success of *Not the Nine O'Clock News* offers a distinct contrast to the other project that Victoria Pile was working on at the same time. *Revolting Women* (BBC 1981) was a feminist sketch show which ran for just one six-episode series. Lynn Webster, the show's producer, saw it as a response to the male-centred comedy of the 1970s and '80s, focussing on women's experience and attempting to avoid gender stereotypes (Lewisohn 2003: 648). Pile recalls that 'it was the first programme by the BBC (I think I'm right in saying) which asked specifically for women writers. And I think if that programme hadn't been there I wouldn't have got started' (cited in Banks and Swift 1987: 208). The cast of *Revolting Women* reversed the gender dynamic of *Not the Nine O'Clock News*, featuring four women and one man, and was slated by the critics. Pile's explanation for the demise of *Revolting Women* is telling:

> All the women were desperate to unload ten years of trying to get their words out, and put them into this half-hour programme. There was too much trying to be done in too little time . . . it was fraught with personal battles, everyone had an axe to grind. And I don't think it should have been like that. We should just have been stepping in to make a comedy programme, and the fact that we were women should have been almost incidental. [...]
>
> There was prejudice right from the start. Again, I was so green, I'd never encountered such blatant sexism until then. I think, because we'd gone in waving banners, some of us, the press was going to be bad from the start. So there was no help, very little money, everything was put in our way. Had it had another series I think it would have been really good. (cited in Banks and Swift 1987: 208–9)

Despite the fact that Pile was working in an era when politically informed 'alternative' comedy was in vogue, this account indicates the struggle of women even within the 'alternative' circuit. Some of the most successful female performers to emerge from that era were well aware of their gendered difference. Dawn French believes that she and Jennifer Saunders were initially hired to perform stand-up at the Comic Strip club in Soho primarily because 'they were desperate for women in the line-up of an all-male comedy group' (French 2008: 255; see also Saunders 2013: 51). French later discovered that she and Saunders were being paid half as much as their male colleagues in the Comic Strip ensemble (French 2008: 268; Saunders 2013: 57).

Pile's account of *Revolting Women* registers the pressure on women in comedy: the pressure to represent their gender, to be 'as funny' as their male peers, and to deal with the internal and external barracking about simply *being* women in comedy. Histories of the 'alternative' circuit in Britain note the limited numbers of women on stage in the early 1980s; many subsequently retreated from writing and performance, sometimes moving into production (Wilmut and Rosengard 1989; Schaffer 2016). Pile's comment also registers the pressure put upon women in 'alternative' comedy to embody feminist politics. Male alternative comedians often espoused a left-leaning worldview on stage but could be casually sexist and racist off stage. Gavin Schaffer argues that 'alternative' comedy may even be read as 'a manifestation of Thatcherite hegemony', producing a few highly successful (mainly male) comedy stars and spawning a generation of popular television shows that did little to challenge the political status quo (2016: 376). This may explain the scarcity of female performers who made careers from the 'alternative' boom; French and Saunders, Jenny Éclair and Jo Brand are among the few that have endured. Morwenna Banks and Amanda Swift's groundbreaking history of women in comedy features a range of performers from the 1980s who have disappeared from view, such as Jenny Lecoat, Rebecca Stevens and Claire Dowie, who now write for stage and screen (1987).

Pile's account of the reception of *Revolting Women* was documented in the late '80s, as the backlash against second-wave feminism began. When *Smack the Pony* was commissioned a decade later, postfeminism was in full swing. The parody music videos that end each episode mimic postfeminist girl bands such as the Spice Girls, B*Witched and Elastica. The brightly coloured aesthetic of *Smack the Pony* is aligned with commercial aspects of 1990s postfeminist consumer culture – chick-flicks, chick-lit and 'girlie' fashions – yet the comedy frequently undermines key assumptions on which postfeminism is founded. Reflecting on the show nearly 20 years after its original broadcast, Sally Phillips, one of its stars and writers, stated:

> We developed rules: no celebrity references, no recurring characters, no catchphrases. We didn't want to be like *The Fast Show*

[BBC 1994–2000]. It meant a lot more work, but it does mean that the show hasn't dated too much. We were definitely coming from a feminist perspective: our characters were the women who would normally be stuck on the sidelines. In a boys' sketch show, you might have guys doing a bank robbery. We were interested in the women in the car park round the back, unaware that the robbery was happening (cited in Barnett 2015)

This approach, representing a view from the margins rather than the mainstream, confounded some early viewers. Doon Mackichan recalls shooting the first sketch with an all-male crew, where she performed an elaborate warm-up by a swimming pool and then belly-flopped into the water:

None of them laughed. I thought: 'This is absolutely dreadful.' But gradually, as we went on, the atmosphere on set changed. I remember doing one of the dating agency videos, and seeing the crews' shoulders shaking with laughter. I thought: 'We've cracked it!' (cited in Barnett 2015)

Reviews of the show were mixed. Andrew Billen in the left-wing *New Statesman* praised its 'brilliant actor-comedians' but criticised the show for 'clumsy, spluttering comedy', comparing it unfavourably with Chris Morris's *The Day Today* (BBC 1994) – in which Doon Mackichan also appeared – and other contemporary mockumentary series (1999: 39).

Smack the Pony was commissioned by Caroline Leddy, head of comedy at Channel 4, who first met Victoria Pile when working in children's television at the BBC. Pile would make Leddy, then an actor, do 'wacky bits of comedy'. Leddy subsequently moved into producing and commissioning work for Channel 4 (Raphael 2006). Billen's ambivalent review is fuelled by statements from the production team, such as Leddy's denial that this is 'a girls' sketch show', Mackichan's statement that 'Hopefully, people won't even notice it's all women' and Pile's suggestion that 'Viewers should be pushed to tell whether they're watching a documentary or a comedy' (Billen 1999: 39). Such refusal to identify the show as by, for or about women, when it self-evidently is, speaks to postfeminist denials of feminist politics but also of the problems that Pile noted in her account of *Revolting Women*. To identify

Smack the Pony as a feminist sketch show would be to make it bear all the weight and expectation which destroyed *Revolting Women*. At the same time, a sketch show with a female cast is still so clearly marked as exceptional that it cannot be 'gender-free' in the way that shows with all-male casts apparently can (Raphael 2006).

This contradictory discourse, which avoids the 'f' word while addressing key feminist precepts, inflects the comedy in *Smack the Pony*. It is a comedy sketch show featuring a predominantly female cast, written and produced almost exclusively by women (albeit with a largely male crew), and addressing topics that primarily address femininity. *Smack the Pony* is by, for and about women but cannot present itself as feminist. The gender politics which run through the series are thus less a political polemic than a grotesque examination of contemporary femininities. In these terms, *Smack the Pony* is feminist not because it makes overtly political jokes but because it examines and queers heterofemininity. As Sally Phillips asserted, this is comedy about 'the women in the car park round the back' rather than the men at the centre of the action (cited in Barnett 2015).

Queer Temporalities

Sketch comedy on television offers an apposite venue for queering gender roles; it is a format embedded in British broadcasting which has often addressed political issues. Neale and Krutnik map the trajectory of sketch shows from 'nineteenth- and twentieth-century theatrical variety', through the kind of comedy 'bits' that appeared in early American television variety shows and from which early sitcoms such as *The Burns and Allen Show* and *I Love Lucy* were developed (1990: 182). These traditions waned on American networks – albeit with notable exceptions, such as *Saturday Night Live* (NBC 1975–) – but were reiterated on British television and have become an established aspect of comedy programming here. Ian Mowatt identifies two different strands of British sketch show: early comedies informed by music hall and variety such as *The Benny Hill Show* (BBC/ITV 1955–89) and *The Dick Emery Show* (BBC 1963–81), and those informed by 'alternative' comedy such as *A Little Bit of Fry and Laurie* (BBC 1987–95) and *The Mary Whitehouse Experience* (BBC 1990–2) (2010: 21). These shows and their successors – such as *Little Britain* (BBC 2003–6) and *The Catherine Tate*

Show (2004–9) – have been hugely successful, often launching longstanding careers in television. Yet there is little academic work on television sketch comedy, and women's sketch comedy is rarely addressed as a discrete topic. The emergence of academic volumes on *Little Britain* and Chris Morris (Lockyer 2010b; Leggott and Sexton 2013) make the lack of work on *French and Saunders* (BBC 1987–96) or Victoria Wood all the more evident.

British sketch shows tend to follow a standard format: a half-hour slot broken down into longer and shorter sketches: 'Sketches on social, sexual, political or current mores last for up to four minutes: shorter sketches, usually 10–15 seconds, known as quickies, usually connect the sketches to each other' (Mowatt 2010: 20–1). This is a format where performers are often also writers, offering a space where women can both create and deliver a character role (Mowatt 2010: 21). Its medium is brevity:

> The convention that a sketch will be a miniature work entire (set up its own premise, establish ground rules, settle its own little drama) encourages us to survey and savour its emerging shape (for instance, a pattern of escalation) with an eye towards its imminent completion (Clayton 2013: 85–6)

Above all, the sketch format inhabits a *little* world, often a particular aspect of the everyday skewed in some way to reveal, through techniques such as exaggeration and escalation, its particular peculiarities. As Alex Clayton notes, the 'little drama' of the sketch is usually structured with an eye to a visual or verbal punchline, the laugh that offers viewers a final satisfaction. Despite this miniaturised structure, the brevity of the sketch format means that it relies on reiterated characters or types of character as shorthand in order to tell a story in the shortest possible time. The shortness of sketch comedy thus contradicts the ontological draw of sitcom narrative which I observed in *The Big Bang Theory*. It is a format which evades the heteronormative romance plot and is frequently drawn to ridicule the standard tropes of romantic narrative. Many television sketches by women, like their colleagues in stand-up comedy, address the script of heterosexual romance in order to critique it, so that shows such as *Wood and Walters* (Granada 1981–2) and *French and Saunders* refer to heterofemininity as a norm which their comedy exposes and undercuts.

The sketch show is thus prime territory for queering gender and sexual roles. British sketch shows have historically featured men cross-dressed as women or camping it up as 'gay' characters, from *Monty Python's Flying Circus* (BBC 1969–74) to *Little Britain* (Mowatt 2010: 26–30). Despite the often misogynistic and homophobic tenor of such performances, they nonetheless denote the carnivalesque arena which sketch comedy affords, reaching back to the vaudeville and variety traditions at its root. Further than this, however, is the temporal structure of the sketch itself:

> The expectation that the sketch's resolution, as convention demands, will be laughably expedient, without further consequence, fosters a mode of perception less geared to 'what will happen next' and more attentive to comic patterns, repetitions and variations (Clayton 2013: 86)

This lack of narrative teleology, that structure which is 'laughably expedient', aligns sketch comedy with queer refusals of heteronormative temporality that Judith Halberstam addresses in *In a Queer Time and Place* (2005) and returns to in *The Queer Art of Failure* (2011). Queer temporality refuses or satirises the linear imperative of heteronormativity: 'birth, marriage, reproduction and death' (Halberstam 2005: 2). Applying 'low theory' to popular examples such as *50 First Dates* (Peter Segal 2004), Halberstam proposes that the motif of forgetting that runs through such films inadvertently exposes the politics of romance:

> ultimately it reveals heterosexual romance to be nothing more than the violent enforcement of normative forms of sociality and sexuality: heterosexuality is literally reduced to a visual text which installs the national narrative as a basis for the personal narrative of marriage and childbearing. Within such a structure, where the heroine forgets to get married and have kids (as a Barbara Kruger cartoon would have it), forgetting surprisingly stalls the implantation of heteronormativity and creates a barrier to the conventional progress narrative of heterosexual romance (2011: 77)

The structure of sketch comedy is similarly forgetful as it proceeds through a repertoire of sketches and quickies that depend on 'patterns, repetitions and variations' rather than the teleology of narrative (Clayton 2013: 86). Halberstam's 'low theory', grounded in Stuart Hall's work, is proposed as a queer approach to popular culture: 'Low theory tries to locate all the in-between spaces that save us from being snared by the hooks of hegemony and speared by the seductions of the gift shop' (2011: 2). In these terms *Smack the Pony* offers an 'in-between space' regarding its aesthetic as a sketch show, but it is also produced and broadcast at an in-between moment in media culture.

Contexts: Postfeminism, Femininity and the 'Norm'

First broadcast in the late 1990s and early 2000s, *Smack the Pony* corresponds with three significant moments: the transition from mobile phones to smartphones, the subsequent explosion of social media, and the emergence of the 'entrepreneurial subject' (Scharff 2016). These shifts prompted a wave of academic debate. Work on postfeminism and popular culture blossomed in response to new contradictions and complexities in the relation between Western femininities and feminisms (Gill 2016; see, for example, Whelehan 2000; McRobbie 2004, 2009; Gill 2007; Tasker and Negra 2007). Much of this work interrogates the increasingly mediatised emphasis on appearance and self-regulation which undermines feminist advances even as young white middle-class women reap the benefits of the second wave. At the cusp of the millennium, Myra Macdonald observed how 'postfeminism takes the sting out of feminism' and Michèle Roberts described it as 'unthreatening, nice. Less a politics than a behaviour' (cited in Whelehan 2000: 92). These voices from the second wave register postfeminism's return to a girlishly normative femininity: a return to being pleasant, polite and uncontroversial in contrast to that media-generated monster of confrontation, the feminist. Such '"girling" of femininity' also indicates the generational aspect of postfeminism's attention to the young, white, able-bodied, straight-identified, middle-class woman, as it attempts to encourage all women to be 'nice girls' (Tasker and Negra 2007: 18).

'Hegemonic femininities' established in the late twentieth century took on a specifically regulatory aspect: a 'sensibility' centred on the body (Gill and Scharff 2011: 2–4). Work on postfeminism and popular television has examined the proliferation of makeover formats as a means of critiquing that postfeminist sensibility (see for example Roberts 2007; Smith 2011). Angela McRobbie describes the new sexual contract which emerged in the postfeminist era:

> In the language of health and well-being, the global fashion-beauty complex charges itself with the business of ensuring that appropriate gender relations are guaranteed. This field of instruction and pleasure oversees the processes of female individuation which requires the repudiation of feminism which is frequently typecast as embodying bodily failure, hideousness or monstrosity (2009: 61–2)

Feminism is thus aligned with the grotesque and the monstrous as a *spoiled* or *queered* femininity in a postfeminist context. Yet even in the regulatory environment of makeover television there can be moments of resistance. Hannah McCann argues that the British makeover show *Snog, Marry, Avoid* (BBC 2008–13) offers a space for participants to speak back to and actively refuse such regulation, even as it disciplines its working-class subjects into more acceptable middle-class femininities. McCann proposes the hyperfemininity of many participants on *Snog, Marry, Avoid* as a visible form of 'queening' which problematises the 'normal' femininities that such shows attempts to impose. She suggests that rather than reading femininity as a form of gendered oppression, we should ask *'What does femininity do and how can some forms of femininity queer gender?'* (2015: 250, emphasis in original). That question may productively be applied to sketch shows such as *Smack the Pony*, as its female stars perform extreme and excessive characters that work to queer white middle-class heterofemininity. More recent examples can be seen in the work of Julia Davis and Morgana Robinson. Such comedy can thus be read as delivering a feminist grotesque through performances that work to queer gender by exaggerating and exposing the bizarre performativity of heteronormative identity: making it *funny* and making it *visible*.

Queer theory draws attention to the fragility of gender norms and the potential for their disruption. Judith Butler's account of gender as 'a practice of improvisation within a scene of constraint' could almost be taken as a description of television sketch comedy, each performance rendered within the constraints of the sketch format, but she is in fact referring to the social dynamics through which gender identities are summoned and regulated (2004: 1). Butler proposes the norm as a key means by which gender is *made* 'regular': 'A norm is not the same as a rule, and it is not the same as a law. A norm operates within social practice as the implicit standard of *normalization*' (2004: 41). The norm is here constituted as a social construct and thus is not immutable. It is a discursive form of regulation that has power in its implicit ordinariness − that it is just *common sense* − but which is situated culturally and historically through its embodiment in social practice and thus retains the possibility of change: 'the norm in its necessary temporality is opened to a displacement and subversion from within' (Butler 2004: 47). This is not to underestimate the pervasive hegemonic power of normalisation:

> The norm governs intelligibility, allows for certain kinds of practices and action to become recognizable as such, imposing a grid of legibility on the social and defining the parameters of what will and will not appear within the domain of the social (Butler 2004: 42)

If gender identity is made intelligible, readable, through its relation to a norm, then even identities that are constituted as 'deviant' or 'other' are regulated through that 'grid of legibility' because they are understood in normative terms. Butler, however, proposes gender norms as simultaneously a form of regulation *and* the means of its exposure: 'Gender is the mechanism by which notions of masculine and feminine are produced and naturalized, but gender might very well be the apparatus by which such terms are deconstructed and denaturalized' (2004: 42). This is what sketch comedy can do. In their exaggeratedly grotesque account of postfeminist femininities, these performances can make evident how monstrous such femininities have become. Comedy can expose the inherent anxieties and weaknesses which sustain normative femininities and their dependence on loosely reiterative acts to shore up 'natural' appearances:

> The norm has no independent ontological status, yet it cannot be easily reduced to its instantiations; it is itself (re)produced through its embodiment, through the acts that strive to approximate it, through the idealizations reproduced in and by those acts (Butler 2004: 48)

This embodiment of an elusive norm is satirised in the first episode of *Smack the Pony*. During the closing credit sequence Doon Mackichan and Fiona Allen stand side by side over the hand basins in the women's toilet of a club or restaurant (Figure 4.1). It is an everyday scene performed to a diegetic soundtrack of flushing toilets and running water. The two women ignore each other and check their make-up in the mirror. Allen applies her dark red lipstick and Mackichan does the same. Allen applies more and Mackichan follows suit, each surreptitiously glancing at the other's reflection but not speaking. The competitive application of lipstick continues, as they alternately trace larger and larger red mouths across their faces. Eventually, with mouths outlined in a clownish sea of red, they each gaze approvingly at their reflection and head out of the toilet to the public area. The reiterative status of gender performance is enacted here, but in such an exaggerated and ridiculous manner that femininity becomes clownish. The extreme femininities which women are encouraged to pursue in a postfeminist era are on show in this sketch. The self-regulation and constant inspection of their own, and other women's, appearance within the private/public space of the toilet is performed repeatedly and thus made *funny*. The norm is 'deconstructed and denaturalized' through grotesque performance (Butler 2004: 42). Tracing the genealogy of normalisation through Levi-Strauss, Lacan, Foucault et al., Butler addresses how it might be disrupted, arguing that

Figure 4.1 Competitive lipstick application in *Smack the Pony* (1:1, Talkback Productions, 1999–2003).

in order to evade the 'grid of legibility' we need to think beyond heterosexual hegemony. While normative histories of what constitute the human are embedded in binary understandings of gender, as masculine *or* feminine within a heterosexual 'grid', a queer perspective can work 'to show possibilities for gender that are not predetermined by forms of hegemonic heterosexuality' (Butler 2004: 54).

Academic work on unruly performances by pretty *and* funny women in television and stand-up comedy since the millennium has noted the queer potential of that dynamic: how it exposes postfeminism's reiteration of heteronormative understandings of gender. Marusya Bociurkiw argues that Ellen DeGeneres's performance in *Ellen* (ABC 1994–8), before the character and star famously 'came out' on screen, is comparable to that of Lucille Ball in *I Love Lucy* in its skilful depiction of failing heterofemininity: 'Ellen's and Lucy's ineptitude, expressed via physical movement, was a gag that spoke where the (gagged) mouth couldn't – the plot, turning on these bodily attributes, turned also on a silent rage, grotesque excess, and a kind of productive disequilibrium' (2005: 177). Both Ellen and Lucy queer the 'natural', 'common-sense' heterofemininities of their times, a queering that arguably became less destabilising once DeGeneres and her sitcom alter ego were officially classified *as* queer (Bociurkiw 2005).

In a similar vein, Hannah Ballou argues that women in contemporary comedy can exploit the pretty/funny paradox 'via the particularly incongruous instrument of their poised and privileged bodies. [...] There is a certain pleasure (comic or otherwise) when a person subverts a system that in some ways privileges her' (2013: 183–4). For Ballou, examining the work of Olivia Côte in France and Olivia Lee in Britain, it is the grotesque juxtaposition of 'pretty' heterofemininity and comic situations that has the potential to expose femininity as performative rather than a natural category. Linda Mizejewski likewise notes how contemporary American women comedians queer gender through their comic performances, citing 'the queerness implicit in a comedy based on rage against gender norms' (Mizejewski 2014: 16). In *Pretty/Funny: Women Comedians and Body Politics* she demonstrates how Kathy Griffin, Tina Fey, Sarah Silverman, Margaret Cho, Wanda Sykes and Ellen DeGeneres deploy configurations of 'pretty/funny' in their performances to queer femininity, addressing celebrity culture, racism and homophobia. Employing a Deleuzian approach, Mizejewski recuperates

DeGeneres's post-*Ellen* career as a celebrity talk-show host by arguing that her normalising performance of lesbian identity is most disconcerting for homophobic viewers: 'DeGeneres's predictable wholesomeness and upbeat nature are indeed disturbing elements for a conservative audience that would prefer to make butch lesbianism invisible or at least abjected. DeGeneres instead makes lesbianism itself incoherent for such a worldview' (2014: 215).

Smack the Pony plays upon that queered incoherence in the reiterative format of the sketch show, troubling the 'grid of legibility' that binary accounts of gender requires in order to function (Butler 2004: 42). The grotesque application of bloody red lipstick, so that the mouth becomes a smear of pigment rather than a neatly bounded bow, can be read in many ways: as an expression of feminine rage or as a feminist refusal of 'the global fashion-beauty complex' (McRobbie 2009: 61). At its root, however, it is hilariously *in*coherent and *il*legible, offering 'grotesque excess and a kind of productive disequilibrium' (Bociurkiw 2005: 177). As the two women finally consider their ridiculous reflections in the mirror, they appear satisfied, even pleased, with this bizarre new look, inviting the viewer to wonder if this is no more peculiar than the ordinary rituals we perform each day. Such comedy offers a grotesque intervention by drawing attention to newly normalised postfeminist practices regarding grooming and self-presentation.

The Grotesque, the Queer, the Monstrous

The grotesque has a standard reading list in academic work. In their overview of the field, for example, Justin Edwards and Rune Graulund cite Mikhael Bakhtin, Wolfgang Keyser and Mary Russo, as well as the work of Peter Stallybrass and Allon White on the politics of transgression. At the same time, Edwards and Graulund note the fluidity and indeterminacy of the grotesque as a term which 'does not inhabit a stable or predetermined ground' (2013: 4). In this regard the grotesque stands alongside the queer and the monstrous as a concept which is always in transition: 'For if there is one thing that defines "the" grotesque it is precisely that it is hybrid, transgressive and always in motion' (Edwards and Graulund 2013: 15). Alice Mills also remarks on the grotesque as a term which evades legible categorisation and, in doing so, aligns the grotesque with comedy: 'Like nonsense, like humour, the grotesque is annihilated by definition' (1999: 2). The power of the grotesque lies in its indefinable, transient status; it is thus a useful lens through which to examine queered femininities.

Mary Russo's foundational study of the female grotesque continues to resonate across feminist debates regarding femininity and performance. Russo proposes the alignment of the grotesque and the feminine as terms which shadow each other through abjection and marginality, superficiality and bodily excess (1995: 2–6). She defines the grotesque as a carnivalesque public performance but also as an uncanny private fantasy, contrasting the abjection of the grotesque body with the classical body, where the latter is figured as a contained, 'perfect' object (1995: 7–8). Most pertinently, Russo offers a critique of the normalising imperative, noting its presence within feminist discourse:

> With the best intentions (which include prominently the wish to be maximally inclusive) this normalizing strategy cannot conceal its class bias and attachment to an 'upward mobility' which depends upon leaving others behind. Furthermore, it concedes much to the misogyny which permeates the fear of 'losing one's femininity', 'making a spectacle of oneself', 'alienating men' (meaning powerful men) or otherwise 'making errors'. Most importantly, it leaves uninterrogated the very terms and processes of normalcy. I begin this study on the side of the freak and the uncanny (1995: 12)

In this passage Russo dissects the inherent power dynamic of being 'proper' – as a woman, as an academic, as a professional in the public sphere – and the constraints that entails. Privileged white middle-class women who remain within the norms of femininity, who accede to the imperative to remain silent and polite in the face of unfeasible behaviour by those in positions of power, accede to the hegemony of heteronormativity. In these postfeminist times, silence is the price of privilege: 'the new female subject is, despite her freedom, called upon to be silent, to withhold critique, to count as a modern sophisticated girl, or indeed this withholding of critique is a condition of her freedom' (McRobbie 2004: 260). Through grotesque performance, women in British sketch comedy can expose such restrictions, undermining the 'natural' presentation of postfeminist girls and women, making heterofemininity both visible and *un*intelligible.

Judith Butler contends that in order to be oppressed the subject of oppression 'must first become intelligible', so that those in power can identify and regulate their oppressed others (2004: 30). Grotesque performances of femininity, even within the densely regulated and commodified environment of television comedy, mess up that core intelligibility by exposing its particular peculiarities. As Linda Mizejewski argues in her analysis of Sarah Silverman's work, grotesque speech acts or routines by a 'totally cute white girl' undercut the romantic fictions of normative heterofemininity, exposing its limitations and constructed reiterations (2014: 104). Such performances may be understood as an enactment of fantastic possibilities:

> The critical promise of fantasy, when and where it exists, is to challenge the contingent limits of what will and will not be called reality. Fantasy is what allows us to imagine ourselves and others otherwise; it establishes the possible in excess of the real; it points elsewhere, and when it is embodied, it brings the elsewhere home (Butler 2004: 29)

This is a utopian premise and there are clear limitations to comedy as a medium for challenge because the comic arena is a space in which transgression is licensed, even expected. Nevertheless, grotesque and ridiculous performances of heterofemininity harbour a potential to render the normal and everyday strange and unusual. Jane Arthurs remarks the extreme responses that grotesque performance of the feminine can evoke and proposes that television comedy is one place where angry women can be seen:

> This is why comedy is an important arena for the expression of female fantasies of physical aggression. The ambivalence of the 'licensed transgression' institutionalized by comedy – a cultural form within legitimized public spaces, where the unthinkable and the undoable can be thought and done without retribution from society in general or the individual psyche – has allowed for a growing cultural expression of women's anger, especially the anger generated by their experience of subordination. Dressed up in

jokes and comedy, this aggression can find a place in popular culture which is sufficiently unthreatening to gain a space in the mainstream without much controversy. For a while, in the early nineties, Friday nights on Channel Four [UK] was [*sic*] taken over by stroppy, unruly women who literally and metaphorically 'took up space' in the schedules (1999: 141)

Arthurs follows Kathleen Rowe's work in addressing women who are physically unruly; her examples are Jo Brand's stand-up and sketch show *Through the Cakehole* (Channel 4 1994–6) and Joanna Lumley's performance as Patsy Stone in *Absolutely Fabulous* (BBC 1992–6). *Smack the Pony* follows a similar trajectory, where comedy routines such as the competitive lipstick sketch offer grotesque exaggerations of 'normal' femininities in a postfeminist frame, suggesting that a feminist anger fuels such performances and informs the show's aesthetic. That feminist perspective may have emerged from the conditions of *Smack the Pony*'s production, from the cultural and professional contexts in which it was produced. In these terms one can see the production process of the show itself as a form of feminist praxis.

Feminist Praxis: The Production of *Smack the Pony*

Nearly 20 years after *Smack the Pony* was first broadcast, Doon Mackichan remembers how working on this show differed from other experiences:

It was refreshing to have women in the lead. We'd all done years of 'feeding' for various sketch shows – playing the foil to set up the joke, so that the male comic could take the laugh. My first sketch show was called *Five Alive*, with Brian Conley and Peter Piper [TVS 1987–8]; from the beginning, we women were told in no uncertain terms that the show was to launch the men's careers. For *Smack the Pony*, we'd get sent stacks of sketches from writers who had often been turned down by male comics, such as Mel and Griff [Mel Smith and Griff Rhys Jones of *Smith and Jones* (BBC 1989–98)], and rework them, turning the straight female characters into the funny ones. (cited in Barnett 2015)

Mackichan charts the secondary status of women in much television comedy during the 1980s and '90s, as 'feeders' for male stars. Mark Lewisohn confirms her account of *Five Alive*, describing it as 'a wham-bam sketch show' built around its male stars, with a 'high babe-count' in the opening episode that was toned down in the subsequent series (2003: 289). *Smack the Pony*, then, reversed the gender dynamic of many sketch shows at the time, putting women in the starring roles and reworking material written for men. This – together with the ambivalent definition of the show by Pile, Mackichan and Phillips at the time and in subsequent interviews as feminist and/or not feminist – indicates the contradictory postfeminist discourse regarding gender politics which informed the production of *Smack the Pony* and which its comedy addressed.

Such contradictions continue in the lived experience of women within the neoliberal workplace. Christina Scharff's examination of women working in classical music demonstrates how these professionals constitute themselves as 'entrepreneurial subjects' (2016). Like television performers, classical musicians seek work within a predominantly white middle-class profession as freelancers engaged in pursuing and securing short-term temporary contracts. Scharff's in-depth interviews with 64 young female classical musicians reveal how they negotiate a physically and emotionally challenging environment, concealing injuries and vulnerabilities. The self is regarded as 'a business' or a product, as is the case for actors and increasingly for academics and other professionals (Scharff 2016: 111–12). Scharff's interviewees navigate the risks inherent in their work with individuated strategies such as 'positive thinking', which enable them to function but also depoliticise the conditions under which they operate: 'According to [Barbara] Ehrenreich (2009: 8), "positive thinking has made itself useful as an apology for crueller aspects of the market economy"' (Scharff 2016: 113).

The vulnerability of freelance actors who operate within such neoliberal environments offers one way of understanding how the identification of *Smack the Pony* as feminist or even primarily for and about women was problematic in the late 1990s, a time when the 'f' word was decried as limiting or outdated. In the 2010s, however, feminism has become 'cool', as we are in 'a moment in which feminism has seemingly moved from being a derided and repudiated identity among young women [...] to becoming a desirable, stylish, and decidedly fashionable one' (Gill 2016: 611). Sally Phillips and Doon Mackichan now characterise *Smack the Pony* as explicitly feminist, which may have as much to do with their established careers in television and a more public engagement with politics, as with discursive shifts regarding the term's popularity. In 2016 Phillips presented *A World Without Down's Syndrome?* (BBC 2016), a controversial documentary about prenatal testing, and Mackichan fronted *Body Count Rising* (BBC 2016), a half-hour programme for BBC Radio 4 addressing the prevalence of violence against women in television drama. In an interview to promote *Body Count Rising*, Mackichan recalls her early feminist activism at Manchester University and with Violence Against Women in London. She advocates against being 'nice': 'I've stopped being afraid of saying the wrong thing, or trying to be a good girl. We're overdomesticated: there's a whole other side of our natures [...] On the surface, I'm quite nice – but underneath, I'm no longer tame' (cited in Williams 2016).

Such undomesticated, untamed femininities infuse *Smack the Pony*. Whether categorised as feminist or not, this show addresses women's consciousness in a man's world. Whelehan notes how in postfeminist discourse 'Feminism becomes something "we" must be liberated from in order to explore the endless possibilities of free-floating desire – desire which is almost always linked to consumption and sexuality' (2000: 92–3). *Smack the Pony* addresses that tension between feminist politics and postfeminist culture with deliberate silliness. Clowning techniques predominate, with the show's stars often assuming ridiculous appearances, voices or bodily quirks. Mackichan has an extensive career in comedy, as has Fiona Allen, while Sally Phillips has had regular roles as the best friend in *Miranda* (BBC 2009–15) and in the *Bridget Jones* film series. In contrast to most of their other work in television and film, however, *Smack the Pony* enabled and encouraged its female cast to workshop and write their own material. Victoria Pile stated at the BFI event in 2012: 'we played, we fought, we explored' (BFI 2012a). Workshopping material is a common technique in the theatre and some forms of film-making – Mike Leigh's work, for example – but is less common in television production with its rapid turnover of material and professionals. Kay Stonham and Sue Teddern, writers with extensive careers in British radio and television comedy, have both experienced the

American model of the 'writers' room', where individuals compete to produce jokes and storylines for collaborative scripts: 'For Teddern this mode of working is one that she aligns with masculinity as "blokey", with the implication that such creative spaces do not welcome women' (Mills and Ralph 2015: 105). Such working practices produce a 'masculine', gag-based style of humour in a production context that is predominantly male and formed around gendered divisions of labour where secretaries and production assistants are mostly women and directors and writers are mostly men (Mills and Ralph 2015: 106–9). While the collaborative model that Mackichan describes on *Smack the Pony* is not exclusive to women, in this context it is an example of feminist praxis.

Like most collaborative work, the process was not straightforward: playing, fighting and exploring are not linear methods with a specific teleology. That exploratory aesthetic shapes the comic style of the series. Sally Phillips recalls that the show became something of a diary project as the performers incorporated aspects of their lives at the time (BFI 2012a). In this respect they followed a strategy already mapped out by two major female stars to emerge from the 1980s alternative stable, Dawn French and Jennifer Saunders. *French and Saunders* created an alternate world which exploited the performers' skills in clowning, mimicry and satire. Jennifer Saunders also describes their methodology as that of play: 'We play. We make up characters and voices and use people we have seen and lines we have heard and then we play them into a sketch' (2013: 100). *French and Saunders* is manifestly not 'a wham-bam sketch show' like *Five Alive*. Similarly, *Smack the Pony* attends to surreal aspects of the everyday rather than working to the 'wham-bam' of a punchline.

That dilatory approach was carried through in *Smack the Pony*'s visual aesthetic. The show differed from other British sketch comedies in the late 1990s, such as *The Fast Show*, which tended to be filmed in multiple-camera studios under high-key lighting. The series was filmed on video tape, using filters and low-key lighting to effect a more natural appearance. Pile recalls the decision – at times problematic – to keep the camera at eye level, using long lenses and Steadicam in an attempt to have all the performers visible within the frame, as a means of capitalising on their reactions and any background business. Viewers were invited to watch everything that was happening in a scene rather than focus on the central business of a star performer. The production process involved two weeks of workshopping the sketches, followed by two weeks of filming. As Mackichan states, the three leads had longstanding careers as 'feeds' for male stars, and were determined to '[make] the straight person funny', with a policy of 'not having a punchline, which is a very male thing' (BFI 2012a). If there was a punchline it was often overheard as the camera moved away from the action. Mobile, eye-level camerawork together with naturalistic lighting was designed to echo the 'observational' comedy. *Smack the Pony* thus worked to make the everyday ridiculous through visual jokes or clownish behaviour as the audience 'eavesdropped' on the action. In this way the 'straight person' did indeed become 'funny' and women usually consigned to the background took centre stage (BFI 2012a). The format, visual aesthetic, production regime and division of labour thus fostered a comedy which targeted the silliness of the everyday.

Smack the Pony did not always remain true to this feminist praxis. Parody advertisements were a regular feature of the second series, including straplines such as 'Not getting enough sex? Become a prostitute' (2:2), or a scenario depicting a woman whose life is 'rubbish' and the strapline is 'get a cleaner', as a woman in a business suit hugs her new employee (2:2). While these scenarios touch upon serious issues such as sexual politics and domestic labour, they do so clumsily. The quality of the sketches is uneven, evidencing the uncertainty that the show's writers and performers felt at the time regarding its production and their chances of success (BFI 2012a; Barnett 2015). Some sketches indicate that the show expects its viewers to have a politically sophisticated worldview. A dating agency sketch in the second season features Fiona Allen and Sally Phillips as a lesbian couple 'looking for a man' who recite stereotypical male fantasies about lesbian sexuality: they want a man who 'could teach us how to pleasure him' (2:2). They finally agree that it is unlikely any man will want to do this. The joke is dependent on understanding that lesbians do not search for heterosexual men who want to teach them how to 'pleasure him' but that this is often a feature of heterosexual pornography. While these are not the most successful sketches, they betray a rage about social expectations which remain for even the most privileged women in a postfeminist environment: to have 'enough' sex, to attain a lifestyle that is not 'rubbish' or to address pornographic fantasies about women's sexuality. Their awkwardness and clunky delivery betrays a discomfort with the contexts within which the show was produced, indicating a mismatch between the neoliberal arena of popular television and the political aesthetic of *Smack the Pony*. The show's depiction of new media in the dating agency sketches exemplifies that discomfort but deals with it in a more productive manner, so that the characters' unintelligible desires gesture toward queer possibilities.

Queerly Desiring Subjects

The dating agency sketches were a regular and highly successful aspect of the show, featuring members of the cast as various outrageous characters. This is one of the first sketches that made the crew laugh and they have achieved an afterlife through fans uploading the sequences on YouTube (Barnett 2015). The dating agency sketches speak to and anticipate the impact of new technologies on gender and sexual identity. *Smack the Pony* precedes the explosion of social media and online dating apps in the early twenty-first century but was broadcast at a moment when such new media were on the horizon.

The sketches are filmed in low-fi video, with a fixed camera and an 'amateur' style. The actors are placed in what appears to be a booth, against a plain background, initially framed within the screen by a thick black border (Figure 4.2). Performers speak directly to camera in the manner of webcam footage. The format is both intimate and public in that the 'dates' are advertising for a partner. The sketches mimic dating agency videos, the 1980s version of contemporary online apps such as Tinder. These videos would be watched by clients who signed up to dating agencies looking for a potential partner; often they would be watched in the agency's offices. In the 2010s a YouTube upload of video dating clips from 1987 went viral with its combination of awkward statements, odd body language and dated fashions (Mulshine 2015). In the *Smack the Pony* sketches, the 'dates' are almost all female and anticipate the prevalence of online footage on sites such as Match.com. The number of dating agency sketches in the show (often quickies lasting less than a minute) indicates the format's adaptability, limited only by the number of characters the show's writers and performers could create. The sketches thus inadvertently anticipated the proliferation of identities now visible on social media.

The dating sketches offer a queered atlas of unexpected and inexplicable feminine desires, as the 'dates' are remarkably specific in their requirements and requests. One woman has heard of a man whose name is 'Clive Bosoms' and is so aroused by this idea that she appears in the dating video solely to contact him (2:5). Another is a Welsh beautician 'looking for a bloke with a stammer and a ginormous beard', who draws a picture of the latter to illustrate what she wants (2:4). Others offer a surreal take on heterosexual desire:

Figure 4.2 The dating agency sketches (*Smack the Pony*, Talkback Productions, 1999–2003).

Bernadette, 42: I'm looking for someone with a kitchen-come-lounge. I'm not interested in someone with a separate lounge. I have to be able to watch *you* cook, or have *you* watch *me* cook. I am prepared to look at the lounge through a hatch initially but long term I am looking for someone with a through lounge or a through kitchen. I can't be having one of those men who lock themselves up in the kitchen and leave me in the lounge not knowing what's going on. It's not that I believe the kitchen is better than the lounge, or that the lounge is better than the kitchen; it's just that I believe the walls between those two areas should be knocked down if that's architecturally viable. So ideally my ideal man would have no need for privacy in either the kitchen or the lounge areas. He will be a man, and he will have a kitchen-come-lounge area, all in one. [places her hand on her heart] Because I believe that dividing those two areas up is wrong, and causes a lot of wars (2:5)

This monologue is delivered in a heartfelt, deadpan manner by Sally Phillips in a Mancunian accent. Hand gestures are used throughout to emphasise each point. What are we to make of this? Clearly the comedy emerges from a surreal and specific form of desire, where watching someone cook becomes an erotic spectacle.

Recent work by Helen Wheatley demonstrates that such unexpected erotic spectacle is characteristic of the television experience: 'the visual pleasures of television are widespread and diverse, subjectively defined according to personal tastes and preferences, and present throughout the medium's broadcast flows' (2016: 222). In this regard the specificity, variety and comically unexpected nature of the dating sketches are entirely consonant with the medium. Television is 'a privileged site for the articulation of female desire', and the dating sketches both enact and satirise this dynamic (Wheatley 2016: 212). The designation of normative heterosexual desire in the kitchen/lounge sketch – this is clearly a woman looking for a man – is compromised by the bizarre demand for a specific domestic space and also by the lack of boundaries between those spaces. A mere hatch is not enough! The closing statement, ridiculously hyperbolic in its claim that 'dividing up those two areas is wrong, and causes a lot of wars', reflects upon the many equally arbitrary forms of difference – gender, sexual, ethnic and religious – that do indeed evoke violence. These short comedy bits expose the specificity of desire: its queer potential even within a heteronormative frame. Heterosexuality is queered, satirised and made peculiar through such close examination and deliberate silliness.

Speaking and Stunting

Smack the Pony frequently deploys silliness to expose the grotesque requirements of heteronormative relationships. Several sketches are based around the behaviour of straight couples in public spaces such as bars, cafés and clubs. In one scenario a man and woman sit in a restaurant after a meal and she nervously asks him where he sees the relationship going: 'What are your *intentions*, haha?', to which he bluntly replies 'I want to see your tits' (Figure 4.3). He then clarifies that it is just her breasts that he wants to see, and that he does want to get married, but not to her. Distressed, she asks why he has been taking her out and buying her presents, to which he replies 'You have to, otherwise you'd never get to see any tits at all' (2:3). This blunt exchange makes manifest the economic power relations which underpin heteronormative romance: that the man is expected to pay for gifts, meals and so on, and in return expects a sexual pay-off. The joke echoes work by Gayle Rubin and Luce Irigaray which examines the economy of heterosexual romance (Rubin 1975; Irigaray 1985). In the same episode, a sequence of sketches shows Sally Phillips clinging to Darren Boyd's leg as he goes to work, has a meeting and goes to a bar on a date with another woman, dragging her along the ground. She literally clings to him, refusing to believe that their relationship is over and discussing it, saying 'I'm prepared to give it another go', while the man remains silent on the topic, ignoring the embodied emotional baggage attached to his leg (2:3).

These sketches exemplify a significant aspect of *Smack the Pony*'s comedy, where the figurative is made manifest to humorous ends.

Figure 4.3 'I want to see your tits' (*Smack the Pony*, 2:3, Talkback Productions, 1999–2003).

Mary Russo asks 'In what sense can women really produce or make spectacles out of themselves?', arguing that 'in the everyday indicative world, women and their bodies, certain bodies, in certain public framings, in certain public spaces, are always already transgressive – dangerous, and in danger' (1986: 217). In *Smack the Pony* the always already transgressive spectacle of femininity is made manifest through grotesque conversation and physical comedy: a man who expressly regards romance as a financial transaction and a woman who embodies the refusal to let go of a relationship. In the restaurant sketch the woman is exposed to danger through her horror at his crude request. The man is financially invested but emotionally disinvested in the relationship, stating his voyeuristic desire bluntly and without shame. Phillips's clinging woman is emotionally overinvested in her now-defunct relationship with a former lover and has thus become dangerous. In the final sequence of the clinging woman sketches, she sits on the floor of a nightclub, still hugging his leg while sipping a drink and talking about their relationship as he ignores her and flirts with another woman. What is lacking in both scenarios is the shame of transgression. In neither sketch does the woman remain silent. She continues to speak, to question, to hold on, despite cruel and unusual behaviour by the male characters. These women do not accede to the postfeminist requirement 'to be silent, to withhold critique, to count as a modern sophisticated girl' (McRobbie 2004: 260); rather they embody a feminist grotesque in refusing to comply with the logics of heteronormative romance. This is the *comedy* but it is also one aspect of the show that has remained powerful and politically relevant in the years since *Smack the Pony* was originally broadcast. While this show is not polemic or unitary in its approach to gender norms, it addresses heterosexual hegemonies, exposing them as bizarre, grotesque and monstrous.

Much of *Smack the Pony* is surreal, aligning that uncanny category with humour through juxtapositions which address the silliness of hegemonic femininities. Shorter sketches often rely on visual jokes, such as a bride in full wedding regalia shopping in a supermarket or going swimming (1:2). More elaborate sequences construct a whole narrative, such as a female matador's romance with her bull which is shot as an art-house film (1:5). The first season features repeated quickie sketches, where a woman in an everyday setting is suddenly intercut with a random still image – of a horse, a pair of cowboy boots, a man's chest, male bodybuilders, an astronaut – and falls over (1:3, 1:7). This is elaborated with a variation where a woman or two women together encounter a naked man who is casually walking past them on the street, getting off a bus or entering a lift (1:3, 1:4, 1:5). They fall over. The collapsing women are ridiculously unintelligible: do they fall over through distraction? Do they faint with fear or desire? Like the kitchen/lounge dating sketch these sequences defy explanation. Female desire cannot be ordered within the normative grid of intelligible behaviour and thus becomes queered, both funny and peculiar. That these sketches are situated in everyday locations – the restaurant, the supermarket, the bar and the street – is significant, reminding viewers that in these public spaces women 'are always already transgressive – dangerous, and in danger' (Russo 1986: 217).

Large sections of *Smack the Pony* were filmed on location for comic effect and this is most evident in several choreographed routines featuring the three stars in public spaces. The first of these is located in front of an advertising hoarding which states 'Wandsworth: The Brighter Borough' (Figure 4.4). The sequence is filmed with a fixed camera from across the street at a busy interchange. Cars can be heard on the soundtrack beeping their horns as the women perform. Sally Phillips, Doon Mackichan and Fiona Allen walk into shot dressed in

Figure 4.4 The public dance routine (*Smack the Pony*, 1:3, Talkback Productions, 1999–2003).

short macs and sunglasses, with backcombed 1960s-style hair and handbags; they are initially filmed in black and white, recalling '60s realist cinema and television. Sally Phillips carries a tape recorder which she places on the ground. They casually take off their coats to reveal substantial bikinis, then assume a starting position with one hand in the air and the other on one hip as Phillips presses play. To a tinny '60s burlesque tune, they mechanically perform a short dance routine as the scene shifts from black and white to colour, returning to monochrome once the music stops. When the performance is over, the women abruptly put on their macs and walk out of shot. The traffic noise and the passing cars may be heard and seen throughout.

This sketch is reiterated. Later sequences include a routine with water hoses performed in front of a municipal fountain where Phillips, Allen and Mackichan emerge from a van with the insignia 'South London Water Works'; a sequence with the women dressed as cheerleaders on the back of a flatbed lorry chanting 'Vegetarians can't dance' and 'Eat more mince' as they drive back and forth past 'Greens Meat Packers'; and a burlesque routine where the women are lit up by strategically placed lampshades on their costumes in front of a sign that says 'Brentford is Brilliant'. While the Water Works and Brentford routines appear staged, the other locations seem to be guerrilla activities, hijacking municipal hoardings or local businesses with 'glamourous' routines. These happenings adopt a Dadaist tactic, juxtaposing resolutely mundane environments with ridiculously kitsch performances. All of them are filmed in long shot using a fixed camera, so that the public street assumes the role of theatrical stage with the three women framed within the *mise en scène*.

The *risk* of the Wandsworth routine is tangible. Allen, Mackichan and Phillips perform in a deadpan manner facing the camera but their bodies are exposed to the elements and the gaze of passing traffic. They look cold. They are literally making a spectacle of themselves. Mary Russo talks about the concept of 'stunting', applying it specifically to female stunt pilots and aerialists but also to any performance which portrays a queered femininity:

> A stunt may be thought of more theoretically as a tactic for groups or individuals in a certain risky situation in which a strategy is not possible. Strategies depend upon a proper place, a place of one's

own from which a certain 'calculus of force' can be organized and projected outward. [...] As a temporal category, the tactic, or [...] the practice of stunting, belongs to the improvisational, to the realm of what is possible in the moment (1995: 22)

These sequences from *Smack the Pony* embody stunting tactics and their sheer silliness is aligned with a bravery on the part of the performers that exemplifies queered femininity. This is not proper and not logical but it *is* funny and peculiar. The camp heritage on which the sketches are based, with Allen, Mackichan and Phillips effectively performing routines in female drag, speaks to the dangers of not being properly feminine. It is a practice which is lodged in the moment, not in a feminist future or a political praxis. The sketches offer a demonstration about and against the gender politics of popular culture. These are women on the margins making fun of marginality: making it a party, camping it up, stunting for all they are worth.

Legacies

Reflecting on the making of *Smack the Pony* in 2015, Doon Mackichan said:

I still get younger women saying they started out in comedy because of *Smack the Pony*. What's distressing is that it didn't produce a raft of other shows. What else have we got apart from *Miranda*? Women are out there, writing, but they're not getting commissioned, or seeing their shows dropped after one series. It's still a battle (cited in Barnett 2015)

This is evidently the case: while there are occasional pilots or initial seasons of shows with predominantly female casts, they rarely last. The closest inheritors to *Smack the Pony* may be *Titty Bang Bang* (BBC 2005–7), which featured a female cast with a predominantly male writing team, or *Beehive*, which aired five episodes on Channel 4 in 2008 and was not commissioned for a second series. There have been some notable successes by British women in television comedy but they have tended to be individual stars who headline sitcom narratives, such as Julia Davis's darkly bizarre *Nighty Night* (BBC 2004–5) and *Hunderby*

(Sky Atlantic 2012–15), Phoebe Waller-Bridge's *Fleabag* (BBC/Amazon 2016) or *Miranda* (BBC 2009–15).

Smack the Pony was produced and broadcast when digital television was becoming a reality. In 1998 the BBC launched its first digital channel, BBC Choice, with Sky and ITV following suit in the same year. In 2002 CBBC and CBeebies were launched alongside BBC4, and Freeview heralded a new era of digital provision for most British viewers, in the form of a set-top box for a one-off payment (Lewisohn 2003: 867). When *Smack the Pony* ended its original run on Channel 4 in 2002, digital programming was beginning to become available via smart technologies, on televisions, computer screens and mobile phones. This may be a more likely venue for comedies which queer gender: an online space with low-cost production values which invites a direct interaction with viewers. BBC3 was launched in 2003 and quickly became a forum for testing out new British comedy, such as *Little Britain*, *Gavin and Stacey* (BBC 2008–10) and *Him and Her* (BBC 2010–13) (Mills 2009: 53). When it moved to online-only provision in early 2016, BBC3 developed a series of webcasts called *Top Tens* by new British comedians, many from the burgeoning stand-up scene:

> Each *Top Ten* is a few minutes long and will be published by BBC Three every Thursday morning at www.bbc.co.uk/bbcthree and www.youtube.com/bbcthree with each *Top Ten* being made available so it can be embedded on third party sites. [...] *Top Ten* fans will be able to add their own funnies based on that week's subject immediately after by using the BBC's creativity platform www.mixital.co.uk. [...] Using a range of assets including characters, sets, visual and sounds effects, users can create their own comedy content, as well as being able [to] re-mix other people's sketches. They can also share their creations on social media, rate others, comment, and follow each other on Mixital so the creators with the most creative flair can build their reputation
> (SB 2016)

This is clearly a cost-effective means for broadcasters to distribute material in a multi-platform environment while generating user content. Although it offers a forum for new stars, writers and creatives, it also de-professionalises the industry. The message is that anyone can do this. Broadcasting, like many professions, has become increasingly fragmented, outsourced and wedded to the short-term freelance economies of consumer capitalism. Nevertheless, it is interesting to note that, as of November 2016, there were 11 'Top Tens' episodes listed on the BBC3 site, six of which featured women writers and performers. These include Holly Walsh on online dating ('Ten reasons to swipe left') and Mae Martin on gender and sexual fluidity ('Things I find attractive regardless of gender'). The examination of extreme and ridiculous heterofemininities continues in 'Lou Sanders tips to become a beauty model' and the 'Lazy Susans' make up tips', which draw upon the clowning techniques deployed in *Smack the Pony*. Online provision may prove more amenable to voices from the margins, offering a platform for stunting and speaking.

It is also interesting to note what the team which produced *Smack the Pony* have done since the show ended. Victoria Pile's subsequent work on *Green Wing* breached the generic boundaries of sitcom, comedy drama and sketch show, as indicated by its IMDb listing as a 'Funky hospital-based sketch-comedy-drama type show'. Set in an NHS hospital, the reality-television-style camerawork floats from character to character, often speeding up or slowing down footage to mark transitions. The hour-long show is loosely structured around a burgeoning romance between Dr Caroline Todd (Tamsin Greig) and Dr Guy Secretan (Steven Mangan), but the performances of the cast as a whole are bizarrely exaggerated. The highly strung office manager, Joanna Clore (Pippa Haywood), is engaged in a sadomasochistic affair with the deranged Dr Alan Statham (Mark Heap); Harriet Schulenberg (Olivia Colman) is a chaotic office worker who often forgets where she has left her children; and the misanthropic staff liaison officer, Sue White (Michele Gomez), does everything she can to confuse and humiliate her colleagues. Much of the comedy is surreal and inexplicable, employing a sketch-show aesthetic to disrupt the ongoing romantic narrative. There is a notable reprise of the competitive lipsticking sketch from *Smack the Pony*, with Clore and White competitively rearranging their cleavage in a hospital toilet. Like the characters in *Smack the Pony*, the women in *Green Wing* are clownish in their rendering of professional middle-class desires and anxieties.

Sally Phillips, Fiona Allen and Doon Mackichan now represent an older generation of women in comedy and continue to forge successful careers. In most interviews with the press, *Smack the Pony* is mentioned. In 2013 Sally Phillips told *The Independent* that she now works 'with women 10 or 15 years younger who all grew up watching it' (Gilbert 2013). In the same interview Phillips stated that she was waiting for the BBC to green-light a new sitcom with Allen and Mackichan called *Stick or Twist*, a show which has never come to fruition.

The question of how women in comedy preserve and foster their legacy remains unresolved. This is a thorny issue for women who work behind the scenes too:

> [Kay] Stonham notes that for women writers age becomes particularly significant, as whenever commissioners and executives look for more female writers they think this means new and young, thus ignoring the talent of those with experience. For Stonham this means that men are able to have a career in the industry because their age is seen as evidence of authority, whereas younger women inevitably replace older women (Mills and Ralph 2015: 106)

The legacy of *Smack the Pony* is most visible on YouTube: a form of unofficial archive allowing fans to post material and curate their favourite sketches. This is probably where younger women see the show for the first time. While this affords a means of sharing that history, it does not offer its stars a *profitable* heritage. As Doon Mackichan states: 'Even when we'd won two Emmys, we still didn't get our *Smack the Pony* DVD. I just don't know what that's about' (cited in Williams 2016). Women's access to power within the industry and to the profits that that power brings remains a problem because feminism still has work to do. *Smack the Pony* is an important series because it makes that necessity clear, disrupting any notion that the late 1990s and early 2000s were an apocalyptic moment for feminist politics, when postfeminism reigned.

This chapter has traced the potential of a millennial sketch show to address the exigencies of postfeminist popular culture at a moment when feminism was allegedly on the wane. In the queered temporal space of sketch comedy, *Smack the Pony* examined the ridiculous fictions which underpin heterosexual hegemony. By satirising the excessive millennial emphasis on grooming and self-presentation, the show critiqued postfeminist sensibilities which continue to shape popular understandings of femininity. Through its comedically freakish characters, *Smack the Pony* delivered an uncanny reflection upon Western popular culture in the late twentieth and early twenty-first century. Finally, in its fantastically *un*intelligible sketches, the show gestured toward queer possibilities through camp performance, clownish stunts and spectacular interrogations of gendered economies. While this sketch show put postfeminism and younger women in the spotlight, the next chapter turns to older women in television sitcom to examine the different ways in which such comedies challenge heteronormative models of feminine behaviour.

CHAPTER 5

QUEERING AGE: OLDER WOMEN IN BRITISH TELEVISION COMEDY

Older women tend to inhabit the margins of television programming as wives, widows, grandmothers or spinsters, often relegated to supporting roles or, conversely, key figures in 'feminine' genres such as soap opera (Fiske 2011: 181–99). In this chapter I examine two examples of older women in British sitcom, arguing that they offer a commentary on how popular culture addresses ageing femininity and, indeed, ageing and gender per se. Representations of ageing women are particularly pertinent in the current social context of an ageing Western population where women tend to outlive male partners, and a media culture which continues to privilege youth with its narrow regime of heterofeminine 'beauty' (Gullette 2004; Woodward 1999). In British television these issues have gained notoriety through a number of high-profile news stories regarding recruitment and representation in the industry, not least of which is the Miriam O'Reilly case. In 2008 O'Reilly was ejected from *Countryfile* (BBC 1988–) in favour of younger presenters. She subsequently took the BBC to court and won (Jermyn 2013).

I have written elsewhere about the ambivalent representation of older women in British television comedy by cross-dressed younger women or men (White 2014b). Here I focus on older women playing characters who are often close to their own age, in a location which offers the comedic structure of a sitcom but is haunted by the melodrama of soap opera: the retirement home. *You're Only Young Twice* (Yorkshire

Television 1977–81) is set in a private retirement home, Paradise Lodge – a 'superior residence for retired gentlefolk' – and features a female cast drawn from the ranks of British character actors with longstanding careers on stage and screen. *Waiting for God* (BBC 1990–4) is set in Bayview Retirement Village, with a central couple who have a late-life romance. These two series mark different moments on television regarding the aesthetics of British sitcom and the representation of ageing in popular culture. Moving from the theatrical style of traditional three-camera studio-set sitcom in the 1970s, to a more realist, multi-camera mode in the 1990s, these two comedies reflect upon social change regarding ageing and gender in Britain. *You're Only Young Twice* seems to precede second-wave feminism but was made at its height. In this respect it combines pre-feminist and feminist depictions of ageing femininity. *Waiting for God* was produced in the early 1990s, an allegedly postfeminist era, yet it features a female protagonist who declares herself an atheist feminist. Both shows engage in debates about what it meant to be old in the late twentieth century.

Sitcom traditionally requires a confined 'situation' such as the family home, and in these series the institutional community becomes a substitute for the family with all its attendant tensions. A show set within a retirement home might logically lend itself to the melodrama traditionally associated with soap opera, because any narrative featuring older protagonists necessarily refers to the perils of ageing and the inevitability of death. *You're Only Young Twice* and *Waiting for God*, however, exploit the juxtaposition of melodrama and comedy as a means of exploring the uncanny discomforts of ageing in a manner which disrupts key discourses around heterofemininity. Margaret Morganroth Gullette and Kathleen Woodward have noted the ways in which we are 'aged by culture': how women's ageing bodies are policed, made *in*visible across a variety of popular media, and how that invisibility may be challenged or resisted (Gullette 2004; Woodward 1999, 2006). These comedy series set within old people's homes examine the processes by which older women's bodies and behaviours are policed and constrained, while offering the pleasures of seeing older female characters made visible and ageing disreputably, as unruly protagonists. These British television comedies thus examine Western discourses of age and ageing, often questioning and queering the hegemonic position of more youthful femininities.

Queer Times

Sitcoms set in retirement homes depict a queer institutional temporality, beyond the time of work, family and reproduction (Halberstam 2005). Because the retirement home is often seen as a last resort, a dumping ground for the old and unproductive, it represents a space beyond the heteronormative family. These institutional spaces and times are situated outside the temporal imperatives of romantic narrative, nuclear families or enduring coupledom, as much of the comedies' humour is grounded in eccentric alliances and mutual support. Judith Halberstam lists 'queer subjects' who live in queer times and spaces as 'outside the logic of capital accumulation: [...] ravers, club kids, HIV-positive barebackers, rent boys, sex workers, homeless people, drug dealers, and the unemployed' (2005: 10). I would add the very old to that list, as subjects who step outside the neoliberal economy. The elderly in these comedies are cast adrift from nuclear families and work environments. These are not the active, youthfully ageing 'young old', but the 'old old' who are living with what their younger peers may dread: infirmity, loss of independence and the range of chance encounters that such a state entails (Blaikie 1999: 97).

Amy Holdsworth and Karen Lury suggest that the dependent states experienced during childhood and old age represent a radical refusal of the neoliberal focus on the individual-as-consumer. They argue that children and old people expose the spurious claims of neoliberal discourses of 'choice', so that television programming which centres on such figures may be understood as positioning the elderly, children and the disabled 'as integral to a more diverse and fluid understanding of subjectivity over the life-course' (2016: 189). The dependent moment of old age, like childhood, is a queer time, and television comedies situated within the space of a retirement home make such queerness visible. These late-life communities, with all their limitations and tensions, problematise any progressive account of ageing and propose old age as a time for renewed playfulness.

The sitcom format inadvertently embodies this stalling of the life-as-journey, with its notoriously static aesthetic, where each 30-minute episode returns its protagonists to their initial situation. Like the circular plots of traditional sitcom, time is cyclical in the retirement home, following a daily routine which is insistent in its repetition.

This chimes with Holdsworth and Lury's account of the repetitive aesthetic of children's programming:

> The resistance of these narratives to the linearity of time passing is further underpinned by the way in which episodes within these series are structurally repetitive: beginnings and endings are echoed, while the actual episodes themselves may be repeated on air, on demand or online. The pattern or rhythm of television, its 'ebb and flow', therefore allows these television series (as opposed to film-based narratives such as *Boyhood* [Richard Linklater 2014]) to challenge the unidirectional movement or the aspiration of stories of childhood to be chronological and teleological and instead reimagines such narratives as simultaneously folding and unfolding, looping between times and spaces that pull together the experiences and tales of those at 'opposite' ends of the life course. (2016: 193)

In contrast to children's programming, which centres upon looping and repetitive narratives, sitcoms set in care homes offer a tension between time as finite (ageing and death) and infinite (moments of play). There is an ever-present teleology in these shows. Any 'looping' between childhood and old age is played out *through* the characters in late-life sitcoms, such as *One Foot in the Grave* (BBC 1990–2001), who act in a childlike manner, producing the necessary comedy. This uncanny depiction of the old/child and the child/old is enacted within a form that, like children's series, lends itself to repeat viewing in a manner often regarded as comforting rather than stimulating. The half-hour structure of traditional sitcom is easily consumed via online, on-demand viewing, or inserted into television schedules, as on the British digital channel E4, as blocks of episodes.

How sitcoms about the elderly deal with that most evident marker of time – death – is telling. When one of the central elderly characters in *The Last of the Summer Wine* (BBC 1973–2010) died in 1999, both character and actor were replaced by their sons: Compo Simonite (Bill Owen) was replaced by Tom Simonite (Tom Owen) (Lewisohn 2003: 457). This solution is unusual. Whereas in soap operas it is not unheard of for a character (particularly a child) to be played by different actors through their life course on the show, in comedy a star performer's death usually kills the series. That *The Last of the Summer Wine* resolved this by casting the actor's own son, who looked remarkably similar and performed an identical character part, is indicative of the reiterative aesthetic of sitcom and its investment in character performance.

How sitcoms deal with the exigencies of ageing is also significant. The retirement home often represents a dreaded future in wealthier Western nations: an indicator that one is dependent and thus no longer a functioning subject. The glossy lifestyle of *The Golden Girls* (NBC 1985– 92) was haunted by such a future. When the 'girls' are distressed following a visit to an unprepossessing care home, Blanche states that if they do have to move into such a facility they should 'all go together' but Rose asks 'what happens when there's only one of us left?' (Gray 1994: 76). This exchange aligns the retirement or care facility with death itself. Better health care and medical advances are ensuring that many of us are living far longer than our grandparents or even our parents. At the same time, financial crises and lack of investment in health services are raising anxieties about the ability of the state and the individual to provide adequate support in an era of extended old age. We may survive our spouses, partners, friends and colleagues – what happens then? *You're Only Young Twice* and *Waiting for God* attempt to imagine a *life* in late life, and those imaginings take us into a queer realm which gestures beyond binary accounts of gender and sexuality.

Queering Ageing

Margaret Morganroth Gullette and others have identified a discourse of 'successful ageing' in Western media, together with its normative subject: white, bourgeois, heterosexual (Cruikshank 2003; Gullette 2004; Sandberg 2008; Dolan and Tincknell 2012). Josephine Dolan argues that 'We are living through a hegemonic struggle for the meaning of old age: a struggle between the pathologised old age of the clinical gaze and the emergent discourse of youthful aging' (2010: 9). Dolan cites Foucault's *The Birth of the Clinic*, where subjects are divided into the healthy and the well, the 'normal and the pathological', so that 'the aging body is *always already* a problem, *always already* pathologised and in need of treatment' (Dolan 2010: 3, emphasis added). Older women and men are undoubtedly subject to such a pathological gaze, perceived as always already 'failing' by not being healthy, youthful, *normal*.

Other work on ageing has taken this failure as a moment to be seized. Barbara Macdonald, in an early book about women and ageing written with Cynthia Rich, proposes age as offering particular opportunities:

> It seems to me that whether we choose it or not, age in our society gives us a second opportunity (or places the demand on us, if that is how it feels), to finally deal with our difference if we have not done so before; to move out of the safe harbour of acceptability. (Macdonald and Rich 1984: 1–2)

Ageing here is perceived as opening up a range of responses and behaviours that may have been seen as too risky or impossible in earlier years. It also gestures toward the arguments Halberstam presents in *The Queer Art of Failure* – that failing may be a queer strategy in the face of late Western capitalism's imperative to 'succeed' (2011). To be old is to be unacceptable, so why not embrace that possibility? This introduces another stereotype, that of the eccentric older woman, famously celebrated in Jenny Joseph's much-cited poem 'Warning' (1961), which relates the bad behaviour of an elderly spendthrift who wears purple and drinks too much. This poem and the stereotype it evokes indicate the connection between ageing and queer identity. 'Warning' notes how old age allows for non-normative gender performance. The older woman is imagined dressing as she pleases rather than conforming to notions of taste and appropriate behaviour. She is noisy, greedy, drunken, a thief. The poem maps a femininity that is unbound and angry. As the poem continues it reveals that the speaker, the 'I' of the poem, is looking forward to becoming old from the point of view of a younger self that is feeling the pressure to be properly heterofeminine; looking forward to an older self no longer restrained by the proper. In this reading, wearing purple is heavy with queer connotations.

The parallels between lesbian identity and old age are noted by Macdonald, who remarks the silences that have historically existed regarding sexuality and ageing (Macdonald and Rich 1984: 5). In a similar vein, Linn Sandberg cites Judith Butler's account of abjection regarding queer identity and extends that queerness to ageing and becoming old: 'To Butler, the abject serves the very promise of subversion in how [...] despite its impossibility and unintelligibility

[it] continues to exist; the abject is the disruption to the ongoing reiteration of heterosexuality (Butler 1990, 1993)' (2008: 126). Sandberg argues that the negative discourse of shame which circulates around queer identities confounds any attempt to make old age a concrete and identifiable category – to *become* or to *be* old – to solidify it as *proper* within a neoliberal economy. Queer ageing thus means refusing to be shamed, refusing to be proper and refusing to be *placed*. By embracing the exigencies of ageing, Sadie Wearing argues that we can refuse to see age as simply decline, trauma and disintegration but as also entailing the possibility of 'accumulation and growth' (Wearing 2007: 280). She deploys Halberstam's work on queer time to disrupt the trajectory of heteronormative temporalities: 'Queer subcultures produce alternative temporalities by allowing their participants to believe that their futures can be imagined according to logics that lie outside of those paradigmatic markers of life experience – namely, birth, marriage, reproduction, and death' (Halberstam 2005: 2). The British comedy series examined in this chapter similarly imagine such other trajectories, establishing the community of the retirement home as an alternative to heteronormative paradigms.

Setting a sitcom in a retirement home is significant in this regard, as television narratives which focus on younger groups of women often close down any challenge to normative scripts of femininity by having romance or marriage always in sight. Vicky Ball notes how class and sexuality are re-normalised through such happy endings in British female ensemble dramas:

> whilst the F[emale] E[nsemble] D[rama] embodies and disrupts discourses of respectability by taking working-class women out of their traditional maternal roles and positioning them as career women, footballers and lesbians in texts such as *Real Women* [BBC 1998–9] and *Playing the Field* [BBC 1998–2002], they also stave off the threat of unruly and dangerous working-class subjectivities by posing marriage as *the* life choice of these female characters which, in turn, safely returns them to spaces and discourses associated with wives and mothers. (2012: 257)

Retirement-age comedies do not often feature this curtailment of women's queer alliances because ageing, post-menopausal women are not regarded as valid candidates for romance. Many of the characters have been through marriage and maternity and are now returned to themselves, relinquishing the guilt that many women still feel about prioritising their own interests. In *You're Only Young Twice* and *Waiting for God*, older women's lack of respectability, their distance from marriage and maternity, is mobilised to demonstrate that, without such policing mechanisms, women might indeed become unruly in their later years. Before addressing those sitcoms, however, it is necessary to review two of the most significant shows about ageing on Britain and American television.

The Young Old: *The Golden Girls* and *Last of the Summer Wine*

It is impossible to discuss ageing in British and American television comedy without reference to two key sitcoms from either side of the Atlantic. *The Golden Girls* and *Last of the Summer Wine* offer different accounts of gender and ageing from those provided by *You're Only Young Twice* and *Waiting for God*. *The Golden Girls* is particularly notable for its female cast. Bea Arthur, who played Dorothy Zbornak, came to the show trailing a history of work in Lear sitcom, most notably as the groundbreaking *Maude* (CBS 1972–8), a spin-off from *All in the Family* (CBS 1971–9). Betty White, who played Rose Nylund, has had a remarkable career in television comedy, and continues to break new ground in her 90s (Rawitsch 2014). The premise of *The Golden Girls* is that Dorothy and Rose become Blanche Devereaux (Rue McClanahan)'s housemates, with Dorothy's elderly mother, Sophia Petrillo (Estelle Getty), also moving in after a fire at her retirement home. Dorothy, Rose and Blanche are all in their 50s (hence 'golden') and thus middle-aged, while Sophia is in her 70s or 80s with a sharp and uninhibited turn of phrase. Despite the house-share being driven by (Devereaux's) financial need, there is little sense that the 'girls' want for anything. Dorothy and Rose both have jobs, the former as a supply teacher and the latter as a grief counsellor, but this has little impact on the storylines.

Like the more youthful ensemble in *Friends*, *The Golden Girls* is based upon the 'girls' friendship. As Frances Gray notes: 'their particular importance to one another; the embraces round the table among the four of them are visible, while those with their "dates" are not' (1994: 76).

That prioritising of same-sex friendship underpins the show's LGBTQ cult status (Doty 1993: 41–4; Rawitsch 2014: 185; Patterson 2016). Nevertheless *The Golden Girls* is a comedy of the middle years, rather than the old. The series ended when Bea Arthur decided to leave the show, and in the final episode Dorothy marries Blanche's uncle and moves to Atlanta (Lewisohn 2003: 324). This female ensemble comedy is thus curtailed by a very conventional romantic conclusion. The remaining three characters continued in a spin-off series, *The Golden Palace* (CBS 1992–3), but only lasted one season. While *The Golden Girls'* 'smutty' dialogues represent queer moments of transgression, they were consistently framed within the terms of heteronormativity by the girls' 'dates' (Gray 1994: 76–8). Rose's ridiculous misunderstandings and bizarre references to traditional practices in her home town of St Olaf, Minnesota, together with Sophia's age-inappropriate language, also opened up a queer potential, but it is neatly contained by a raised eyebrow from Dorothy. *The Golden Girls* casts a long shadow across late-life sitcoms with a female cast, but its queered community is undermined by the dominant discourse of 'success' in American network comedy terms. The girls do *not* end up in a nursing home together but fragment, as if to finally ratify the heteronormativity that Blanche's campily overstated desire satirised throughout the show (Küpper 2016).

On this side of the Atlantic, *Last of the Summer Wine* was the longest-running British television sitcom, featuring a core trio of elderly men in rural Yorkshire who spend their days wandering about the town and countryside in an imitation of youth. The rural location is a key feature of the show and the protagonists' adventures often take place in beautiful Yorkshire countryside. The series had a significant impact on the local economy in and around Holmfirth, where much of the show was shot (Lewisohn 2003: 457). This location denotes a peculiar timelessness which is reflected in the show's longevity and aesthetic. *Last of the Summer Wine* is situated within a discourse of British rural 'northern-ness', outside the gritty realism of northern cities such as Manchester or Leeds, in a pastoral geography weighted with literary tradition. The original trio – Compo (Bill Owen), Foggy (Brian Wilde) and Clegg (Peter Sallis) – are like the rude mechanicals of *A Midsummer Night's Dream* in their magical ability to remain unharmed despite such youthful pranks as the notorious ride in a bathtub careering down a hill. In contrast to the juvenile antics of the male leads, female characters are more concretely situated within the show. Many of the performers arrived in *Last of the Summer Wine* trailing television and comedy heritage. Jean Alexander as Auntie Wainwright (1988–2010) linked the series with Britain's longest-running television soap via Alexander's longstanding role as Hilda Ogden on *Coronation Street* (Granada, 1960–). Thora Hird as Edie Pegden (1986–2003) drew upon Hird's extensive career in comedy and drama, most notably her work with Alan Bennett (Medhurst 2007: 159–60). *Last of the Summer Wine* became a form of 'retirement home' for ageing performers but the female supporting actors, like their character parts, are more heavily *placed* than the male leads. If the old men are puckish Peter Pans, the old women who surrounded them are ageing Wendies, weighted with responsibility and the job of policing their juvenile male peers. It is never their role to jump into the careering bathtub but rather to look on disapprovingly as the old men have their fun.

Once again, these are the active 'young old', still fit and mischievous, and once again this ensemble comedy *precedes* the retirement home. Frances Gray proposes that the carefree childlike comedy of the three leads is licensed and framed by the older women, most notably Norah Batty (Kathy Staff) and Ivy (Jane Freeman) (1994: 85). Gray reads these characters as stereotypical battleaxes but the longevity of the series allowed more eccentric details to emerge. As the show continued through the 1970s, '80s and '90s into the twenty-first century, the female cast expanded and some scenes focussed solely on the interactions of female characters, albeit always gathered in a domestic space, often for a coffee morning. Although this does not stray too far from the stereotypes which Gray critiques, such moments allowed for more textured characterisations and there is much work to be done on gender and ageing in this under-examined comedy.

Both *The Golden Girls* and *Last of the Summer Wine* position their female characters in domestic spaces. The ageing female ensemble is evidently designed for the traditional domestic arenas of situation comedy. The retirement home may be understood as an aspect of this, with all the gendered connotations that 'home' entails. Traditional sitcoms are filmed on theatrical sets, to allow for the three-camera style of shooting and to accommodate a studio audience who provide the laughter (Mills 2009: 39). Sérgio Dias Branco notes how traditional sitcom formats *situate* comedy in a specific space and time: 'grounding and inscribing the comic idiosyncrasies and rapport of a small group of characters in a defined and regular spatial and temporal context' (2013: 95). The retirement home comedy with a predominantly female cast, or a female star, is both traditional in its domestic habitus and non-traditional in its institutional setting. It is both a private and a public space. In many ways the retirement or care home is a logical situation for comedy centred on a group of women. Women tend to outlive male partners and any brief survey of retirement facilities will show that women outnumber men. This is not, however, the kitchen in *The Golden Girls* or a coffee morning in *Last of the Summer Wine*. The institutional aspect of these series is fundamental to their queer potential – their uncanny combination of domestic and public arenas. Much like their sister genre, the hospital or medical fiction, the institutional setting means that these sitcoms 'repeatedly work through issues of shared space, social behaviour/difference, and state service provision' (Piper 2016: 175). Through this combination of care and (un)homeliness, elderly inhabitants in these sitcoms queer gender and sexuality, undermining conventional accounts of femininity in favour of a situated comedy about getting *really* old and confronting the end of life.

You're Only Young Twice

You're Only Young Twice stars Peggy Mount (1915–2001) and Pat Coombs (1926–2002), with Lally Bowers (1917–84) and Diana King (1918–86). The show offers a platform for a generation of female character actors who began their careers in theatre, moved into film and radio, and then established a presence on the small screen as the British television industry developed during the 1950s and 1960s. On television they frequently played older women, as this generation were by then in their 40s or 50s, but actors like Peggy Mount had performed older roles on stage and screen throughout their careers. Rarely cast as romantic leads, they tended to be comic sidekicks or comedy characters within a larger ensemble piece. In this regard the character comedy actor kicks against popular discourses of the star as an exceptional individual in favour of a performance that is located within an onscreen community (Dyer 1979; Roof 2002). Such performers are ideally suited to the ensemble form of the television sitcom. A number of British actors are notable in this tradition, such as Irene Handl (1901–87), Esma Cannon (1905–72), Dandy Nichols (1907–86), Patricia

Hayes (1909–98), Thora Hird (1911–2003), Liz Smith (1921–2016) and Jean Alexander (1925–2016). Most of these women were character actors on the British stage, in variety shows and provincial repertory theatre, before moving into radio, film and television work, and there is much work to be done to acknowledge their legacy (Williams 2011). These actors often became identified with stereotypical character parts: the confused and confusing old lady, the battleaxe, the gorgon. What they did with those roles went beyond stereotype, however, into the realm of the 'eccentric', queering notions of how older women could or should behave. Peggy Mount and Pat Coombs are part of this generation. Like many of the actors cited above they played older parts for much of their careers, so that age and ageing was always already written into any role they took on. In this respect they embody both ageing and agelessness, disrupting linear teleologies through their performances.

The very title of *You're Only Young Twice* interrupts the progressive account of heteronormative time. To say that you are young *twice* is to imply that the trajectory from youth to old age and death is not absolute. It also indicates the cultural alignment of youth and old age – those looping paradigms that Amy Holdsworth and Karen Lury described. A 'second youth' is thus constituted as a time for play and playfulness, which this comedy series plays upon. Beyond this queer temporality, however, *You're Only Young Twice* is haunted by queer sexualities. Peggy Mount as Flora Petty is a domineering stone butch figure, paired with Pat Coombs as a dithering femme. Both performances are based on character parts established through the actors' longstanding careers on stage and screen: *You're Only Young Twice* was effectively a showcase for their talents. Mount and Coombs are supported by Lally Bowers as the faded, dipsomaniac actress Dolly Love and Diana King as the unlikely motorbike enthusiast Mildred Fanshaw. The notable absence of male leads distinguished this show from Mount's and Coombs's earlier work which was often set within a dysfunctional heterosexual marriage. In the ATV comedy *Lollipop Loves Mr Mole* (1971–2), Maggie Robinson, aka 'Lollipop' (Peggy Mount), embarked on a late-life marriage with Reg, 'Mr Mole' (Hugh Lloyd), and their suburban haven was invaded by Reg's brother, Bruce (Rex Garner), and his wife, Violet (Pat Coombs). Mount's television career had been secured by her performance as the booming matriarch Ada

Larkin in the first British family sitcom, *The Larkins* (ATV 1958–60, 1963–4) (Mortimer 2015).

In *You're Only Young Twice* the frame of the marital or family-based sitcom is broken by situating Flora Petty (Peggy Mount) and Cissie Lupin (Pat Coombs) in Paradise Lodge, where they effectively operate as a queer couple. Lally Bowers and Diana King as Dolly and Mildred are similarly configured, often depicted sitting side by side on the sofa, with both taking the femme role even as Mildred's motorbiking outfits situate her as butch. If this queer reading of a prime-time ITV sitcom appears overstated, it is worth remembering the success of *The Killing of Sister George* on stage and screen in the 1960s (Robert Aldrich 1968). While this is not the most positive depiction of lesbian sexuality, it did offer mainstream audiences some insight into lesbian subcultures in London's Soho (White 2014a). Lally Bowers is the material link between *Sister George* and *You're Only Young Twice*, as she played Mercy Croft in the touring production of *The Killing of Sister George*, which, like the film version, starred Beryl Reid in the title role (University of Bristol n.d.). The play debuted at Bristol Old Vic in 1965, moving on to great success in the West End and on Broadway, where it won a Tony. *You're Only Young Twice*, first broadcast a decade after the Sexual Offences Act 1967 which began the process of decriminalising homosexuality in the UK, is part of an ongoing debate about queer identities during the 1970s and 1980s.

Mildred, symbolically costumed predominantly in purple in series one and green in series two, is characterised by her constant reference to motorbikes. She often arrives on set with a helmet (also purple or green), sometimes in leathers, and usually heading for a nip from her personal bottle of Wincarnis tonic wine. Mildred's relationship with her son, Damien, is a reminder of the gay lifestyle that exists outside the retirement home for a younger generation. Damien lives with his boyfriend, Norman, and is a frequent but invisible presence within the comedy, summoned only in dialogue, never on screen. In the first season Damien is implicitly gay, and by season two the inference is made explicit when Roger (Johnny Wade), the Paradise Lodge handyman and only regular male character, arrives with a phone message for Mildred from Damien, saying: 'I wrote it down because he [...] sounded queer to me – no offence Mrs F', at which Mildred smiles and nods ('The Foundling', 2:5). In this way queer identities haunt

You're Only Young Twice, problematising heteronormative families and romantic scripts.

The show's queer account of heteronormativity is evident in season two's 'The Foundling', which centres on a baby that has been abandoned at the door of Paradise Lodge. Mildred's message from Damien, which mentions a surprise delivery, leads the residents to think that Damien might be the father. A horrified Mildred exclaims 'Oh Damien, Damien, how could you do it?' to which Dolly dryly retorts: 'That's got us all guessing' ('The Foundling', 2:5). The ensuing comedy is structured around misunderstandings and the repurposing of objects. A wheelbarrow becomes a pram, Mildred's motorbike helmet is proposed as a potty and towels become nappies. Kathryn Bond Stockton remarks on such repurposing in her account of childhood as a queer time: 'Not uncommonly children are shown as having a knack for metaphorical substitutions, letting one object stand for another, by means of which they reconceive relations to time' (2009: 15). Such substitutions disrupt linear narratives of time, identity and teleology.

The arrival of the baby might seem to put the residents of Paradise Lodge back into place as grandmotherly, maternal figures but if anything it underlines their lack of 'natural' mothering abilities. Flora is the first to find the child and claims authority in its care while also acknowledging 'I'm not very good with babies'. She offers it tea. Mildred announces that she is 'not frightfully baby-minded', having told her husband that she was 'shutting up shop' following the birth of Damien. When it appears that Damien might be the father, Mildred faints and then downs a bottle of Wincarnis. In one scene all the women are sitting in a row knitting baby clothes (Figure 5.1) but the activity seems more a collective hobby than an assertion of maternal abilities. The baby itself (which for much of the time is clearly a prop doll) is initially christened with Lucozade by Cissie as 'Margaret Rose' until he is found to be a boy and Flora rechristens him 'Charles Andrew'. The women try to conceal the baby from Miss Milton (Charmian May), the manager of Paradise Lodge, but once it is discovered Mildred, as the presumed grandmother, is asked to leave. Cissie, however, takes the baby on the run and is found 'causing an obstruction in Mothercare' by the local police, whom she verbally confounds in a style comparable to that of Gracie Allen. Motherhood and maternal care is denaturalised and satirised throughout.

Figure 5.1 Knitting for the baby in 'The Foundling' (*You're Only Young Twice*, 2:5, Yorkshire Television, 1977–81).

This comedy about the mismatch between mothering and older women might deny them agency, yet the residents of Paradise Lodge *do* care for the child, in their own way. For them, motherhood is not work but rather a welcome distraction from the tedium of their daily routine. Maternal care becomes a game, something to be played at, as the comic repurposing of objects implies. The game ends when the child's grandfather, Mr Handy (Joe Gladwin), appears and reveals that he had to take his wife to hospital at short notice and left the baby on the doorstep of Paradise Lodge because he knew Cissie was a kind woman – behaviour which itself questions the 'natural' facility of families to take care of their children. Mr Handy is so impressed with their care for 'Paul-Starsky' that he asks the residents to care for his other grandchildren until their parents return. The women are visibly horrified as five more children, all different ages and all named after television detectives, charge into Paradise Lodge's day room. Mothering is once again *labour*.

This female community in the retirement home sitcom thus offers a commentary on the heteronormative family, demonstrating other possibilities beyond such limited social scripts. *You're Only Young Twice* is not a political comedy but it is politicised in its attention to *different* understandings of the everyday. From the first episode, heteronormative scripts are queered. In 'Stranger in Paradise' (1:1) one of the protagonists' fellow residents, Mrs Willis, has been hospitalised, and Miss Milton reiterates her standard tenet that she 'does not nurse'. Any resident who needs personal or medical care is asked to leave. While Mrs Willis's swift expulsion from Paradise might be taken as a traumatic warning of their own vulnerability, Flora, Cissie, Dolly and Mildred instead attend to her newly vacant and desirable room. Just as Flora Petty asserts her right to the room, however, they discover that an elderly gentleman, Mr Whittaker (Robert Raglan), has taken it. In most sitcoms of this era such a situation would lead to competition between the women for the attentions of a rare man about the house. This is initially signalled as Cissie engages Mr Whittaker's help in the day room to undo her necklace. Flora, whose regular chair is now occupied by the new arrival, is disgusted, denouncing such behaviour: 'Grown women acting like teeny boppers. It will be woolly hats and posters over the bed in no time' (1:1). The proximity of age and youth is once more evinced. It is not Mr Whittaker who is the object of desire in this episode, however, but the room he occupies. Flora subsequently enlists Cissie in a honeytrap operation to get Cissie into his room so that she can create a scandal. Cissie cannot remember the set script that Flora has composed, so they have to role-play outside Mr Whittaker's door, each taking different roles to the point where Cissie cannot keep track of who is playing whom: 'Are you being him or you or me now?' (1:1; Figure 5.2). Gender is constituted as performative and fluid. Although Mount and Coombs perform a double act, it is staged differently, pairing two older women rather than two men or a heterosexual couple. This early sequence sets the tone for the series: in the heterotopic space of Paradise Lodge all things are queerly possible.

The residents of Paradise Lodge exhibit a range of sexualities. Flora is constituted as asexual, perhaps agender in contemporary parlance, and Cissie is a nervous spinster who claims to be 'untouched', at which Flora retorts 'And likely to remain so' ('The Royal Visit', 1:6). Such dialogue positions these older women as both innocent and knowing, loading their exchanges with camp innuendo. Flora claims that her magazine astrologer is 'bisexual' as he's only an astrologer for part of the week

Figure 5.2 Flora and Cissie rehearse their roles in 'Stranger in Paradise' (*You're Only Young Twice*, 1:1, Yorkshire Television, 1977–81).

('One of Life's Winners', 1:3), while Dolly wistfully asserts that, although porcelain ornaments depicting old men on park benches are expensive, 'The young [men] aren't cheap' ('The White Elephant', 2:4). This style of comedy borrows directly from music hall in its reference to non-normative identities and behaviours within a carnivalesque arena (Medhurst 2007: 63–86). In the visual aesthetic of the series, however, other juxtapositions are jarring.

The first season is set almost exclusively within Paradise Lodge, a stage set which all but contains a proscenium arch. The style of performance is theatrical and structured accordingly. Actors project out to the camera and the studio audience, with the chairs in the day room set in a semicircle facing the fourth wall. This is standard for 1970s sitcoms, with brief forays into other studio sets such as Flora's bedroom, the hallway or Miss Milton's office. The décor in each case is 'tasteful', if not fashionable for the time, with chintzy patterns and pastel colours.

The sets, like the sign which features in each title sequence (Figure 5.3), signal Paradise Lodge as a 'superior residence for retired gentlefolk'. Yet while the implication is that this is a home for the respectable middle class, none of the main characters fit the profile. Flora and Cissie have the working-class accents of those born and bred in and around London, and, although Dolly and Mildred enunciate their lines in Received Pronunciation, their backgrounds (a faded actress and a reluctant mother/wife) set them outside the terms of the proper. Class is invoked here only as a totem. The 'superior residence for retired gentlefolk' could be construed as the wishful thinking of Miss Milton, who is characterised as an upper-middle-class manager, well-meaning but foolish. Although she refuses to 'nurse' she is largely benevolent, meeting each crisis with the catchphrase 'What are you saying? What are you telling me?' as if to underline her inability to understand or manage the residents of Paradise.

When Miss Milton has a fall and is incapacitated, Flora offers herself as a prospective leader, citing her experience as Chief Warden for Chingford in the London Blitz. Milton, however, has already appointed a stand-in: Rex King (David Lodge), an ex-teacher at the local comprehensive school with a background in the military. His regime is in direct contrast to that

Figure 5.3 The opening title sequence of *You're Only Young Twice* (Yorkshire Television, 1977–81).

of Miss Milton, as he confronts Flora and asserts 'I'm running this institution' ('The Deputy', 2:6). Paradise Lodge thus becomes temporarily *institution*alised with the introduction of a rigorous and disciplined regime, in contrast to the normal state of affairs where the residents manage their own time. Under Mr King's orders the women are forced out of their usual clothes and into track suits for a cross-country run. This attempt to enforce patriarchal order is repeatedly undermined:

> Mildred: Don't speak to me! I said, don't speak to me ...
> Dolly: Why not?
> Mildred: I'll tell you. I've just been on the phone to my son Damien. Damien, I said, we are at the mercy of a *BRUTAL* man.
> Cissie: What did he say Mildred?
> Mildred: That you should be so lucky and was he free for parties ... [laughter] *Honestly*, young men these days ... ('The Deputy', 2:6)

Mr King is thus lampooned as a fetish object, underlining the permeable boundary between military masculinities and queer sexualities.

During his regime of enforced exercise Flora, Cissie, Mildred and Dolly appear dishevelled in their assorted track suits. The costumes are deliberately ill-fitting and clearly *wrong* (Figure 5.4). This is a rare occasion where the sitcom takes its cast outside the studio space; the actors appear paler and more vulnerable than under the studio lights. Mr King lines them up and plans to make them play football, but the residents resist. Flora takes a taxi as a means of circumventing a cross-country run and the football match elicits a further protest where they all take to the roof of Paradise Lodge (once more in a studio) to evade Mr King. The women slip down the roof and catch each other in a fantastic piece of physical comedy until Cissie reveals that Mr King has already left and Miss Milton is once again in charge. There is an odd contemporary relevance, however, to this moment of revolt, as when the episode was broadcast (10 July 1978) blanket protests by republican prisoners in Northern Ireland's Maze Prison were at their height. The retirement home sitcom thus reflects upon power relations between dominant and subordinate groups, not only the elderly but also other disenfranchised communities.

Figure 5.4 The residents of Paradise Lodge under Mr King's regime in 'The Deputy' (*You're Only Young Twice*, 2:6, Yorkshire Television, 1977–81).

In a recent collection on ageing and old age in television narratives, Anita Wohlmann and Maricel Oró-Piqueras draw upon Deleuze to argue:

> If it is true that TV series, due to their repetitive make-up, give us 'chance after chance' to understand and experience the magic of time as something that continually opens up 'possibilities of becoming,' TV series emerge as a promising medium to study new, non-stereotypical, radical and inspirational representations of age and ageing. (12)

This may be the case for some television series, but comedies set in retirement homes must inevitably also address the conflict between the home as an institution and the desires of its residents. The contradictory public/private space of the retirement facility or care home is productively explored in these sitcoms. After the cardiganned campery of *You're Only Young Twice*, the hegemonic struggle between residents and management becomes more evident and central to the comedy in *Waiting for God*.

Waiting for God

When Stephanie Cole was offered a leading role in *Waiting for God* she was 50 and had already made a career playing older women. At 16 she was cast as a 90-year-old in *The Woodcarver* at Bristol Old Vic Theatre, and proceeded to play a succession of older roles in repertory theatres across the UK (Cole 1998: 61, 65). Even as Dr Beatrice Mason in *Tenko* (BBC 1981–4) she played a woman in her 50s when she herself was in her 40s (Cole 1998: 184). This performance of old(er) age underpins an extremely successful career in television. Since starring in *Waiting for God* in the early 1990s, Cole has taken the lead role in a controversial and less successful sitcom about elderly care – *Keeping Mum* (BBC 1997–8) – and has had substantial character parts in *Doc Martin* (ITV 2004–), *Coronation Street*, *Still Open All Hours* (BBC 2013–) and *Man Down* (Channel 4 2013–).

By the time that *Waiting for God* came along Cole was well versed in how to *perform* being old. As Diana Trent (Figure 5.5) she dons a grey wig (a notably shabby one in the first series) and adopts a limp and a stick:

> I think we all felt that it was highly unlikely that a series about two elderly people, one completely loopy and the other chronically crotchety, living in an old people's home, could capture the imagination of the great British public. The BBC didn't think so either. It was the last of several pilots they had made, but none of the others had really worked, and they were left with ours. They looked at it, and within a fortnight, the first series was in production. This meant that the wig I had worn for the pilot, which had come out of stock and looked like nothing so much as a lank tea cosy, had to be used for the whole of the first series because there wasn't time to have a proper one made. To everybody's surprise, it took off. (The series, not my wig.) (Cole 1998: 184)

The dowdy wig is echoed in the first season by costumes that are largely baggy and nondescript. Cole had used padding and various 'tricks' to

Figure 5.5 Tom Ballard first catches sight of Diana Trent (*Waiting for God*, 1:1, BBC, 1990–4).

develop an older appearance in her repertory days: 'You wound lavatory paper round and round your legs, and then you put your lisle stockings over the top – bingo – swollen ankles and varicose veins' (Cole 1998: 65). This repertoire of costuming the body as older, together with the limp and the stick as a means of performing age, are unpicked as the series progresses. By the second season, with a significantly more flattering grey coiffure, Cole appears more youthful and vital. She is not aged through make-up so that her performance skills and previous roles on stage and screen stand in for 'being old'. Cole's success with *Waiting for God* made her a spokesperson for the elderly: she became a patron of the British charity Age Concern while working on the series and was in great demand as a speaker at nursing homes and charity events (Cole 1998: 221, 187). This is significant, as *Waiting for God* self-consciously navigates debates around 'successful ageing'.

Cole and her character, Diana Trent, become increasingly youthful during the series, as if to defy the discourse of old age as a process of decline. *Waiting for God* thus disturbs a linear notion of time as it posits a *life* in late life as possible, albeit a life only available to the privileged middle classes. The residents of Bayview are candidates for 'successful ageing' because they are – without exception – white, bourgeois and heterosexual. There is little that is visibly queer here. Yet *Waiting for God* addresses its protagonists' later years as a site of struggle regarding ageing, identity and economics. Whereas *You're Only Young Twice* was a sitcom *set* in a retirement home, *Waiting for God*'s comedy is *about* ageing and the retirement home; it queers the cultural and economic contexts in which the comedy is set. In many ways it shadows academic work that was beginning to emerge on gender and ageing in the 1990s.

While Bayview is far more middle class than Paradise Lodge, it does not allow its residents to rest easy. Bayview's manager, Harvey Baines (Daniel Hill), defines it as 'a retirement village, a new concept in elderly care' (1:3); it is far more clearly privatised and commercial than Paradise Lodge. *Waiting for God* thus engages in a critical discussion regarding the *costs* of 'successful ageing'. As Margaret Cruikshank notes: 'When success is proposed as an ageing model [...] a competitive or business standard measures a complex human process and a white, male, middle-class professional outlook is taken for granted' (2003: 2). That competitive business agenda is embodied by Harvey Baines, the neoliberal manager who is Bayview's putative Gordon Gecko. His attempts to make the retirement business turn a profit are central to the plotlines of most episodes. Where Miss Milton represented a benevolently liberal regime, Baines is constantly trying to cut costs and exert control. *Waiting for God* centres on his inability to do so, as his plans are inevitably foiled by Diana Trent and Tom Ballard (Graham Crowden). The show extends the debate about ageing to reflect upon changes in British public and private sectors during the late 1980s and early 1990s. These included significant shifts in British broadcasting, so that *Waiting for God* not only comments upon health and social care but also on the television industry itself.

You're Only Young Twice was produced when there were three terrestrial channels on British television, which broadcast at limited times. *Waiting for God* inhabits a very different moment in British television history. The 1990s saw the beginning of 24-hour television, there were the first signs of now-endemic reality formats, and government legislation about satellite broadcasting was signalling a brave new world of digital broadcasting. The Broadcasting Act 1990 (HMSO 1990) was the latest in a series of legislative interventions which began in the 1970s, shifting television production away from an ethos of public service broadcasting towards a market-led, outsourced structure. These changes were particularly visible within the BBC, who produced *Waiting for God* in the early 1990s:

> The use of temporary contracts and the outsourcing of production to independent producers, and the introduction of an internal market at the BBC, have shifted decision-making powers from programme-makers to schedulers and commissioners and made the career paths of programme-makers much more unstable. When John Birt led the BBC in the 1990s the sweeping changes he introduced weakened the independence of the producer by centralising power in London and giving more control to commissioners, schedulers and controllers. The same process affected the commercial channels. The BBC sold off many of its programme production and technical facilities in the early 1990s, and increased the proportion of programmes commissioned from independent producers rather than made in-house. (Bignell and Lacey 2014: 10–11)

This neoliberal ethos is replicated at Bayview, which offers 'luxury bungalows and apartments for the retired'. Bayview represents high-end retirement but its costs are fought over. When Tom first arrives he complains about the food, to be told by Baines that the menu is a matter not of pleasure or nutrition but of 'budgets'. Baines is a shareholder in Bayview, as are Tom's son and daughter-in-law. He cynically asserts that 'shareholders are people too' (1:1) and explicitly states that the restricted menu is due to the need for the care home to make a profit from its occupants. Tom goes on hunger strike and rallies support among the other residents, eventually pointing out that Baines is their employee. By the second episode the catering budget has doubled. This opening storyline establishes the central conflict of the series, between Baines's profit-driven management and Diana and Tom's revolutionary desire for a more pleasurable life. *Waiting for God* can thus be understood as a series which addresses a moment when the interests of private corporations and individual wealth are visibly taking over state services and social care:

Harvey Baines:	As you know, Bayview is run by a group of dedicated doctors, in conjunction with fiscal resource development analysts –
Diana Trent:	Tax dodgers.
Harvey Baines:	Taxation specialists.
Diana Trent:	A band of middle-class cowboys.
Harvey Baines:	Now, Diana ... (1:4)

Despite its anti-capitalist script this revolutionary dialogue is situated within a white, bourgeois, heteronormative community. In contrast to the camp comedy of *You're Only Young Twice*, *Waiting for God* is avowedly straight and visibly privileged. Even as the show queers ageing and gender it demonstrates that retirement facilities like Bayview are only affordable by the few.

Before arriving at Bayview, Diana Trent has been a photojournalist, working in war zones, while Tom has been an accountant, creating a Walter Mitty fantasy world to make up for the boredom of his career. Their pre-retirement existence is referred to frequently throughout the series, so that Diana and Tom are effectively haunted by their younger selves. *Waiting for God* depicts their struggle to come to terms with the realities of ageing and living within an institution, albeit a relatively luxurious one. Their different strategies for dealing with the situation are telling. Tom embraces eccentricity as a means of combating the boredom and the disempowered environment of Baines's Bayview: 'They all think you go barmy after seventy – exploit it, that's what I say' (1:1). Diana, however, rages against the dying of the light, bluntly stating 'We're born, we consume, we die' (1:1), and asserting that 'Conflict is what keeps you alive' (1:4). In the first season Diana's angry misanthropy is given full rein, but in subsequent seasons Tom's whimsical influence softens her as they work together against Harvey Baines.

The contradiction between Bayview's financial imperative and the possibilities of ageing communities is made evident in a second season episode, 'Foreign Workers' (2:8), which features two significant storylines. Baines's latest plot is to employ illegal immigrants as cheap labour. More than this, he has calculated that because Asian immigrants are physically smaller than English employees they will need less food, heat and space to house them. As he tells his assistant Jane: 'I'm a percentage man' (2:8).

This storyline exposes the reality of care work in the West, where staff are poorly paid, under-resourced and exploited:

> The bad image of nursing homes results from widespread abuses and unnecessary regimentation, but irrational fear about them impedes creative thought about their possibilities. Major problems of nursing homes are low pay and extremely high worker turnover, as much as 100 per cent a year in some homes. Many aides are recent immigrants. A sensible nursing home plan would be to offer English as a Second Language classes to workers, who would be encouraged to practice their skills by talking to residents and writing down some of their stories. Workers would then have the incentive to pay attention to the individuality of residents and to keep their jobs at least until completing their classes. (Cruikshank 2003: 12)

Baines, of course, does not want the staff to communicate with the residents of Bayview but Tom undermines this divide by involving the new staff in his keep fit exercises. Tom attempts to include the disenfranchised workforce in Bayview's community but Baines regards both workers and residents as units of income, in line with the dysfunctional and unimaginative management of care homes that Cruikshank describes.

In this episode Tom is on a health kick, arguing that 'Age is merely a state of mind' (2:8). This is one of many episodes that directly engage with debates about ageing. The notion of ageing as merely 'a state of mind' is lampooned: Tom dresses incongruously in designer leisure wear and collapses when he overdoes it, but the idea is shown to be an exaggeration of academic insights. Suspicious of Tom's new enthusiasm, Diana gets his son and daughter-in-law to follow Tom's taxi to the Bournemouth Community Centre, where he is seen sitting on the floor listening to a female 'guru'. When Diana challenges Tom about joining a cult he takes her to visit the 'guru', Susan Speed (Carol Macready), who is a professor of geriatric medicine. Professor Speed argues that 'old age is a relatively new concept' and that we need to work towards an 'ageless society' where age is not discriminated against (2:8). Diana approves of her account, which both historicises and politicises ageing, agreeing that 'old age is in its infancy'. This sequence is not integrated within the comedic narrative of *Waiting for God*. It functions as an infomercial within the show, communicating the terms of 'ageing comfortably' rather than successful or positive ageing (Cruikshank 2003: 3). That public information aspect is evident in later episodes too.

'The Estate Agent' (3:5) makes the politics of ageing even more explicit, as Baines is encouraged by a local estate agent, Janet Follett (Caroline Harding), to exploit Bayview residents by raising costs so that they can no longer afford to lease their rooms. As Baines and Follett drive away from Bayview after a meeting, she deliberately tries to knock Diana over, stating: 'They're a bloody nuisance, these old gits. They never used to live this long. Now they just clog up decent properties and slow down the whole process of estate management' (3:5). Diana and Tom, however, volunteer at the local branch of 'Age Action' and meet an elderly woman who has been scammed by Follett into letting her a flat at a ridiculously low rent. Diana calls on her contacts in the press to expose both Baines and Follett as they attempt to legally establish occupancy so that she cannot be evicted. In a subsequent feature on the local news, Diana turns to the camera and delivers a speech about the avaricious character of the younger generation, warning elderly viewers to sign nothing until it has been checked by a solicitor. Bayview residents watching on the television in the dining room applaud, endorsing the public service announcement as well as the political tenor of her speech.

The rights of the old to decide how to live are thus situated within *Waiting for God* as a conflict between right- and left-leaning politics. Baines, the arch-capitalist, is thrilled when a new resident, Daisy Williams (Jane Bowns), arrives and, like Mr King in *You Only Live Twice*, decides to reorganise Bayview along military lines (2:2). While Diana identifies Daisy as a 'fascist', Daisy describes Diana as a 'fifth columnist' and 'free thinker' who 'lost us the empire' through lack of 'team spirit' (2:3). To Baines's delight Daisy convinces the residents to follow a regimented regime, with Tom as her errant second-in-command. When the elderly Basil (Michael Bilton) tells Tom he is being a fool, Tom recognises that the new order has gone too far, and addresses Daisy in front of the whole community:

> Sorry old thing, but you see the people here have *survived* not just because they are old but because they have been made with the right stuff. Independence, self-reliance – being an *individual*.

There's a time and a place for armies and teams and pulling together and I'm sure they've all done that but this is *their* time now. *Our* time. Not the time to be bullied or dragooned [camera cuts to Harvey Baines] but a time to enjoy, a time to reflect. A time to *smile*. Haha! [the residents applaud] (2:3)

In this moving speech, Tom significantly reclaims the residents' *time*. He refuses the 'logic of capital accumulation' (Halberstam 2005: 10) and the concept of time as progressive, regimented and productive within heteronormative terms. Despite the heterosexual tenor of *Waiting for God* it calls upon a queer temporality which is set against the neoliberal economies voiced by Harvey Baines. Time as pleasure, thoughtfulness and laughter all work against the dominant discourse of time in Western capitalism as a consumable, marketable *commodity*. Baines embodies market-driven political policies established during the 1980s which continue to affect health and social care in Britain. Any attempt to argue for a more liberal regime within Bayview is seen as politically aggressive. When Baines catches Diana reading material from Age Concern (now Age UK), he dismisses the charity's work as that of 'communist agitators' and 'pinkos' (2:10).

This political debate extends to the show's representation of heterosexuality. *Waiting for God* is framed by the uneven progress of a late-life romance between Diana and Tom, together with the comedic (and eventually consummated) desire of Jane Edwards (Janine Duvitski), deputy manager of Bayview, for the oleaginous Baines. These narratives are distinct from the queer female community visible in *You're Only Young Twice*, yet they are central to debates about ageing and sexuality within the show, problematising media discourses of romance as reserved for the young. In a survey of ageing on American network television in the early 1990s John Bell notes: 'Sexuality [...] is an important absence in the lives of most elderly television characters, and especially in the lives of elderly women' (1992: 309). While the women of Paradise Lodge were not afforded a sexual life, Bayview's occupants are clearly sexually active. Basil is the resident lothario, enthusiastically seducing a range of older women. Diana's response to Basil's and Tom's advances is ambivalent but she does not deny that she has had a sexual past and the series offers her a sexual present.

In season three Diana and Tom's sexual relationship is established following a drunken wake for a fellow resident, when Diana falls asleep in Tom's bed and then instigates sex (3:6). This is reported in comedic detail by Tom and Diana, and the response of residents, staff and relatives is telling. Tom suddenly becomes very popular with the other older women at Bayview, to the extent that Diana has to warn them off, and Basil tells Tom to stop 'muscling in on my turf' (3:6). Marion Ballard (Sandra Payne), Tom's daughter-in-law, is horrified when she walks in on Diana and Tom having sex the following morning: 'I've never seen anything so disgusting! They're *old*!' (3:6). Such disgust is cognisant of the shame surrounding older women's sexuality (Wearing 2011). Diana and Tom's sexual relationship is in this regard revolutionary, working against taboos which are often enforced through institutional over-medication because sexuality is seen as aberrant in the elderly (Cruikshank 2003: 65–6). From the outset, Diana and Tom's sexuality is part of the ongoing political debate in *Waiting for God* about the rights of the elderly. When Harvey's assistant Jane expresses her disgust at Diana and Tom's new relationship she is taken to task:

> Jane, how do you see me? [...] Thanks to some cheap plonk and a fully functioning Tom Ballard I am rediscovering the fact that I am firing on all cylinders and still going off like the proverbial rocket. (3:6)

Diana argues strongly for sexual rights, recommending that Jane read *Living, Loving and Ageing* by Age Concern. *Waiting for God* thus makes older women's sexuality *visible* because, as Kristyn Gorton states: 'It is not simply a matter of ageing women being seen as undesirable, it is more a problem of them being unseen' (2016: 243). Once again the show acts as public service announcement, addressing an issue and raising awareness of the resources available for further information.

While Diana's sexual renaissance is liberating, corresponding with the overall tenor of *Waiting for God*'s depiction of a life in late life, it also appears to align the series with debates about 'successful ageing': 'Increasingly [...] the neo-liberal project of "successful ageing" extends to notions of successful or active later sex life' (Jennings and Oró-Piqueras 2016: 79). Certainly in the eyes of fellow residents and possibly their elderly viewers, Diana and Tom's sexual congress is a sign of 'success'. Their newly sexual relationship denotes that they are still *alive*, still 'firing on all cylinders' within the neoliberal terms of a productive, active and heteronormative old age. That trajectory is problematised in *Waiting for God*, however, as the series shows Diana and Tom's subsequent problems with sharing space. They move in together but then immediately separate, each claiming that the other is 'driving [them] nuts' (4:3). The emotional implications of sexual intimacy are thus unpacked in a manner that works against conventional narratives of heterosexual romance. Despite *Waiting for God* apparently moving towards a heteronormative happy ending in the late-life marriage of Diana and Tom, that trajectory is repeatedly commented upon and compromised:

> Diana [to Tom]: Marriage – what a weird concept. Two people meet, spark off an emotional explosion, which is probably the most intense feeling they will ever have in their entire lives. They rush off to church, swear they will keep it up forever, then when the steam of lust has cleared they see each other's blackheads and nasal hair with *pustular* clarity. They realise they are joined at the legal hip and are condemned to years of sullen compromise, bitterness, despair, depression, futility and – only if they're lucky – the blessed release of an early death.
>
> Tom: I never realised it was such fun. (2:10)

This cynical summary can be read as emerging from Diana's personal history. She had been the mistress of a married man for 30 years and never married, whereas Tom was happily married until his wife died. What these different histories also denote, however, is the range of possibilities regarding sexual practices and trajectories, queering the hegemonic homogeneity of heterosexuality. In *Waiting for God* heterosexuality is repeatedly queered as 'weird' and exceptional rather than a given of the normative life course. Even in their enactment of a 'successful' late-life sexual relationship, the dynamic between Diana and Tom is not a Hollywood story. From their first night together, Diana is represented as the one to instigate sexual activity, with Tom the delighted recipient, undermining the allegedly passive role of women within heterosexual couples.

The unpicking of mythologies around heterosexual behaviour is part of the show's comedy and offers an interesting reflection upon Linn Sandberg's recent work on the sexuality of older men and women. Sandberg describes dominant accounts of late-life sexuality as 'a discourse of decline and of increasing asexuality as one ages'. In particular she remarks how the language of 'successful ageing' is loaded with binary gender stereotypes where 'successful' sexual activity is seen in terms of a 'masculinist and heterosexual discourse in which most of the focus is placed on restoring men's potential for penile-vaginal penetration', while the declining or failing body is characterised in feminine terms as leaky and abject (2013: 13–14). This binary model is notably disrupted in Diana and Tom's late-life relationship, with regard to both their sexuality and their various health problems. During the series Tom has a heart attack and is diagnosed with prostate cancer while Diana is treated for rheumatoid polymyalgia, has a hip replacement, and develops diabetes in the final season. Tom is frequently hospitalised, indicating that he too possesses a failing body, although Graham Crowden's performance as Tom is more physically active than Stephanie Cole's depiction of Diana Trent. Crowden often deploys a funny walk, demonstrating clowning techniques similar to those of John Cleese in *Monty Python's Flying Circus*, whereas Diana moves slowly and painfully, often using a stick. The ageing body is thus shown to be various: not immune to illness and decline, but not defined by it either.

Sandberg proposes the concept of *'affirmative old age'* as an alternative to terms such as positive or successful ageing which invoke sexist and neoliberal ideologies, arguing that this is a better way of representing the 'complex lived experience of ageing' (2013: 14–15). More pertinently, her doctoral research on embodiment and sexuality in older men discovered that they had a dialectical relation to their changing physicality: 'When the men's bodies changed due to ageing, and not only in terms of erectile function, several men in my study narrated a (re)discovery of other body parts, practices and pleasures' (2013: 23). One participant, called Gustav, noted that when his breasts began to grow following hormone treatment for prostate cancer he and his wife treated them as a new and delightful innovation, rather than a failure of masculinity: 'Gustav's story is interesting in how it presents the agency and capacity of ageing bodies to shape new subjectivities and experiences of pleasure. But it is also interesting in how it opens up ways of rethinking masculinity' (2013: 24). In this way the ageing body can be understood as a means of challenging binary models and queering gender.

The queering of heteronormativity in *Waiting for God* extends to the long-heralded resolution of the sitcom: the marriage of Tom and Diana in the show's fifth and final season. The narrative of their engagement and wedding runs alongside the bizarre romance between Harvey Baines and his assistant Jane. Both couples raise questions about heteronormative practices. Throughout the series the central married couple – Tom's son, Geoffrey (Andrew Tourell), and daughter-in-law, Marion – are shown to be entirely mismatched and dysfunctional, separating several times. Geoffrey is ineluctably boring, obsessed by shelving and his job in a dairy products company, while Marion is an alcoholic nymphomaniac, only showing any attraction to Geoffrey in the final season when he assumes the persona of a leather-clad Hell's Angel called 'Fatboy Higgins'. In season five Baines and the besotted Jane take holy orders. Baines becomes a Reverend of the Church of the Flaming Sword, Las Vegas, in a final attempt to be accepted as a member of the local golf club, while Jane becomes a novitiate nun in the belief that he will never love her. Despite this radical shift, Baines does finally propose to Jane (albeit largely for the tax breaks) in front of all the residents (5:6). Although his feelings towards Jane appear to border on the genuine, Baines remains largely unchanged, economising on costs as they approach a double wedding with Tom and Diana.

Diana and Tom's romance also questions the institution of marriage. Even as the narrative steams toward a happy ending, *Waiting for God* resists that magnetic pull. At Tom's first proposal Diana collapses and is hospitalised (5:4). When she recovers she refuses him and continues to do so for much of the final season. When Jane asks Diana why, she bluntly responds: 'I didn't accept Tom's offer for the same reason I didn't accept about fifty other lunatics; because I have never wanted to get married. I've never wanted to be Mrs Somebody Else and I still don't' (5:6). Tom is adamant that this is what they should do, however, arguing that the natural life course is to pair off and reproduce:

Diana: If you don't wed or breed you lose out, is that it?
[... he gets into her bed, the lights go out]
Diana: Are you sitting comfortably?

Tom: Yes Diana!
Diana: Then I'll begin ... (5:7)

Waiting for God thus continues to disrupt the progressive teleology of heteronormativity. Diana's objections to marriage challenge the hegemony of heterosexual romance. The final episodes of the series feature her resistance to the cultural imperatives of heteronormativity. As the dialogue above indicates, Diana retains the active role in her relationship with Tom. While he has popped the question and introduced the marriage script, she continues to refute it, appearing to go along with the process for his sake (5:8).

The final sequence at the church is darkly comic, with a confused vicar uncertain as to who is marrying whom or even if this is a wedding, christening or harvest festival. Most significantly, a funeral has been mistakenly booked into the church at the same time. The mourners and coffin hover by the door, even coming into the church as Harvey and Jane take their vows. The progressive future which heterosexual marriage is purported to depict is haunted by the spectre of death, ironically gesturing toward the queered potential that ageing offers (Port 2012: 3). This queering of time and teleology may appear to chime all too well with stereotypical accounts of both ageing and queer identities as negatively unproductive, but Cynthia Port, citing the work of Lee Edelman and Judith Halberstam, argues that such intimations of mortality offer a different understanding of time. She proposes that heteronormative trajectories that are predicated on a future happy ending, such as romance and marriage, close down other ways of imagining the here and now: 'The attempt to achieve duration and chase meaning into the future denies the potential for the identification of other modes of being in the present' (2012: 4). What this might mean in practice is demonstrated in the final scenes of the last episode of *Waiting for God*.

To Diana's evident delight, Tom suddenly has a change of heart: refusing to take her as his wife during the ceremony, he says 'I think it's a bad idea – I think it would ruin everything' (5:8). This calls a halt to the progressive narrative of the wedding. By refusing their vows, Tom and Diana accede entirely to the moment and its present possibilities – *living* in sin. Just as their age contradicts the reproductive futurity of their union, so this final refusal of cultural legitimation asserts that there are other ways of living together *in the present*. During the photos outside the

Figure 5.6 Tom and Diana after they refuse to marry (*Waiting for God*, 5:8, BBC, 1990–4).

church (which they continue with as they are already paid for), Diana promises Tom the 'best Saturday night in' of his life, once again indicating her active role (5:8; Figure 5.6).

Although the potential of heterosexual marriage is not dismissed – Jane surprises Harvey with an enthusiastic kiss when they take their vows – the priority of Diana and Tom's romantic liaison is unequivocally foregrounded. *Waiting for God*'s final season, like the final season of many popular sitcoms, 'jumps the shark' but it also offers a satisfying *lack* of resolution to a sophisticated comedy about ageing, gender and sexuality. In effect, Diana and Tom's non-marriage refuses the temporal logics of heterosexuality, neoliberal capital and the cultural imperatives of Western discourse regarding ageing, in favour of playfulness, pleasure and the present. This conclusion contradicts the title of the show: they are not *waiting*.

Going Forward?

You're Only Young Twice and *Waiting for God* are both set in private retirement homes, indicating the privileged demographic of these comedies. Although the residents of Paradise Lodge and Bayview Retirement Village challenge the boundaries of their age, class, sexuality and gender, they have the time and economic power to do so. Two recent British comedies which address late-life care offer a far bleaker vision. Jo Brand's three-episode series *Going Forward* (BBC 2016) offers a salutary reflection upon my argument regarding *You're Only Young Twice* and *Waiting for God*. It is a darker and less optimistic vision of getting old in contemporary Britain. *Going Forward* is a sequel to *Getting On* (BBC 2009–12), an award-winning sitcom which Brand wrote with her co-stars, Vicki Pepperdine and Joanna Scanlan. An American version of *Getting On* was subsequently produced by the BBC and HBO (2013–15) starring Laurie Metcalfe as Dr Jenna James. The British *Getting On* is set in the geriatric ward of a National Health Service hospital, and focusses primarily on the lives of its staff, Nurse Kim Wilde (Jo Brand), Sister Den Flixter (Joanna Scanlan) and Dr Pippa Moore (Vicki Pepperdine). *Going Forward* follows Kim Wilde into the private sector, where she works for a company which provides domiciliary care, and once again the primary focus is not the elderly 'clients' but Wilde and her family as they struggle to get by. This sitcom offers a useful conclusion to my discussion as *Going Forward* represents a dark reversal of the queered communities which *You're Only Young Twice* and *Waiting for God* celebrate. In *Going Forward* the elderly are marginalised and atomised. Their experience of late-life care is shown to be a direct result of a fragmented and crumbling welfare state.

Hannah Hamad argues that the current popularity of medical dramas which centre on nursing is indicative of a culture which is both reassessing the value of women's work and anxious about the financial and political contexts in which it is set. Television shows about nursing and care work are thus at the frontline of 'a culture war over the NHS' (Hamad 2016: 142–3). Series such as *Getting On* and *Going Forward* offer a bleak disavowal of the optimistic futures that were imagined in Britain after World War II, when the establishment of the NHS and the expansion of National Insurance following the positive reception of the Beveridge Report (1942) marked a moment where the state was seen as responsible for the welfare of its citizens. *You're Only Young Twice* and *Waiting for God* feature a generation which has grown old under the welfare system. By the time *Getting On* was broadcast in 2009, Britain had seen 30 years of government that had withdrawn funding from health and education while outsourcing many aspects of NHS services. As Beth Johnson states, *Getting On* offers a 'weighty, substantial and radical' commentary on getting old in Britain in the twenty-first century (2016: 191). From the traditional three-camera studio-set sitcom in *You're Only Young Twice*, via a multi-camera, drama format in *Waiting for God*, to the pseudo-documentary single-camera style of filming in *Getting On* and *Going Forward*, these comedies reflect upon cultural and political discourse around ageing and gender in British culture.

Getting On's social commentary is taken a step further in its sequel. *Going Forward* begins with a documentary-style announcement that 'Nurse Kim Wilde left the NHS two years ago. She is now working for independent health care providers Buccaneer 2000' (1:1). Although a 'buccaneer' might indicate a piratical, go-getting agenda, one step removed from the dubious implications of a 'cowboy' operator, it also smacks of the team names thought up on reality shows such as *The Apprentice* (NBC 2004–, BBC 2005–), where the voracious greed of young entrepreneurs is made evident. Buccaneer *2000* also denotes that this private care provider is already past its sell-by date. This was a business set up in the fever of millennial ambition but it is now in decline, packing up its offices and rationalising its resources. If the patients in *Getting On* were marooned in their beds, rarely speaking to each other or to the staff, the 'clients' in *Going Forward* are atomised in their own homes. They represent a fragile array of individuals with different demands and needs which Kim attempts to address, despite an apparent lack of support from her employers. *Going Forward* makes the precarious vulnerability of its elderly characters evident, acknowledging the realities of ageing bodies without resorting to such 'cruel optimism' as neoliberal discourses of rejuvenation – such as '70 is the new 50' – which shifts the responsibility for care onto individuals and away from the state (Woodward 2006; Berlant 2011; Shildrick 2015).

Going Forward demonstrates that there is *no* 'going forward' in the terms of that bastardised managerial discourse. Kim's clients, like Kim herself, are just getting by, dependent on brief and often unreliable visits from Buccaneer 2000 care workers. They are isolated and lonely. Kim's first home visit in the opening episode is to Mrs Jenkins (Vivien Bridson), who has had a packet of biscuits for breakfast because the morning carer did not turn up (Figure 5.7). As Mrs Jenkins says: 'When it was the council [who provided care] they always came.' She asks Kim to post her son's birthday card: 'I haven't seen him for a couple of years but he'll be round like a shot when I pop my clogs to sell the house' (1:1). Mrs Popat (Lalita Ahmed) is on a nebuliser and wishes she could have a later visit: 'It's so long until bed time without company' (1:2). Mrs Bishop (Hazel Godfrey) is not taking her medication and Kim learns from an inquisitive neighbour that she is booked to go into a hospice as she has now been diagnosed with cancer; there she will at least 'have some company' (1:3). Kim is monitored and reprimanded on the phone by staff at central office for not keeping up with her appointments. She is allowed 15 minutes with each client, which is clearly not enough. This is care at a minimal level. As Kim attends to their emotional needs with kind words, jokes and a cup of tea, she is also dealing with personal hygiene, incontinence pads and colostomy bags.

Kim's struggle to provide care in *Going Forward* exposes the extent to which private care providers are 'uncaring' (Cruikshank 2003: 204). Margaret Cruikshank suggests that the elderly should be allowed to manage their own care or at least contribute to how it is shaped, as was the case in *You're Only Young Twice* and *Waiting For God*. In *Going Forward*, care is imposed on Buccaneer 2000's 'clients' so that, while it might address basic medical needs, it does not offer them any sense of agency. Where Harvey Baines was confounded by Diana and Tom in *Waiting for God*, the managers in *Going Forward* are evasive and care*less*,

Figure 5.7 Kim Wilde and Mrs Jenkins in *Going Forward* (1:1, BBC, 2016–).

supporting neither their 'clients' nor their staff. When Kim discovers that the man who managed her ward when she worked in the hospital is now the 'Head of Special Projects' for Buccaneer 2000 she retorts that he is the 'Angel of Death' for any organisation, a phrase which has grim resonance in this context (1:3). There is little hope in either *Getting On* or *Going Forward*, in the absence of a potential queer community or a politically mobilised older citizenry. The elderly are disempowered, disenfranchised and either imprisoned within their own homes in *Going Forward* or marooned in an under-resourced NHS ward in *Getting On*.

The question of elderly care has also come home for Kim Wilde. In *Going Forward* Kim and her sister Jackie discuss the care of their elderly mother. In the first episode Jackie wants to sell their mother's house as a means of clearing her own credit card debts. Just as Buccaneer 2000 regards its workers and clients as monetary units, so Jackie regards her mother as a potential source of income. By the second episode, three months later, their mother has had a stroke and is in a care home which costs £870 a week. The house has been sold and Jackie has spent all her share on clearing her debts, but their mother is not ill enough to qualify for 'full medical needs' NHS support. Jackie is horrified to discover that the money they received from the house can be retrieved by the council to pay for their mother's care. In the third episode it is six weeks later; their mother has had another stroke and is now being tested to 'see if she is seriously ill enough to qualify for care' (1:3). Jackie is elated at the news that she will not have to return the money and Kim is disgusted at her attitude: 'Our mother has had a serious stroke and could die any day now' (1:3). These conversations between two middle-aged sisters make evident the financial, political and affective costs of care but at no point do we see their mother or hear what she has to say. She is written out of the conversation, remaining only as a central topic which causes a furious row between the sisters in the final episode. The invisible presence of Kim and Jackie's mother, together with the frail appearances of Kim's clients, underlines the danger of getting old and being poor. *You're Only Young Twice* and *Waiting for God* make a comedy of queer ageing, of life in late life, but *Going Forward* is a startling wake-up call. If there is a queer aspect to *Getting On* and *Going Forward* it is in these series' refusal to accede to the neoliberal discourse of productive, positive, *happy* decline. As Margrit Shildrick states, living into advanced old age is not about 'getting better':

living on is always measured against an impossible scene of fulfilment, a fantasy of full capacity that is ever beyond reach. It invokes both an underlying ontological anxiety and a futile desire to resolve that anxiety through strategies of self-realization directed towards happiness – a privileged trope of western neo-liberalism [...] – and, more generally, well-being. To be debilitated – to never reach the putative security of corporeal, affective and cognitive standards of flourishing – just is the condition of life. (2015: 14)

The power of *Getting On* and *Going Forward* is thus their dogged resistance to neoliberal fantasies of 'successful ageing' and the manner in which they problematise even Sandberg's 'affirmative old age' or Cruikshank's 'comfortable old age' by bluntly asserting the political and financial issues which shape how we get old.

CONCLUSION

This book has, I hope, demonstrated how strategies afforded by queer theory provide useful equipment with which to deconstruct the complex iterations of gender in television comedy. The programmes examined in this study, from early American television variety and sitcom to recent hit shows and British sketch comedy, indicate the diversity of approaches which a queer lens affords. In the introduction I noted the paradox of analysing comedy – that such close scrutiny often destroys the joke – yet by destroying the laughter it is possible to expose uncertainties regarding gender identity which much comedy plays upon. In this sense queer readings of television comedy take the joke further, by examining the complexity of its workings and the contradictions it relies on. The examination of comedy does not make it funnier but unpicking the certainties of gender makes these comedies *richer*. Deploying queer strategies to do that unpicking renders identity more visibly complex, mutable and provisional. There are no certainties here and there is much more work to be done.

In a 2016 conversation with Sara Ahmed, Judith Butler looks back at the reception of *Gender Trouble* (1990): how it was initially received and how that volume helped to shape the emerging discipline of queer studies:

> People now say, 'I am queer' and at the time that queer theory began, I am pretty sure that nearly everyone thought that 'queer' should *not* be an identity, but should name something of the uncapturable or unpredictable trajectory of a sexual life. [...]

I understand that in certain contexts the demand for recognition within institutional and public structures is great, and that one way to achieve that is by establishing an identity. But since a fair amount of queer theory has been directed against the policing of identity, the demand to have one and to show one upon demand, it has been a bit startling to me. But then again, I have to ask myself: why should we not be startled by the directions that a term like 'queer' takes? It has travelled far and wide, and who knows what next permutation it will have. (cited in Ahmed 2016: 489)

In this discussion of women – and men – in television comedy, I have been drawn to figures that represent queer indeterminacies, to performances that indicate 'the uncapturable or unpredictable trajectory of a sexual life'. The years it has taken to produce this book have at times seemed like a long struggle to nail down the queerness of television comedy. I have been trailing queer accounts of gender in television comedy as they travel, mapping early trajectories and tracking their potential in the neoliberal context of twenty-first-century Western academia. Of course the queerness of television comedy – as of television as a medium – cannot be finitely captured, as the very aspect of these comedies that drew me to examine them is their refusal to be defined. The 'demand' to have an identity and to capitalise upon it, politically or economically, which Butler describes above, is the precise demand that these comic works tend to resist. And why not? Isn't comedy itself a queer medium, forged across derogated cultural tropes such as silliness, misunderstanding and failure? In this regard the process of writing this book has been educational in every sense. Comedy, like the term 'queer', is constantly on the move, and the chapters which constitute this volume are, like any writing process, adventures in failure.

If television comedy has anything to tell us about gender and sexual identity it is that these categories are never simple or static, but always in transit and transitory. Television comedy is a dense, rich and inchoate field, and there is much work to be done on successful shows that have barely been glanced at by academic scholarship. In my discussion I have called for further work on shows such as *Last of the Summer Wine* and *French and Saunders* but that barely scrapes the surface of the unexamined archive. The account of queer gender and sexual identities which television comedy offers may gesture toward other possibilities beyond

CONCLUSION

the heteronormative tropes we are so used to seeing on our screens, but it is not a road map. Where television comedy intersects with feminist politics, queer accounts of gender demonstrate the limitations of models which propose a series of 'waves' or depend upon notions of 'triumph' or 'failure'. During my discussion I have charted how 'successful' sitcoms such as *The Big Bang Theory* fail to live up to their queer potential and how different models of success may be found in more queerly marginal programmes such as *Smack the Pony*.

In *The Queer Art of Failure*, a work that has haunted this project, Judith Halberstam proposes:

> The history of alternative political formations is important because it contests social relations as given and allows us to access traditions of political action that, while not necessarily successful in the sense of becoming dominant, do offer models of contestation, rupture, and discontinuity for the political present. These histories also identify potent avenues of failure, failures that we might build upon in order to counter the logics of success that have emerged from the triumphs of global capitalism. [...] failure's by-ways are all the spaces in-between the superhighways of capital. (2011: 19)

Television comedy does not offer a 'history of alternative political formations' but it does address them, even as it denies their direct influence. Thus, in *Smack the Pony*, by making work that addresses 'the women in the car park round the back', rather than the men at the front of the action, women in comedy reference the *different* perspectives that feminist and queer politics have offered us (Barnett 2015). These are the 'spaces in-between' (Halberstam 2011: 19). Likewise, by portraying queered and politicised older people in *You're Only Young Twice* and *Waiting for God*, television comedies can represent imagined communities that draw upon an unacknowledged history of socialist, feminist and queer politics. Dominant models of success, such as *The Big Bang Theory*, are instructive, demonstrating how a liberal agenda focussed myopically on masculinity and a heteronormative 'logics of success' works to confine its characters. This is not to say that my positive readings of Burns and Allen, Raye and Ball, *30 Rock* and *Parks and Recreation*, together with the British comedies, constitute a canon of *properly* queer comedy. Subversion and gender perversion are never unconfined.

Butler, again, addresses the limits of subversion at the end of *Bodies That Matter*, noting the temporal and geographic specificity of the term 'queer' within contemporary popular and academic discourse. She reflects on Jennie Livingston's 1990 documentary about 1980s drag balls in New York:

> As *Paris is Burning* made clear, drag is not unproblematically subversive. It serves a subversive function to the extent that it reflects the mundane impersonations by which heterosexually ideal genders are performed and naturalized and undermines their power by virtue of effecting that exposure. But there is no guarantee that exposing the naturalized status of heterosexuality will lead to its subversion. Heterosexuality can augment its hegemony *through* its denaturalization, as when we see denaturalizing parodies that reidealize heterosexual norms *without* calling them into question. (Butler 1993: 176, emphasis in original)

As with the drag performances in Livingstone's documentary, comedy does not inevitably queer femininity but contains the potential to do so. Through its denaturalisation of heteronormative gender roles, comedy can offer a subversive vision regarding the explosive deconstruction of gender and identity, but that potential is always provisional. Its provisional and temporal limits are visible because subversion and radical political acts are themselves provisional and temporary. Queering is always a process, not a destination – hence Butler's discomfort with the claim of a 'queer' identity. Once subversive or radical politics are naturalised and become orthodox, they relinquish their destabilising potential.

Television comedy could be seen as the most effective means of naturalising subversion, by placing subversive acts within a comic script, putting them on the small screen, broadcasting them into the domestic sphere. Yet the effects of comedy are unknown and unknowable. Who is laughing? Why? At what? The incommensurable quality of comic effects constitutes the appeal and continuing power of television comedy narratives and performance: an appeal which often relies upon the inability of dominant discourses to keep to the heteronormative script, to police its own systems and to manage the binary matrix upon which it relies. As Butler argues, with regard to *Paris is Burning*, 'The critical promise of drag does not have to do with the proliferation of genders [...] but rather with the exposure or the failure of heterosexual regimes ever fully to legislate or contain their own ideals' (1993: 181). *30 Rock* and *Parks and Recreation* are constantly pecking away at those failures, while *You're Only Young Twice* and *Waiting For God* reimagine gender, sexuality and community in old age, forming other ways of *living* life in late life. They do so by demonstrating that 'the heterosexual matrix proves to be an *imaginary* logic that insistently issues forth its own unmanageability' (Butler 1993: 183, emphasis in original).

This book is not intended as an historical overview of how television comedy has worked to queer gender. Rather my eccentric trajectory though British and American television comedy tracks the potential of particular shows to expose how gender is always queering itself in comic work. In this respect television comedy has much to say about gender politics and the ongoing work of feminist and queer theory. For me, and hopefully for you as a reader, this examination of television comedy evokes a history of queer and feminist politics that endures, despite being repeatedly told that it is irrelevant, invalid and unnecessary. These are politics that are manifold and manifest: 'Feminism lives variously, even vicariously, across the multiple enunciations that it embodies as, alternatively and collectively, a political project, analytical perspective, interdisciplinary practice, and historical entity. [...] a living thing' (Weigman 2010: 84). As a living thing, feminist and queer politics remain relevant, valid and necessary.

While I was finishing this book I was invited to present a paper at a Women and Comedy Symposium which took place at the University of Salford in October 2017. The symposium was a launch event for the newly formed *Mixed Bill* comedy and gender research network founded by Ellie Tomsett, Lisa Moore and Kate Fox.[1] The event followed a single programme – no parallel sessions – so that everyone attended the same panels and a continuing conversation developed. It was an inspiring experience, organised on a shoestring but with a wealth of imagination and intent. Effectively, this symposium brought together a range of researchers, archivists and performers working on women and comedy who had, in the main, never encountered each other before. New connections were created and new avenues explored. Sam Beale

(Middlesex University) looked back to London music hall and the spaces that it offered to female performers in the late nineteenth century. Harriet Reed from the Victoria and Albert Museum in London discussed their growing archive of British radio and television comedy. Maggie Inchley (Queen Mary, University of London) examined the performance politics of *Manwatching* (2017), a comedy stage show which requires a male stand-up to read a script by and about an anonymous female playwright. Neslihan Arol (University of Arts Berlin) advocated the use of allegory in women's comedy performance as a form of feminist praxis. Ellie Tomsett (Sheffield Hallam University) spoke passionately on the necessity of ensuring that women's comedy is founded on a more egalitarian and intersectional politics. The closing panel discussion brought together comedy performers, writers, producers and promotors to address the current culture regarding women and comedy in the UK. What this remarkable event made clear was at the very least twofold. First, there is a lot of work being done in a range of disciplines, both within and beyond academia, which addresses women and comedy. That work is hard and continues – often despite the culture within which it operates – to address inequities and absences. Much of it retains a strong sense of its relation to a long history of feminist politics and activism. Second, this event demonstrated, again, that there is more work to be done.

Women's comedy on television and on the live circuit is prone to disappearance and discontinuity. As I noted regarding *Smack the Pony*, there is no DVD box set, nor an edited collection of essays which secures the show's place within a history of British sketch comedy. In this respect Morwenna Banks and Amanda Swift's *The Joke's on Us* offers a salutary reminder of the gaps and elision in recent histories of women and comedy. Published in 1987, this book maps a history of 'women in comedy from music hall to the present', with chapters on stand-up, radio, character performers, film, revue and television comedy. Its historical scope is educational but it is also remarkable as a snapshot of the comedy landscape of the late 1980s and the women who populated it. In this respect the book is an important historical record. Many of the names in that volume have disappeared from screen and stage. Some of the women who started their careers in comedy in the 1980s have subsequently become writers or producers or have moved away from comedy altogether. The book offers a fascinating account of the early career of performers such as Victoria Wood, Dawn French and Jennifer

Saunders, but it is also a catalogue of the disappeared. These figures are hard to track, as comedy, like any performance medium, is tough and demands remarkable quantities of strength, stamina and luck to sustain a career over any period of time. I am fascinated by the ones who did not continue. Like the 'women in the car park round the back', these are figures whose voices are heard briefly, if at all: women whose work is more likely to be a *job* rather than a career and who may well have regarded comedy as a transitional moment in a life lived otherwise.

The Joke's on Us raises questions about our current ability to record and document women in comedy on television and in live performance – an issue which was also raised towards the end of the *Mixed Bill* symposium. Although YouTube and fan-generated sites such as the British Comedy Guide[2] represent a popular archive, they are not matched by critical and academic work. Professional archives, such as the comedy holdings at the British Library and the Victoria and Albert Museum, are battling for space at a moment when a generation of comedy performers – such as June Whitfield and Sheila Hancock – are coming to the end of long careers. Curators, archivists, academics and historians have much work to do to ensure that there is adequate representation of women's work in comedy. The British Stand-Up Comedy Archive was initiated in 2013 at the University of Kent, following the deposit of the personal archive of the British comedy writer and performer Linda Smith, after her death in 2006.[3] That archive has established links with the British Library and builds upon online archives established by fans, such as *Beyond the Joke*.[4]

Much of the current archival work is thus focussed on digital media and on stage performance rather than television shows – possibly because there is an assumption that in the Web 2.0 era all television is available all the time. The sheer volume of material – if only that which documents recent stand-up and live performance – is overwhelming. Yet this is not just about what is remembered but how we remember it. What are we documenting if we are recording the histories and contemporary work of women in television comedy – and how are we going to preserve it? If you have read this book and thought about all the shows, performers and issues which it does not address, then it is time to pick up a pen, fire up the computer and start writing. Consider this a call for more work about comedy, about television and about the complex iterations of gender and sexual identity in popular culture.

NOTES

Conclusion

1. https://mixedbill.wordpress.com.
2. https://www.comedy.co.uk/.
3. http://blogs.kent.ac.uk/standupcomedyarchive/about/.
4. https://www.beyondthejoke.co.uk/.

BIBLIOGRAPHY

Adkins, Tabetha (2008). 'A label like Gucci, Versace, or Birkenstock: *Sex and the City* and queer identity', in Rebecca Beirne (ed.), *Televising Queer Women: A Reader*, New York and Basingstoke: Palgrave Macmillan, pp. 109–19.
Adorno, Theodor W. (1991). 'How to look at television', in *The Culture Industry: Selected Essays on Mass Culture*, London: Routledge, pp. 136–53.
Ahmed, Sara (2016). 'Interview with Judith Butler', *Sexualities* 19/4, pp. 482–92.
Allen, Robert C. (1991). *Horrible Prettiness: Burlesque and American Culture*, Chapel Hill, NC: University of North Carolina Press.
Andrews, Bart (1976). *Lucy & Ricky & Fred & Ethel: The Story of I Love Lucy*, New York: Dutton.
Andrews, Maggie (1998). 'Butterflies and caustic asides: housewives, comedy and the feminist movement', in Stephen Wagg (ed.), *Because I Tell a Joke or Two: Comedy, Politics and Social Difference*, London: Routledge, pp. 50–64.
Arthurs, Jane (1999). 'Revolting women: the body in comic performance', in Jane Arthurs and Jean Grimshaw (eds), *Women's Bodies: Discipline and Transgression*, London and New York: Cassell, pp. 137–64.
Ausiello, Michael and Andy Patrick (2010). '*Big Bang Theory* mystery: is Sheldon gay?', *Entertainment Weekly*, 9 February, http://insidetv.ew.com/2010/02/09/big-bang-theory-sheldon-gay/ (accessed 3 September 2013).
Auster, Albert (1998). 'Much ado about nothing: some final thoughts on *Seinfeld*', *Television Quarterly* 29/4, pp. 24–33.
Avila-Saavedra, Guillermo (2009). 'Nothing queer about queer television: televised construction of gay masculinities', *Media, Culture and Society* 31/5, pp. 5–21.
Ball, Vicky (2012). 'The "feminization" of British television and the re-traditionalization of gender', *Feminist Media Studies*, 12/2, pp. 248–64.
Ballou, Hannah (2013). 'Pretty funny: manifesting a normatively sexy female comic body', *Comedy Studies*, 4/2, pp. 179–86.
Banks, Morwenna and Amanda Swift (1987). *The Joke's On Us: Women in Comedy From Music Hall to the Present*, London: Pandora.
Barnett, Laura (2015). 'How we made *Smack the Pony*', *Guardian*, 12 January. Available at https://www.theguardian.com/tv-and-radio/2015/jan/12/how-we-

BIBLIOGRAPHY

made-smack-the-pony-sally-phillips-doon-mackichan (accessed 20 October 2016).
Becker, Ron (2009). 'Guy love: a queer straight masculinity for a post-closet era?', in Glyn Davis and Gary Needham (eds), *Queer TV: Theories, Histories, Politics*, London and New York: Routledge, pp. 121–40.
Bell, John (1992). 'In search of a discourse on aging: the elderly on television', *The Gerontologist* 32/3, pp. 305–11.
Bennett, James and Su Holmes (2010). 'The "place" of television in celebrity studies', *Celebrity Studies* 1/1, pp. 65–80.
Berkshire, Geoff (2015). '*Parks and Recreation* finale: Mike Schur on *Sopranos* inspirations, easter eggs and the White House question', *Variety*, 24 February. Available at http://variety.com/2015/tv/news/parks-and-recreation-finale-mike-schur-showrunner-interview-1201441047/ (accessed 20 December 2016).
Berlant, Lauren (2011). *Cruel Optimism*, Durham, NC: Duke University Press.
Best, Amy L. (2005). 'The production of heterosexuality at the high school prom', in Chrys Ingraham (ed.), *Thinking Straight: The Power, The Promise, and The Paradox of Heterosexuality*, London and New York: Routledge, pp. 193–213.
BFI (2012a). 'The making of *Smack the Pony*', Dick Fiddy in conversation with Victoria Pile, Fiona Allen, Doon Mackichan and Sally Phillips. Available at http://www.bfi.org.uk/films-tv-people/51090d377eeec (accessed 31 October 2016).
——— (2012b). 'Trailblazers: queens of comedy', a season of screenings featuring pioneering 'golden girls' of British TV comedy, 14–28 August, BFI Southbank and Hackney Empire, London, press release. Available at http://www.bfi.org.uk/sites/bfi.org.uk/files/downloads/bfi-press-release-trailblazers-queens-of-tv-comedy-at-bfi-southbank-and-hackney-empire-as-part-of-the-london-2012-festival-2012-07-01.pdf (accessed 24 October 2016).
Bignell, Jonathan and Stephen Lacey (2014). 'Introduction', in Jonathan Bignall and Stephen Lacey (eds), *British Television Drama: Past, Present and Future*, 2nd edition, Basingstoke and New York: Palgrave Macmillan, pp. 1–15.
Billen, Andrew (1999). 'Pony tales', *New Statesman*, 26 April, pp. 39–40.
Blaikie, Andrew (1999). *Ageing and Popular Culture*, Cambridge: Cambridge University Press.
Blobel, Corinna (2012). 'The rise of the geek, or when did it become cool to be uncool?', *Clear* brand consultancy, http://web.archive.org/web/20121113232308/http://blog.clear-ideas.com/the-rise-of-the-geek/ (accessed 10 January 2018).
Blundell, Graeme (2010). 'Stop laughing, this is serious', *The Australian*, 13 March, http://www.theaustralian.com.au/opinion/columnists/stop-laughing-this-is-serious/story-e6frg8qo-1225838725834 (accessed 27 June 2010).
Bociurkiw, Marusya (2005). 'It's not about the sex: racialization and queerness in *Ellen* and *The Ellen DeGeneres Show*', *Canadian Woman Studies/Les Cahiers de la Femme*, 24/2–3, pp. 176–81.
Bond Stockton, Kathryn (2009). *The Queer Child, Or Growing Sideways in the Twentieth Century*, Durham, NC and London: Duke University Press.
Bray, James (2010). 'Rise of the geeks', *Soundblab.com*, https://soundblab.com/articles/2672-rise-of-the-geeks (accessed 3 September 2013).
Brook, Vincent (1999). 'The Americanization of Molly: how mid-fifties TV homogenized *The Goldbergs* (and got "Berg-larized" in the process)', *Cinema Journal*, 38/4, pp. 45–67.

Browne, Katherine (2009). 'Queer theory/queer geographies', in R. Kitchin and N. Thrift (eds), *International Encyclopaedia of Human Geography*, London: Elsevier, pp. 39–45.

Buchbinder, David (2008). 'Enter the schlemiel: the emergence of inadequate or incompetent masculinities in recent film and television', *Canadian Review of American Studies*, 38/2, pp. 227–45.

Budgeon, Shelley (2011). 'The contradictions of successful femininity: third-wave feminism, postfeminism and "new" femininities', in Rosalind Gill and Christina Scharff (eds), *New Femininities: Postfeminism, Neoliberalism and Subjectivity*, London: Palgrave Macmillan, pp. 279–92.

Butler, Judith (1990). *Gender Trouble: Feminism and the Subversion of Identity*, New York: Routledge.

—————— (1993). *Bodies That Matter: On the Discursive Limits of 'Sex'*, New York: Routledge.

—————— (2004). *Undoing Gender*, New York and London: Routledge.

Cardwell, Sarah (2007). 'Is quality television any good? Generic distinctions, evaluations and the troubling matter of critical judgement', in Janet McCabe and Kim Akass (eds), *Quality TV: Contemporary American Television and Beyond*, London: I.B.Tauris, pp. 19–34.

Caughie, John (1981). 'Rhetoric, pleasure and art television: *Dreams of Leaving*', *Screen*, 22/4, pp. 9–31.

Clayton, Alex (2013). 'Why comedy is at home on television', in Jason Jacobs and Steven Peacock (eds), *Television Aesthetics and Style*, London and New York: Bloomsbury, pp. 79–92.

Cole, Stephanie (1998). *A Passionate Life*, Cardiff: AvonAngliA.

Conway, Richard J. (2006). 'A trip to the queer circus: reimagined masculinities in *Will and Grace*', in James R. Keller and Leslie Stratyner (eds), *The New Queer Aesthetic on Television*, Jefferson, NC and London: McFarland & Company, pp. 75–84.

Creed, Barbara (1993). *The Monstrous-feminine: Film, Feminism, Psychoanalysis*, London and New York: Routledge.

Cruikshank, Margaret (2003). *Learning to Be Old: Gender, Culture and Aging*, Lanham, MD and Oxford: Rowman and Littlefield.

Davies, Madeleine (2013). 'Thank you, Liz Lemon, for being you', *Jezebel*, 31 January, http://jezebel.com/5980365/thank-you-liz-lemon-for-being-you (accessed 4 November 2013).

Davis, Wendy (2008). 'Playing the television field: *Kath and Kim* and the changing face of TV comedy', *Continuum: Journal of Media and Cultural Studies*, 22/3, pp. 353–61.

Detweiler, Eric (2012). '"I was just doing a little joke there": irony and the paradoxes of the sitcom in *The Office*', *Journal of Popular Culture* 45/4, pp. 727–48.

Deveny, Catherine (2009). '*Two and a Half Men* is no joke', *The Age*, 4 November, http://archive.fo/y7FUk (accessed 10 January 2018).

Dias Branco, Sérgio (2013). 'Situating comedy: inhabitation and duration in classical American sitcoms', in Jason Jacobs and Steven Peacock (eds), *Television Aesthetics and Style*, London and New York: Bloomsbury, pp. 93–102.

Doane, Mary Ann (1991). *Femmes Fatales: Feminism, Film Theory, Psychoanalysis*, London and New York: Routledge.

Dolan, Josephine (2010). 'Firm and hard: old age, the "youthful" body and essentialist discourses', keynote conference presentation at IV SELICUP Conference: Past, Present and Future of Popular Culture: Spaces and Contexts, Palma, Spain, October 2010. Available at http://eprints.uwe.ac.uk/21954 (accessed 7 April 2016).

Dolan, Josephine and Estella Tincknell (2012). 'Introduction', in Josephine Dolan and Estella Tincknell (eds), *Aging Femininities: Troubling Representations*, Newcastle upon Tyne: Cambridge Scholars, pp. vii–xxi.

Doty, Alexander (1990). 'The cabinet of Lucy Ricardo: Lucille Ball's star image', *Cinema Journal* 29/4, pp. 3–22.

——— (1993). *Making Things Perfectly Queer: Interpreting Mass Culture*, Minneapolis and London: University of Minnesota Press.

——— (2000). *Flaming Classics: Queering the Film Canon*, New York and London: Routledge.

Douglas, Susan J. (1994). *Where the Girls Are: Growing Up Female with the Mass Media*, New York: Times Books.

Dratch, Rachel (2012). *Girl Walks into a Bar . . .: Comedy Calamities, Dating Disasters, and a Midlife Miracle*, New York: Avery.

Duncan, Erika (1983). 'The hungry Jewish mother', in Susannah Heschel (ed.), *On Being a Jewish Feminist*, New York: Schocken Books, pp. 27–39.

Dyer, Richard (1979). *Stars*, London: BFI.

Edwards, Justin and Rune Graulund (2013). *The Grotesque*, Abingdon and New York: Routledge.

Eglash, Ron (2002). 'Race, sex, and nerds: from black geeks to Asian American hipsters', *Social Text* 71/2, pp. 49–64.

Ellis, John (1982). *Visible Fictions*, London: Routledge.

Engstrom, Erika (2013). '"Knope we can!" Primetime feminist strategies in NBC's *Parks and Recreation*', *Media Report to Women* 41/4, pp. 6–21.

Feasey, Rebecca (2008). *Masculinity and Popular Television*, Edinburgh: Edinburgh University Press.

Ferraro, Rich (2012). 'Ripped from the headlines: Liz Lemon explains that anti-gay comments "can influence or hurt people" on *30 Rock*', *GLAAD*, 20 January, http://www.glaad.org/blog/ripped-headlines-liz-lemon-explains-anti-gay-comments-can-influence-or-hurt-people-30-rock (accessed 5 November 2013).

Feuer, Jane (1986). 'Narrative form in American network television', in Colin McCabe (ed.), *High Theory/Low Culture: Analysing Popular Television and Film*, Manchester: Manchester University Press, pp. 101–14.

——— (2008a). 'The unruly woman sitcom', in Glen Creeber (ed.), *The Television Genre Book*, 2nd edition, Basingstoke: BFI/Palgrave Macmillan, pp. 82–3.

——— (2008b). '*Will and Grace*', in Glen Creeber (ed.), *The Television Genre Book*, 2nd edition, Basingstoke: BFI/Palgrave Macmillan, p. 87.

Fey, Tina (2011). *Bossypants*, New York: Little, Brown and Company.

Fiske, John (2011). *Television Culture*, 2nd edition, London and New York: Routledge.

French, Dawn (2008). *Dear Fatty*, London: Century.

Freund, Karl (1953). 'Filming the "Lucy" show', *Art Photography* 4/6. Available at http://www.lucyfan.com/freundfilming.html (accessed 16 April 2013).

Galo, Sarah (2015). 'How *Parks and Recreation* served up prime-time feminism amid the laughs', *The Guardian*, 24 February. Available at https://www.theguardian.

com/tv-and-radio/2015/feb/24/parks-and-recreation-prime-time-feminism-laughs (accessed 20 December 2016).
Gerhard, Jane (2005). 'Sex and the City: Carrie Bradshaw's queer postfeminism', *Feminist Media Studies* 5/1, pp. 37–49.
Gilbert, Gerald (2013). 'Always the best friend: Sally Phillips on Christianity, comedians and the class system', *The Independent*, 19 January. Available at http://www.independent.co.uk/news/people/profiles/always-the-best-friend-sally-phillips-on-christianity-comedians-and-the-class-system–8454458.html (accessed 14 February 2017).
Giles, Judy (2004). *The Parlour and the Suburb: Domestic Identities, Class, Femininity and Modernity*, Oxford and New York: Berg.
Gill, Rosalind (2007). *Gender and the Media*, Cambridge: Polity Press.
—— (2009). 'Breaking the silence: the hidden injuries of neo-liberal Academia', in Roisin Flood and Ros Gill (eds), *Secrecy and Silence in the Research Process: Feminist Reflections*, London: Routledge, pp. 228–44.
—— (2016). 'Post-postfeminism? New feminist visibilities in postfeminist times', *Feminist Media Studies* 16/4, 610–30.
Gill, Rosalind and Christina Scharff (2011). 'Introduction', in Rosalind Gill and Christina Scharff (eds), *New Femininities: Postfeminism, Neoliberalism and Subjectivity*, Basingstoke: Palgrave Macmillan, pp. 1–17.
Gill, Rosalind, Hannah Hamad, Mariam Kauser, Diane Negra and Nayomi Roshini (2016). 'Intergenerational feminism and media: a roundtable', *Feminist Media Studies* 16/4, pp. 726–36.
Gillota, David (2010). 'Negotiating Jewishness: *Curb Your Enthusiasm* and the schlemiel tradition', *Journal of Popular Film and Television* 38/4, pp. 152–61.
GLAAD (2016). *Where We Are on TV: GLAAD's Annual Report on LGBTQ Inclusion 16–17*, http://glaad.org/files/WWAT/WWAT_GLAAD_2016–2017.pdf (accessed 12 November 2016).
GLAAD (n.d.). 'Annual GLAAD media awards', http://www.glaad.org/mediaawards (accessed 23 January 2018).
Glenn, Susan A. (2000). *Female Spectacle: The Theatrical Roots of Modern Feminism*, Cambridge, MA and London: Harvard University Press.
Glitre, Kathrina (2011). 'Nancy Meyers and "popular feminism"', in Melanie Waters (ed.), *Women on Screen: Feminism and Femininity in Visual Culture*, Basingstoke: Palgrave Macmillan, pp. 17–30.
Goldberg, Lesley (2016). '*Big Bang Theory* evolution: How TV's nerdy comedy grew into a family show', *Hollywood Reporter*, 24 February. Available at http://www.hollywoodreporter.com/live-feed/big-bang-theory-evolution-how–869049 (accessed 14 November 2016).
Gorton, Kristyn (2016). '"I'm too old to pretend anymore": desire, ageing and *Last Tango in Halifax*', in Maricel Oró Piqueras and Anita Wohlmann (eds), *Serializing Age: Aging and Old Age in TV Series*, Bielefeld: Transcript Verlag, pp. 231–47.
Gray, Frances (1994). *Women and Laughter*, Charlottesville: University Press of Virginia.
Greene, Doyle (2008). *Politics and the American Television Comedy: A Critical Survey from I Love Lucy to South Park*, London and Jefferson, NC: McFarland.
Grote, David (1983). *The End of Comedy: The Sit-com and the Comedic Tradition*, Hamdon, CT: Archon.

Gullette, Margaret Morganroth (2004). *Aged by Culture*, Chicago and London: University of Chicago Press.
Halberstam, Judith (1998). *Female Masculinity*, Durham, NC and London: Duke University Press.
——— (2005). *In a Queer Time and Place: Transgender Bodies, Subcultural Lives*, New York and London: New York University Press.
——— (2011). *The Queer Art of Failure*, Durham, NC and London: Duke University Press.
——— (2012). *Gaga Feminism: Sex, Gender and the End of Normal*, Boston: Beacon Press.
Hallam, Julia (2005). 'Remembering *Butterflies*: the comic art of housework', in Jonathan Bignell and Stephen Lacey (eds), *Popular Television Comedy: Critical Perspectives*, Manchester: Manchester University Press, pp. 34–50.
Halley, Janet E. (1993). 'The construction of heterosexuality', in Michael Warner (ed.), *Fear of a Queer Planet: Queer Politics and Social Theory*, Minneapolis and London: University of Minnesota Press, pp. 82–102.
Halttunen, Karen (1982). *Confidence Men and Painted Women: A Study of Middle-class Culture in America, 1830–1870*, New Haven: Yale University Press.
Hamad, Hannah (2016). 'Contemporary medical television and crisis in the NHS', *Critical Studies in Television* 11/2, pp. 136–50.
Handy, Bruce (2016). 'An oral history of Amy Schumer's "Last fuckable day" sketch', *Vanity Fair*, 3 May. Available at http://www.vanityfair.com/hollywood/2016/05/amy-schumer-last-fuckable-day (accessed 20 December 2016).
Hanke, Robert (1998). 'On masculinity: theorizing masculinity with/in the media', *Communication Theory* 8/2, pp. 183–203.
Haralovich, Mary Beth (2003). 'Sitcoms and suburbs: positioning the 1950s homemaker', in Joanne Morreale (ed.), *Critiquing the Sitcom: A Reader*, New York: Syracuse University Press, pp. 69–85.
Harris, Paul (2011). 'Sexy, sassy, funny: new breed of US sitcoms puts the women in charge', *The Observer*, 23 September, p. 27.
Harrison, Andrew (2013). 'Le geek, c'est chic', *The Guardian G2*, 3 September, pp. 6–9.
Healy, Patrick (2012). 'Stalked by shadows (and a rabbit)', *New York Times*, 23 May. Available at http://www.nytimes.com/2012/05/27/theater/jim-parsons-prepares-for-his-lead-role-in-harvey.html (accessed 12 November 2016).
Heasley, Robert (2005). 'Queer Masculinities of Straight Men: A Typology', *Men and Masculinities*, 7/3, pp. 310–20.
Hibberd, James (2010). 'Why this man has 40,000,000 million [*sic*] viewers', *Hollywood Reporter*, 22 November. Available at http://www.hollywoodreporter.com/news/man-40000000-million-viewers-47805 (accessed 10 January 2018).
Hitchens, Christopher (2007). 'Why women aren't funny', *Vanity Fair*, January. Available at http://www.vanityfair.com/culture/features/2007/01/hitchens 200701 (accessed 8 October 2013).
HMSO (1990). *Broadcasting Act 1990, Chapter 42*. Available at http://www.legislation.gov.uk/ukpga/1990/42/pdfs/ukpga_19900042_en.pdf (accessed 16 August 2016).
Holdsworth, Amy and Karen Lury (2016). 'Growing up and growing old with television: peripheral viewers and the centrality of care', *Screen* 57/1, pp. 184–96.

Horowitz, Susan (1997). *Queens of Comedy: Lucille Ball, Phyllis Diller, Carol Burnett, Joan Rivers, and the New Generation of Funny Women*, Amsterdam: Gordon and Breach.

Howard-Williams, Rowan and Elihu Katz (2013). 'Did television empower women? The introduction of television and the changing status of women in the 1950s', *Journal of Popular Television* 1/1, pp. 7–24.

Hozier-Byrne, Jon (2013). 'An addiction I cured with my mind: Charlie Sheen and the gendered narrative of celebrity mental illness', unpublished paper presented at Console-ing Passions conference, De Montfort University, Leicester, UK, 23–25 June.

Huver, Scott (2016). 'Jim Parsons on *Big Bang Theory*'s future, why he relishes Sheldon's obliviousness', *Variety*, 25 February. Available at http://variety.com/2016/tv/news/big-bang-theory-jim-parsons-sheldon-oblivious-1201715273/ (accessed 12 November 2016).

Ingraham, Chrys (2005). *Thinking Straight: The Power, the Promise, and the Paradox of Heterosexuality*, New York and London: Routledge.

Irigaray, Luce (1985). *This Sex Which Is Not One*, trans. Catherine Porter, Ithaca: Cornell University Press.

Jagose, Annamarie (1996). *Queer Theory: An Introduction*, New York: New York University Press.

Jakobson, Janet R. (1998). 'Queer is? Queer does? Normativity and the problem of resistance', *GLQ: A Journal of Lesbian and Gay Studies* 4/4, pp. 511–36.

Jenkins, Henry (1992). *What Made Pistachio Nuts? Early Sound Comedy and the Vaudeville Aesthetic*, New York: Columbia University Press.

Jenkins, Henry and Kristine Brunovska Karnick (1995). 'Acting funny', in Kristine Brunovska Karnick and Henry Jenkins (eds), *Classical Hollywood Comedy*, London and New York: Routledge, pp. 149–67.

Jenni_Snake (2013). 'Now that we've found love…', Howard and Raj online slash fiction, http://archiveofourown.org/works/870857?view_adult=true (accessed 15 August 2013).

Jennings, Ros and Maricel Oró-Piqueras (2016). 'Heroine and/or caricature? The older woman in *Desperate Housewives*', in Maricel Oró Piqueras and Anita Wohlmann (eds), *Serializing Age: Aging and Old Age in TV Series*, Bielefeld: Transcript Verlag, pp. 69–86.

Jermyn, Deborah (2009). *Sex and the City*, Detroit: Wayne State University Press.

——— (2013). 'Past their prime time? Women, ageing and absence on British factual television', *Critical Studies in Television* 8/1, pp. 73–90.

Johnson, Beth (2016). '*Getting On*: ageing, mess and the NHS', *Critical Studies in Television* 11/2, pp. 190–203.

Johnson, Carla (1994). 'Luckless in New York: the schlemiel and the schlimazl in *Seinfeld*', *Journal of Popular Film and Television* 22/3, pp. 117–24.

Joseph, Jenny (1997). *WARNING: When I Am an Old Woman I Shall Wear Purple*, London: Souvenir Press.

Joyrich, Lynne (2009). 'Epistemology of the console', in Glyn Davis and Gary Needham (eds), *Queer TV: Theories, Histories, Politics*, London and New York: Routledge, pp. 15–47.

——— (2014). 'Queer television studies: currents, flows, and (main)streams', *Cinema Journal* 53/2, pp. 133–9.

Kane, Matt (2011). 'NBC's Tina Fey and Bob Greenblatt respond to Tracy Morgan's rant', *GLAAD*, 10 June. Available at http://www.glaad.org/2011/06/10/nbcs-tina-fey-and-bob-greenblatt-respond-to-tracy-morgans-rant (accessed 5 November 2013).

Kanfer, Stefan (2003). *Ball of Fire: The Tumultuous Life and Comic Art of Lucille Ball*, London: Faber and Faber.

Karpf, Anne (2013). 'Radio silence', *Guardian Saturday Review*, 2 February, p. 18.

Kessler, Kelly (2006). 'Politics of the sitcom formula: *Friends*, *Mad About You* and the sapphic second banana', in James R. Keller and Leslie Stratyner (eds), *The New Queer Aesthetic on Television*, Jefferson, NC and London: McFarland & Company, pp. 130–46.

Kimmel, Michael (2004), 'Masculinity as homophobia: fear, shame, and silence in the construction of gender identity', in Peter Murphy (ed.), *Feminism and Masculinities*, Oxford: Oxford University Press, pp. 182–99.

Knope, Leslie (2011). *Pawnee: The Greatest Town in America*, New York: Hyperion.

Küpper, Thomas (2016). '"Blanche and the younger man": Age mimicry and the ambivalence of laughter in *The Golden Girls*', in Maricel Oró Piqueras and Anita Wohlmann (eds), *Serializing Age: Aging and Old Age in TV Series*, Bielefeld: Transcript Verlag, pp. 249–66.

Landay, Lori (1998). *Madcaps, Screwballs, and Con Women: The Female Trickster in American Culture*, Philadelphia: University of Pennsylvania Press.

―― (2010). *I Love Lucy*, Detroit: Wayne State University Press.

Lang, Brent (2017). 'Natalie Morales calls Christopher Hitchens an "A-hole" for saying that women aren't funny', *Variety*, 29 March. Available at http://variety.com/2017/biz/news/natalie-morales-christopher-hitchens-women-funny-1202018705/ (accessed 24 July 2017).

Lavery, David (2012). 'The state of the American sitcom III: *The Big Bang Theory*', *CST Online*, http://web.archive.org/web/20160419021804/http://cstonline.tv/telegenic-9 (accessed 10 January 2018).

Lavigne, Carlen (2013). 'Two men and a moustache: masculinity, nostalgia and bromance in *The Good Guys*', *Journal of Popular Television* 1/1, pp. 69–81.

Lavin, Suzanne (2004). *Women and Comedy in Solo Performance: Phyllis Diller, Lily Tomlin and Roseanne*, New York: Routledge.

Lawson, Mark (2011). 'Unusual tactics make sense', *The Guardian*, 26 February, p. 3.

Leggott, James and Sexton, Jamie (2013). *No Known Cure: The Comedy of Chris Morris*, London: BFI.

Leitch, Will (2009). 'The Poehler effect', *New York Magazine*, 5 April. Available at http://nymag.com/arts/tv/features/55851/ (accessed 28 November 2013).

Lewisohn, Mark (2003). *Radio Times Guide to TV Comedy*, London: BBC.

Lloyd, Moya (1999). 'Performativity, parody, politics', *Theory, Culture and Society* 16/2, pp. 195–213.

Lockyer, Sharon (2010a). 'Chavs and Chav-nots: social class in *Little Britain*', in Sharon Lockyer (ed.), *Reading Little Britain*, London: I.B.Tauris, pp. 95–109.

Lockyer, Sharon (ed.) (2010b). *Reading Little Britain*, London: I.B.Tauris.

Lotz, Amanda (2006). *Redesigning Women: Television After the Network Era*, Urbana and Chicago: University of Illinois Press.

Macdonald, Barbara and Cynthia Rich (1984). *Look Me in the Eye: Old Women, Aging and Ageism*, London: The Women's Press.

Mann, Denise (1992). 'The spectacularization of everyday life: recycling Hollywood stars and fans in early television variety shows', in Lynn Spigel and Denise Mann (eds), *Private Screenings: Television and the Female Consumer*, Minneapolis and London: University of Minnesota Press, pp. 41–70.

Marc, David (1989). *Comic Visions: Television Comedy and American Culture*, Boston: Unwin Hyman.

Martin, Daniel (2016). '*The Big Bang Theory*: show returns for tenth season but is it time it went bust?', *The Guardian*, 19 September. Available at https://www.theguardian.com/tv-and-radio/2016/sep/19/the-big-bang-theory-season–10-premiere-bust (accessed 21 November 2016).

Martin, Denise (2009). 'Making bureaucracy work: how NBC's *Parks and Recreation* overcame bad buzz', *Los Angeles Times*, 18 November. Available at http://latimesblogs.latimes.com/showtracker/2009/11/parks-and-recreation.html (accessed 28 November 2013).

Martin, Linda and Kerry Seagrave (1986). *Women in Comedy*, Secaucus, NJ: Citadel Press.

McCann, Hannah (2015). 'Pantomime dames: queer femininity versus "natural beauty" in *Snog, Marry, Avoid*', *Australian Feminist Studies* 30/85, pp. 238–51.

McCracken, Allison (2002). 'Study of a mad housewife: psychiatric discourse, the suburban home and the case of Gracie Allen', in Janet Thumim (ed.), *Small Screens, Big Ideas: Television in the 1950s*, New York and London: I.B.Tauris, pp. 50–65.

McIntosh, Heather (2014). 'Representations of female scientists in *The Big Bang Theory*', *Journal of Popular Film and Television* 42/4, pp. 195–204.

McRobbie, Angela (2004). 'Postfeminism and popular culture', *Feminist Media Studies* 4/3, pp. 255–64.

——— (2009). *The Aftermath of Feminism: Gender, Culture and Social Change*, London: Sage.

——— (2011). 'Preface', in Rosalind Gill and Christina Scharff (eds), *New Femininities: Postfeminism, Neoliberalism and Subjectivity*, Basingstoke: Palgrave Macmillan, pp. xi–xv.

Medhurst, Andy (2007). *A National Joke: Popular Comedy and English Cultural Identities*, London and New York: Routledge.

Medhurst, Andy and Lucy Tuck (1982). 'The gender game', in Jim Cook (ed.), *BFI Dossier 17: Television Sitcom*, London: British Film Institute, pp. 43–55.

Mellencamp, Patricia (1992). *High Anxiety: Catastrophe, Scandal, Age and Comedy*, Bloomington and Indianapolis: Indiana University Press.

——— (1999). 'From anxiety to equanimity: crisis and generational continuity on TV, at the movies, in life, in death', in Kathleen Woodward (ed.), *Figuring Age: Women, Bodies, Generations*, Bloomington and Indianapolis: Indiana University Press, pp. 310–28.

——— (2003). 'Situation comedy, feminism, and Freud: discourses of Gracie and Lucy', in Joanne Morreale (ed.), *Critiquing the Sitcom: A Reader*, New York: Syracuse University Press, pp. 41–55.

Merck, Mandy (2005). 'Afterword', in Iain Morland and Annabelle Willox (eds), *Queer Theory*, Basingstoke: Palgrave Macmillan, pp. 187–91.

Meyerowitz, Joanne (1993). 'Beyond the feminine mystique: a reassessment of postwar mass culture, 1946–58', *Journal of American History* 79/4, pp. 1455–82.

BIBLIOGRAPHY

Miller, Julie (2013). 'The Big Bang Theory moves Steve Wozniak to tears', The Hollywood Blog, *Vanity Fair Online*, 12 August, http://www.vanityfair.com/online/oscars/2013/08/steve-wozniak-big-bang-theory (accessed 13 August 2013).

Miller, Margo (2006). 'Masculinity and male intimacy in nineties sitcoms: *Seinfeld* and the ironic dismissal', in James R. Keller and Leslie Stratyner (eds), *The New Queer Aesthetic on Television*, Jefferson, NC and London: McFarland & Company, pp. 147–59.

Mills, Alice (1999). 'Introduction', in Alice Mills (ed.), *Seriously Weird: Papers on the Grotesque*, New York: Peter Lang, pp. 1–11.

Mills, Brett (2008). 'Contemporary sitcom ("comedy vérité")', in Glen Creeber (ed.), *The Television Genre Book*, 2nd edition, Basingstoke: BFI/Palgrave Macmillan, pp. 88–91.

—— (2009). *The Sitcom*, Edinburgh: Edinburgh University Press.

Mills, Brett and Sarah Ralph (2015). '"I think women are possibly judged more harshly with comedy": women and British television comedy production', *Critical Studies in Television* 10/2, pp. 102–17.

Mitchell, Danielle (2006). 'Straight and crazy? Bisexual and easy? Or drunken floozy? The queer politics of Karen Walker', in James R. Keller and Leslie Stratyner (eds), *The New Queer Aesthetic on Television*, Jefferson, NC and London: McFarland & Company, pp. 85–98.

Mittell, Jason (2006). 'Narrative complexity in contemporary American sitcom', *Velvet Light Trap*, 58/Fall, pp. 29–40.

Mizejewski, Linda (2007). 'Queen Latifah, unruly women and the bodies of romantic comedy', *Genders* 46, http://web.archive.org/web/20141105100442/http://www.genders.org:80/g46/g46_mizejewski.html (accessed 10 January 2018).

—— (2012). 'Feminism, postfeminism, Liz Lemonism: comedy and gender politics on *30 Rock*', *Genders* 55, http://web.archive.org/web/20140516201432/http://www.genders.org:80/g55/g55_mizejewski.html (accessed 8 January 2018).

—— (2014). *Pretty/Funny: Women Comedians and Body Politics*, Austin: University of Texas Press.

Modleski, Tania (1986). 'Femininity as mas(s)querade: a feminist approach to mass culture', in Colin McCabe (ed.), *High Theory/Low Culture: Analysing Popular Television and Film*, Manchester: Manchester University Press, pp. 37–52.

Morreale, Joanne (2003a). 'Sitcoms say goodbye: the cultural spectacle of *Seinfeld*'s last episode', in Joanne Morreale (ed.), *Critiquing the Sitcom: A Reader*, New York: Syracuse University Press, pp. 274–85.

Morreale, Joanne (ed.) (2003b). *Critiquing the Sitcom: A Reader*, New York: Syracuse University Press.

Mortimer, Claire (2015). 'Angry old women: Peggy Mount and the performance of female aging in British sitcom', *Critical Studies in Television* 10/2, pp. 71–86.

Mowatt, Ian (2010). 'Analysing *Little Britain* as a sketch show', in Sharon Lockyer (ed.), *Reading Little Britain: Comedy Matters on Contemporary Television*, London and New York: I.B.Tauris, pp. 19–33.

Mulshine, Molly (2015). 'The 80s version of Tinder was "video dating" – and it looks incredibly awkward', *Business Insider UK*, 1 December, http://uk.businessinsider.com/found-footage-awkward-80s-video-dating-2015-12?r=US&IR=T (accessed 25 October 2016).

Mulvey, Laura (1986). 'Melodrama in and out of the home', in Colin McCabe (ed.), *High Theory/Low Culture: Analysing Popular Television and Film*, Manchester: Manchester University Press, pp. 80–100.

——— (1989). 'Visual pleasure and narrative cinema', in *Visual and Other Pleasures*, Bloomington: Indiana University Press, pp. 14–26 (originally published in *Screen* 16 (1975), pp. 6–18).

——— (2017). 'Thoughts on Marilyn Monroe: emblem and allegory', *Screen* 58/2, pp. 202–9.

Munford, Rebecca and Melanie Waters (2014). *Feminism and Popular Culture: Investigating the Postfeminist Mystique*, London and New York: I.B.Tauris.

Murphy, Bernice M. (2009). *The Suburban Gothic in American Popular Culture*, Basingstoke: Palgrave Macmillan.

Murray, Susan (2002). 'Ethnic masculinity and early television's vaudeo star', *Cinema Journal* 42/1, pp. 97–119.

Neale, Steve and Frank Krutnik (1990). *Popular Film and Television Comedy*, London and New York: Routledge.

Needham, Gary (2009). 'Scheduling normativity: television, the family and queer temporality', in Glyn Davis and Gary Needham (eds), *Queer TV: Theories, Histories, Politics*, London and New York: Routledge, pp. 143–58.

New York Times (1964), 'Gracie Allen dead: comedienne was 58', *New York Times*, 29 August, pp. 1, 21.

Nussbaum, Emily (2012a). 'I love Leslie: *Parks and Recreation* and the puzzle of sitcom originality', *New Yorker*, 22 October. Available at http://www.newyorker.com/arts/critics/television/2012/10/22/121022crte_television_nussbaum (accessed 29 November 2013).

——— (2012b). 'In defense of Liz Lemon', *New Yorker*, 23 February. Available at http://www.newyorker.com/online/blogs/culture/2012/02/in-defense-of-liz-lemon.html (accessed 28 October 2013).

——— (2013). '*30 Rock*: I love this dirty sitcom', *New Yorker*, 31 January. Available at http://www.newyorker.com/online/blogs/culture/2013/01/30-rock-i-love-this-dirty-sitcom.html (accessed 24 October 2013).

Olson, Elder (1968). *The Theory of Comedy*, Bloomington and London: Indiana University Press.

Patterson, Eleanor (2012). 'Fracturing Tina Fey: a critical analysis of postfeminist television comedy stardom', *Communication Review* 15, pp. 232–51.

——— (2016). '*The Golden Girls Live*: residual television texts, participatory culture, and queering TV heritage through drag', *Feminist Media Studies* 16/5, pp. 838–51.

Peterson, Latoya (2009). '*The Big Bang Theory*, nerds of color, and stereotypes', *Racialicious*, http://web.archive.org/web/20151003002653/http://www.racialicious.com/2009/03/10/the-big-bang-theory-nerds-of-color-and-stereotypes/ (accessed 10 January 2018).

Petro, Patrice (1986). 'Mass culture and the feminine: the "place" of television in film studies', *Cinema Journal* 25/3, pp. 5–21.

Pilkington, Ed (2011). 'America's favourite sitcom cancelled after rant leaves Sheen looking a proper Charlie', *The Guardian*, 26 February, p. 3.

Piper, Helen (2016). 'Broadcast drama and the problem of television aesthetics: home, nation, universe', *Screen* 57/2, pp. 163–83.

Bibliography

Port, Cynthia (2012). 'No future? Aging, temporality, history, and reverse chronologies', *Occasion: Interdisciplinary Studies in the Humanities* 4, pp. 1–19. Available at http://arcade.stanford.edu/occasion/no-future-aging-temporality-history-and-reverse-chronologies (accessed 10 January 2018).

Projansky, Sarah (2007). 'Mass magazine cover girls: some reflections on postfeminist girls and postfeminism's daughters', in Yvonne Tasker and Diane Negra (eds), *Interrogating Postfeminism: Gender and the Politics of Popular Culture*, Durham, NC and London: Duke University Press, pp. 40–72.

Przybylo, Ela (2011). 'Crisis and safety: the asexual in sexusociety', *Sexualities* 14/4, pp. 444–61.

Rabinovitz, Lauren (1999). 'Ms.-representation: the politics of feminist sitcoms', in Mary Beth Haralovich and Lauren Rabinovitz (eds), *Television, History and American Culture: Feminist Critical Essays*, Durham, NC and London: Duke University Press, pp. 144–67.

Rapf, Joanna E. (2003). 'Comic theory from a feminist perspective: a look at Jerry Lewis', in Frank Krutnik (ed.), *Hollywood Comedians: The Film Reader*, London: Routledge, pp. 145–54.

Raphael, Amy (2006). '*Green Wing*'s midwife and surgeon', *The Telegraph*, 29 March. Available at http://www.telegraph.co.uk/culture/tvandradio/3651213/Green-Wings-midwife-and-surgeon.html (accessed 18 October 2016).

Rawitsch, Elizabeth (2014). 'Silence isn't golden, girls: the cross-generational comedy of "America's grandma" Betty White', in Imelda Whelehan and Joel Gwynne (eds), *Ageing, Popular Culture and Contemporary Feminism: Harleys and Hormones*, Basingstoke and New York: Palgrave Macmillan, pp. 172–86.

Riviere, Joan (1986). 'Womanliness as a masquerade', in Victor Burgin, J. Donald and Cora Kaplan (eds), *Formations of Fantasy*, London: Routledge, pp. 45–61 (originally published in *International Journal of Psychoanalysis* 10 (1929), pp. 303–13).

Roberts, Martin (2007). 'The fashion police: governing the self in *What Not to Wear*', in Yvonne Tasker and Diane Negra (eds), *Interrogating Postfeminism: Gender and the Politics of Popular Culture*, Durham, NC and London: Duke University Press, pp. 227–48.

Roof, Judith (2002). *All About Thelma and Eve: Sidekicks and Third Wheels*, Urbana and Chicago: University of Illinois Press.

Rowe, Kathleen (1995). *The Unruly Woman: Gender and the Genres of Laughter*, Austin: University of Texas Press.

Rubin, Gayle (1975). 'The traffic in women: notes on the political economy of sex', in Rayna R. Reiter (ed.), *Toward An Anthropology Of Women*, New York: Monthly Review Press, pp. 157–210.

Russo, Mary (1986). 'Female grotesques: carnival and theory', in Teresa De Lauretis (ed.), *Feminist Studies/Critical Studies*, Basingstoke: Macmillan, pp. 213–29.

——— (1995). *The Female Grotesque: Risk, Excess, and Modernity*, Abingdon and New York: Routledge.

Sandberg, Linn (2008). 'The old, the ugly and the queer: thinking old age in relation to queer theory', *Graduate Journal of Social Science* 5/2, pp. 117–39.

——— (2013). 'Affirmative old age: the ageing body and feminist theories on difference', *International Journal of Ageing and Later Life* 8/1, pp. 11–40.

Saunders, Jennifer (2013). *Bonkers: My Life in Laughs*, London: Viking.

SB (2016). 'BBC3's top tens put comedians and you in the driver's seat', *BBC Media Centre*, 14 July, http://www.bbc.co.uk/mediacentre/latestnews/2016/bbc-three-top-tens (accessed 14 February 2016).

Schaffer, Gavin (2016). 'Fighting Thatcher with comedy: what to do when there is no alternative', *Journal of British Studies* 55, pp. 374–97.

Scharff, Christina (2016). 'The psychic life of neoliberalism: mapping the contours of entrepreneurial subjectivity', *Theory, Culture and Society* 33/6, pp. 107–22.

Seidman, Steven (1997). *Difference Troubles: Queering Social Theory and Sexual Politics*, Cambridge: Cambridge University Press.

Shaw, Sally (2012). '"Light entertainment" as contested socio-political space: audience and institutional responses to *Love Thy Neighbour* (1972–76)', *Critical Studies in Television* 7/2, pp. 64–78.

Shildrick, Margrit (2015). 'Living on; not getting better', *Feminist Review* 111, pp. 10–24.

Shuttleworth, Rachel (2015). 'Welcome back, Stephen Colbert – honorary smart girl!', *Amy Poehler's Smart Girls*, 8 September, https://amysmartgirls.com/welcome-back-stephen-colbert-honorary-smart-girl-1410fbe8e22d (accessed 8 January 2018).

Silverman, Stephen M. (1999). *Funny Ladies: The Women Who Make Us Laugh*, New York: Harry N. Abrams.

Simpson, Mark (1998). 'The straight men of comedy', in Stephen Wagg (ed.), *Because I Tell a Joke or Two: Comedy, Politics and Social Difference*, London and New York: Routledge, pp. 137–45.

Smit, Alexia (2015). '"On the spectator side of the screen": considering space, gender, and visual pleasure in television', *Feminist Media Studies* 15/5, pp. 892–5.

Smith, Angela (2011). 'Femininity repackaged: postfeminism and *Ladette to Lady*', in Melanie Waters (ed.), *Women on Screen: Feminism and Femininity in Visual Culture*, Basingstoke: Palgrave Macmillan, pp. 153–66.

Spangler, Lynn C. (1992). 'Buddies and pals: a history of male friendships on prime-time television', in Steve Craig (ed.), *Men, Masculinity and the Media*, London: Sage, pp. 93–110.

——— (2003). *Television Women from Lucy to Friends: Fifty Years of Sitcoms and Feminism*, Westport, CT and London: Praeger.

Spanos, Brittany (2015). 'Watch nuns Tina Fey and Amy Poehler help *Broad City* girls', *Rolling Stone*, 15 December, http://www.rollingstone.com/movies/news/watch-nuns-tina-fey-amy-poehler-help-broad-city-girls-20151215 (accessed 20 December 2016).

Spigel, Lynn (1992a). 'Installing the television set: popular discourses on television and domestic space, 1948–1955', in Lynn Spigel and Denise Mann (eds.), *Private Screenings: Television and the Female Consumer*, Minneapolis and London: University of Minnesota Press, pp. 3–38.

——— (1992b). *Make Room for TV: Television and the Family Ideal in Postwar America*, Chicago: University of Chicago Press.

——— (2001). *Welcome to the Dream House: Popular Media and the Postwar Suburbs*, Durham, NC and London: Duke University Press.

Spigel, Lynn and Mann, Denise (1992). 'Introduction', in Lynn Spigel and Denise Mann (eds), *Private Screenings: Television and the Female Consumer*, Minneapolis and London: University of Minnesota Press, pp. vii–xiii.

BIBLIOGRAPHY

Stanley, Alessandra (2008). 'Who says women aren't funny?', *Vanity Fair*, April. Available at http://www.vanityfair.com/culture/features/2008/04/funny girls200804?printable=true (accessed 8 March 2010).
Stober, JoAnne (2007). 'Vaudeville: the incarnation, transformation, and resilience of an entertainment form', in Charles R. Acland (ed.), *Residual Media*, Minneapolis: University of Minnesota Press, pp. 133–55.
Stott, Andrew (2005). *Comedy*, New York and London: Routledge.
Sullivan, Nikki (2003). *A Critical Introduction to Queer Theory*, Edinburgh: Edinburgh University Press.
Tasker, Yvonne (1998). *Working Girls: Gender and Sexuality in Popular Cinema*, London and New York: Routledge.
Tasker, Yvonne and Diane Negra (2007). 'Introduction: feminist politics and postfeminist culture', in Yvonne Tasker and Diane Negra (eds), *Interrogating Postfeminism: Gender and the Politics of Popular Culture*, Durham, NC and London: Duke University Press, pp. 1–25.
Thompson, Ethan (2007). 'Comedy vérité? The observational documentary meets the televisual sitcom', *Velvet Light Trap* 60/Fall, pp. 63–72.
Thompson, Lauren Jade (2015). 'Nothing suits me like a suit: performing masculinity in *How I Met Your Mother*', *Critical Studies in Television* 10/2, pp. 21–36.
Thompson, Robert J. (1996) 'Television's second golden age: the quality shows', *Television Quarterly*, 28/3, pp. 75–81.
Thurm, Eric (2015). 'Why *Parks and Recreation*'s final season was its best ever', *Wired*, 23 February, https://www.wired.com/2015/02/parks-and-rec-ending/ (accessed 17 December 2016).
Tongson, Karen (2011). *Relocations: Queer Suburban Imaginaries*, New York and London: New York University Press.
University of Bristol (n.d.). *University of Bristol Theatre Collection*, http://www.bris.ac.uk/theatrecollection/search/people_sub_plays_all?forename=Lally&surname=BOWERS&job=Actor&pid=5057&image_view=Yesamp;x=19amp;y=17 (accessed 30 June 2016).
Unterbrink, Mary (1987). *Funny Women: American Comediennes 1860–1985*, Jefferson, NC and London: McFarland.
Waddell, Terrie (1999). 'Revelling in dis-play: the grotesque in *Absolutely Fabulous*', in Alice Mills (ed.), *Seriously Weird: Papers on the Grotesque*, New York: Peter Lang, pp. 207–23.
Walsh, Kimberly R., Elfriede Fürsich and Bonnie S. Jefferson (2008). 'Beauty and the patriarchal beast: gender role portrayals in sitcoms featuring mismatched couples', *Journal of Popular Film and Television* 36/3, pp. 123–32.
Warner, Michael (1993). 'Introduction', in Michael Warner (ed.), *Fear of a Queer Planet: Queer Politics and Social Theory*, Minneapolis and London: University of Minnesota Press, pp. vii–xxxi.
Wearing, Sadie (2007). 'Subjects of rejuvenation: aging in postfeminist culture', in Yvonne Tasker and Diane Negra (eds), *Interrogating Postfeminism: Gender and the Politics of Popular Culture*, Durham, NC and London: Duke University Press, pp. 277–310.
——— (2011). 'Notes on some scandals: the politics of shame in *Vers le Sud*', in Rosalind Gill and Christina Scharff (eds), *New Femininities: Postfeminism, Neoliberalism and Subjectivity*, Basingstoke and New York: Palgrave Macmillan, pp. 173–87.

Weigman, Robyn (2010). 'The intimacy of critique: ruminations on feminism as a living thing', *Feminist Theory* 11/1, pp. 79–84.

Weitekamp, Margaret A. (2015). '"We're physicists": gender, genre and the image of scientists in *The Big Bang Theory*', *Journal of Popular Television* 3/1, pp. 75–92.

Wheatley, Helen (2016). *Spectacular Television: Exploring Televisual Pleasure*, London and New York: I.B.Tauris.

Whelehan, Imelda (2000). *Overloaded: Popular Culture and the Future of Feminism*, London: The Women's Press.

White, Rosie (2010). 'Funny women', *Feminist Media Studies* 10/3, pp. 355–8.

——— (2014a). '*Beryl Reid Says ... Good Evening*: performing queer identity on British television', *Journal of European Popular Culture* 5/2, pp. 165–80.

——— (2014b). 'Funny old girls: representing older women in British television comedy', in Imelda Whelehan and Joel Gwynne (eds), *Ageing, Popular Culture and Contemporary Feminism: Harleys and Hormones*, Basingstoke and New York: Palgrave Macmillan, pp. 155–71.

——— (2016). 'Funny *peculiar*: Lucille Ball and the vaudeville heritage of early American television comedy', *Social Semiotics* 26/3, pp. 298–310.

——— (2017). 'Roseanne Barr: remembering *Roseanne*', in Linda Mizejewski and Victoria Sturtevant (eds), *Hysterical! Women in American Comedy*, Austin: University of Texas Press, pp. 233–50.

Winch, Alison, Jo Littler and Jessalynn Keller (2016). 'Why "intergenerational feminist media studies"?', *Feminist Media Studies* 16/4, pp. 557–72.

Wilmut, Roger and Peter Rosengard (1989). *Didn't You Kill My Mother-in-Law? The Story of Alternative Comedy in Britain from the Comedy Store to Saturday Live*, London: Methuen.

Williams, Holly (2013). 'Funny business: meet the women running comedy', *The Independent*, 4 August. Available at http://www.independent.co.uk/arts-entertainment/comedy/features/funny-business-meet-the-women-running-comedy-8742853.html (accessed 9 December 2016).

Williams, Melanie (2011). 'Entering the paradise of anomalies: studying female character acting in British cinema', *Screen* 52/1, pp. 97–104.

Williams, Zoe (2016). 'Doon Mackichan: we were sexy, funny women – perhaps that was a bit much', *The Guardian*, 20 November. Available at https://www.theguardian.com/tv-and-radio/2016/nov/20/doon-mackichan-sexy-funny-women-interview-two-doors-down-smack-the-pony (accessed 13 February 2017).

Wohlmann, Anita, and Maricel Oró-Piqueras (2016). 'Serial narrative, temporality and aging: an introduction', in Maricel Oró Piqueras and Anita Wohlmann (eds), *Serializing Age: Aging and Old Age in TV Series*, Bielefeld: Transcript Verlag, pp. 9–21.

Woodward, Kathleen (1999). 'Introduction', in Kathleen Woodward (ed.), *Figuring Age: Women, Bodies, Generations*, Bloomington and Indianapolis: Indiana University Press, pp. ix–xxix.

——— (2006). 'Performing age, performing gender', *National Women's Studies Association Journal* 18/1, pp. 162–89.

Wyatt, Edward (2009). 'The big surprise of *Big Bang*: the bigger audience', *New York Times*, 4 October. Available at http://www.nytimes.com/2009/10/05/arts/television/05bang.html (accessed 8 November 2016).

Zakos, Katherine (2013). 'Gendering geekiness on *The Big Bang Theory*', *In Media Res*, 23 September, http://mediacommons.futureofthebook.org/imr/2013/09/23/gendering-geekiness-big-bang-theory (accessed 1 October 2013).

Zarum, Lara (2017). 'Why men aren't funny, or, how spectacularly wrong Christopher Hitchens was about women and comedy', *Flavorwire*, 7 February. Available at http://flavorwire.com/599121/why-men-arent-funny-or-how-spectacularly-wrong-christopher-hitchens-was-about-women-and-comedy (accessed 24 July 2017).

INDEX

30 Rock, 21–2, 57–8, 62–5, 67–78, 201, 203

Absolutely Fabulous, 2, 5, 64
Adorno, Theodor, 21, 35
ageing, 23, 159–97
Alexander, Jean, 168, 170
Allen, Gracie, 25, 26, 29–30, 32–4, 37–8, 43, 172
Arden, Eve, 21, 25, 35–7, 43
Arnaz, Desi, 25, 47
asexuality, 113, 115, 174

Ball, Lucille, 16, 21, 25, 35–6, 43–56, 136
BBC, 181–2
Berle, Milton, 38, 49
Big Bang Theory, The, 22, 90–4, 99, 101–21, 201
Bowers, Lally, 169–71
Brand, Jo, 23, 127, 140
Broad City, 89
Burns and Allen Show, The, 21, 26–35, 123, 129
Burns, George, 26–8, 32–3, 37
Butler, Judith, 2–6, 8–10, 12–15, 113, 133–6, 164–5, 199–200, 202–3
Butterflies, 2

camp, 98, 99, 109, 114, 131, 153, 167, 174
Cannon, Esma, 169
CBS, 91–2, 99, 113–14, 120
Cole, Stephanie, 179–80
Coombs, Pat, 169–71
Cooper, Sheldon, 92, 94, 102, 111–18
Coronation Street, 124, 168, 179
Cruikshank, Margaret, 181, 184–5, 195, 197

Daisy Doodad's Dial, 16
Davis, Julia, 153–4
DeGeneres, Ellen, 136–7
Dolan, Josephine, 163
Doty, Alexander, 13–17, 21, 43, 48–9, 51–2

failure, 93, 121, 200–1
feminism, 19, 54–5, 89–90, 119–20, 126–8, 133, 138, 141–2, 156–7, 203–4
and production practices, 140–5
Fey, Tina, 21, 58–9, 69–70, 76, 89–90
Fitzgerald, Ella, 39
Frasier, 94, 96
French and Saunders, 130, 143, 200
French, Dawn, 126–7, 130, 143, 204

Freund, Karl, 35–6
Friends, 65, 96–8, 120, 166

geek, 99, 101–2, 105–6, 111, 114
Getting On, 23, 193–4, 196
Gill, Rosalind, 14, 19, 62, 73, 132
Girls, 67
GLAAD, 76, 113–14
Going Forward, 23, 193–7
Golden Girls, The, 163, 166–7, 169
Golden Palace, The, 167
Good Guys, The, 94–5
Gray, Frances, 1–2, 31, 163, 166–8
Green Wing, 155
grotesque, 16, 40, 44, 64, 107–8, 133–40, 150
Gullette, Margaret Morganroth, 160, 163

Halberstam, Judith, 2, 3, 26, 43–4, 75, 79, 87, 92–3, 119, 121, 131–2, 161, 164–5, 186
Hancock, Sheila, 205
Handl, Irene, 169
Hayes, Patricia, 169–70
Here's Lucy, 25
heterosexuality, 2, 6, 15, 22–3, 26, 66–7, 71–3, 77–8, 80–1, 83–90, 93–4, 115–19, 145–51, 172–4, 186–92, 202
Hird, Thora, 168, 170
Hitchens, Christopher, 11, 59, 69
How I Met Your Mother, 114

I Love Lucy, 21, 25, 27, 35–7, 43–52, 123, 129, 136
Inside Amy Schumer, 89–90
Irigaray, Luce, 149

Jewish American comedy traditions, 49–50, 98, 107–9
Jewish mother stereotype, 22, 107–9
Jewish *toomler* comedy, 38–9
Joseph, Jenny, 164

Killing of Sister George, The, 171

Landay, Lori, 46–7, 51
Larkins, The, 170–1
Last of the Summer Wine, The, 162–3, 166–9, 200
Little Britain, 5, 19, 129–30, 131
Lockyer, Sharon, 19
Lollipop Loves Mr Mole, 170
Lorre, Chuck, 99, 112, 119
Lucille Ball Show, The, 25
Lucy Show, The, 25, 48, 52–4

Macdonald, Barbara, 164
Marc, David, 21, 31, 37, 47
Martha Raye Show, The, 27, 38–43
masculinity, 22, 75–6, 77, 89, 90, 91–21
  hegemonic, 95–6, 98, 101, 104–6, 113, 121
  hypermasculinity, 99–101, 114
McRobbie, Angela, 133,137, 138, 150
Medhurst, Andy, 17–18
Mellencamp, Patricia, 1–2, 20–1, 28, 34
misogyny, 100, 108, 131
Mixed Bill, 203–5
Mizejewski, Linda, 11, 62–3, 136–7
Mount, Peggy, 169–71
Mullally, Megan, 84–6
Mulvey, Laura, 9, 16, 20, 42

Nichols, Dandy, 169

Office, The, 61, 70, 79
One Foot in the Grave, 162
O'Reilly, Miriam, 159
Our Miss Brooks, 35–7

Parks and Recreation, 21–2, 57–8, 62–5, 67, 78–90, 201, 203
Parsons, Jim, 113–14
Pile, Victoria, 124–8, 142–4, 155
Poehler, Amy, 21, 58–9, 69–70, 88, 89

postfeminism, 14, 21–3, 58–90, 124–5, 132–42, 150

queer temporality, 115, 129–32, 161–3, 165–6, 170, 172, 186, 191

racist comedy tropes, 109–10
Raye, Martha, 21, 25, 38–43
Reid, Beryl, 171
Revolting Women, 126
Roof, Judith, 21, 36–7
Roseanne, 60, 64–5, 67, 96, 99
Rowe, Kathleen, 1–2, 60, 63–5, 75, 140
Rubin, Gayle, 149
Russo, Mary, 12, 137–40, 150–3

Sandberg, Linn, 164–5, 189–90, 197
Saunders, Jennifer, 126–7, 130, 143, 204–5
Scharff, Christina, 14, 62, 141
schlemiel, 107–9
Scrubs, 104
Sedgwick, Eve Kosofsky, 2
Seinfeld, 96–8
Sex and the City, 65–9
sidekicks, 36–7, 119–20, 169

Simpson, Mark, 3, 97
sitcom, 21–3, 26–8, 35–7, 43, 46, 48–9, 53–60, 94–101, 160–3, 168–9, 175–7
  and realism, 60–5
sketch comedy, 22, 123–32, 143–8
Smack the Pony, 22, 123–57, 201
Smith, Linda, 205
Smith, Liz, 170
Some Like It Hot, 7–9
Spigel, Lynn, 21, 27, 31–3, 46, 50, 53

Tucker, Sophie, 39
Turner, Florence, 16
Two and a Half Men, 92, 99–103, 113

Waiting for God, 23, 160, 163, 166, 179–94, 195–6, 201, 203
'Warning', 164
Wearing, Sadie, 165
Whitfield, June, 5–6, 205
Will and Grace, 84, 98, 109
Wood, Victoria, 130, 204
Wozniak, Steve, 104

You're Only Young Twice, 23, 159–60, 163, 166, 169–79, 181, 192–4, 195–6, 201, 203

INDEX

Freund, Karl, 35–6
Friends, 65, 96–8, 120, 166

geek, 99, 101–2, 105–6, 111, 114
Getting On, 23, 193–4, 196
Gill, Rosalind, 14, 19, 62, 73, 132
Girls, 67
GLAAD, 76, 113–14
Going Forward, 23, 193–7
Golden Girls, The, 163, 166–7, 169
Golden Palace, The, 167
Good Guys, The, 94–5
Gray, Frances, 1–2, 31, 163, 166–8
Green Wing, 155
grotesque, 16, 40, 44, 64, 107–8, 133–40, 150
Gullette, Margaret Morganroth, 160, 163

Halberstam, Judith, 2, 3, 26, 43–4, 75, 79, 87, 92–3, 119, 121, 131–2, 161, 164–5, 186
Hancock, Sheila, 205
Handl, Irene, 169
Hayes, Patricia, 169–70
Here's Lucy, 25
heterosexuality, 2, 6, 15, 22–3, 26, 66–7, 71–3, 77–8, 80–1, 83–90, 93–4, 115–19, 145–51, 172–4, 186–92, 202
Hird, Thora, 168, 170
Hitchens, Christopher, 11, 59, 69
How I Met Your Mother, 114

I Love Lucy, 21, 25, 27, 35–7, 43–52, 123, 129, 136
Inside Amy Schumer, 89–90
Irigaray, Luce, 149

Jewish American comedy traditions, 49–50, 98, 107–9
Jewish mother stereotype, 22, 107–9
Jewish *toomler* comedy, 38–9
Joseph, Jenny, 164

Killing of Sister George, The, 171

Landay, Lori, 46–7, 51
Larkins, The, 170–1
Last of the Summer Wine, The, 162–3, 166–9, 200
Little Britain, 5, 19, 129–30, 131
Lockyer, Sharon, 19
Lollipop Loves Mr Mole, 170
Lorre, Chuck, 99, 112, 119
Lucille Ball Show, The, 25
Lucy Show, The, 25, 48, 52–4

Macdonald, Barbara, 164
Marc, David, 21, 31, 37, 47
Martha Raye Show, The, 27, 38–43
masculinity, 22, 75–6, 77, 89, 90, 91–21
 hegemonic, 95–6, 98, 101, 104–6, 113, 121
 hypermasculinity, 99–101, 114
McRobbie, Angela, 133, 137, 138, 150
Medhurst, Andy, 17–18
Mellencamp, Patricia, 1–2, 20–1, 28, 34
misogyny, 100, 108, 131
Mixed Bill, 203–5
Mizejewski, Linda, 11, 62–3, 136–7
Mount, Peggy, 169–71
Mullally, Megan, 84–6
Mulvey, Laura, 9, 16, 20, 42

Nichols, Dandy, 169

Office, The, 61, 70, 79
One Foot in the Grave, 162
O'Reilly, Miriam, 159
Our Miss Brooks, 35–7

Parks and Recreation, 21–2, 57–8, 62–5, 67, 78–90, 201, 203
Parsons, Jim, 113–14
Pile, Victoria, 124–8, 142–4, 155
Poehler, Amy, 21, 58–9, 69–70, 88, 89

postfeminism, 14, 21–3, 58–90, 124–5, 132–42, 150

queer temporality, 115, 129–32, 161–3, 165–6, 170, 172, 186, 191

racist comedy tropes, 109–10
Raye, Martha, 21, 25, 38–43
Reid, Beryl, 171
Revolting Women, 126
Roof, Judith, 21, 36–7
Roseanne, 60, 64–5, 67, 96, 99
Rowe, Kathleen, 1–2, 60, 63–5, 75, 140
Rubin, Gayle, 149
Russo, Mary, 12, 137–40, 150–3

Sandberg, Linn, 164–5, 189–90, 197
Saunders, Jennifer, 126–7, 130, 143, 204–5
Scharff, Christina, 14, 62, 141
schlemiel, 107–9
Scrubs, 104
Sedgwick, Eve Kosofsky, 2
Seinfeld, 96–8
Sex and the City, 65–9
sidekicks, 36–7, 119–20, 169

Simpson, Mark, 3, 97
sitcom, 21–3, 26–8, 35–7, 43, 46, 48–9, 53–60, 94–101, 160–3, 168–9, 175–7
  and realism, 60–5
sketch comedy, 22, 123–32, 143–8
Smack the Pony, 22, 123–57, 201
Smith, Linda, 205
Smith, Liz, 170
Some Like It Hot, 7–9
Spigel, Lynn, 21, 27, 31–3, 46, 50, 53

Tucker, Sophie, 39
Turner, Florence, 16
Two and a Half Men, 92, 99–103, 113

Waiting for God, 23, 160, 163, 166, 179–94, 195–6, 201, 203
'Warning', 164
Wearing, Sadie, 165
Whitfield, June, 5–6, 205
Will and Grace, 84, 98, 109
Wood, Victoria, 130, 204
Wozniak, Steve, 104

You're Only Young Twice, 23, 159–60, 163, 166, 169–79, 181, 192–4, 195–6, 201, 203